PyTorch 1.x Reinforcement Learning Cookbook

Over 60 recipes to design, develop, and deploy self-learning
AI models using Python

Yuxi (Hayden) Liu

BIRMINGHAM - MUMBAI

PyTorch 1.x Reinforcement Learning Cookbook

Copyright © 2019 Packt Publishing

Commissioning Editor: Amey Varangaonkar
Acquisition Editor: Devika Battike
Content Development Editor: Athikho Sapuni Rishana
Senior Editor: Ayaan Hoda
Technical Editor: Utkarsha S. Kadam
Copy Editor: Safis Editing
Project Coordinator: Kirti Pisat
Proofreader: Safis Editing
Indexer: Rekha Nair
Production Designer: Shraddha Falebhai

First published: October 2019

Production reference: 1311019

Published by Packt Publishing Ltd.
Livery Place
35 Livery Street
Birmingham
B3 2PB, UK.

ISBN 978-1-83855-196-4

www.packt.com

Packt.com

Subscribe to our online digital library for full access to over 7,000 books and videos, as well as industry leading tools to help you plan your personal development and advance your career. For more information, please visit our website.

Why subscribe?

- Spend less time learning and more time coding with practical eBooks and Videos from over 4,000 industry professionals

- Improve your learning with Skill Plans built especially for you

- Get a free eBook or video every month

- Fully searchable for easy access to vital information

- Copy and paste, print, and bookmark content

Did you know that Packt offers eBook versions of every book published, with PDF and ePub files available? You can upgrade to the eBook version at www.packt.com and as a print book customer, you are entitled to a discount on the eBook copy. Get in touch with us at customercare@packtpub.com for more details.

At www.packt.com, you can also read a collection of free technical articles, sign up for a range of free newsletters, and receive exclusive discounts and offers on Packt books and eBooks.

Contributors

About the author

Yuxi (Hayden) Liu is an experienced data scientist who's focused on developing machine learning and deep learning models and systems. He has worked in a variety of data-driven domains and has applied his expertise in reinforcement learning to computational problems. He is an education enthusiast and is the author of a series of machine learning books. His first book, *Python Machine Learning By Example,* was a #1 bestseller on Amazon India in 2017 and 2018. His other books include *R Deep Learning Projects* and *Hands-On Deep Learning Architectures with Python,* published by Packt. He has also published five first-authored IEEE transaction and conference papers during his master's research at the University of Toronto.

About the reviewers

Greg Walters has been involved with computers and computer programming since 1972. Currently, he is extremely well versed in Visual Basic, Visual Basic .NET, Python, and SQL using MySQL, SQLite, Microsoft SQL Server, Oracle, C++, Delphi, Modula-2, Pascal, C, 80x86 Assembler, COBOL, and Fortran. He is a programming trainer and has trained numerous people in many pieces of computer software, including MySQL, Open Database Connectivity, Quattro Pro, Corel Draw!, Paradox, Microsoft Word, Excel, DOS, Windows 3.11, Windows for Workgroups, Windows 95, Windows NT, Windows 2000, Windows XP, and Linux. He is currently retired and, in his spare time, is a musician and avid cook, but he is also open to working as a freelancer on various projects.

Robert Moni is a PhD student at Budapest University of Technology and Economics (BME) and is also a Deep Learning Expert at Continental's Deep Learning Competence Center in Budapest. He also manages a cooperation project established between and BME with the goal of supporting students in conducting research in the field of deep learning and autonomous driving. His research topic is deep reinforcement learning in complex environments, and his goal is to apply this technology to self-driving vehicles.

Packt is searching for authors like you

If you're interested in becoming an author for Packt, please visit `authors.packtpub.com` and apply today. We have worked with thousands of developers and tech professionals, just like you, to help them share their insight with the global tech community. You can make a general application, apply for a specific hot topic that we are recruiting an author for, or submit your own idea.

Table of Contents

Preface

The surge in interest in reinforcement learning is due to the fact that it revolutionizes automation by learning the optimal actions to take in an environment in order to maximize the notion of cumulative reward.

PyTorch 1.x Reinforcement Learning Cookbook introduces you to important reinforcement learning concepts and implementations of algorithms in PyTorch. Each chapter of the book walks you through a different type of reinforcement learning method and its industry-adopted applications. With the help of recipes that contain real-world examples, you will find it intriguing to enhance your knowledge and proficiency of reinforcement learning techniques in areas such as dynamic programming, Monte Carlo methods, temporal difference and Q-learning, multi-armed bandit, function approximation, deep Q-Networks, and policy gradients—they are no more obscure than you thought. Interesting and easy-to-follow examples, such as Atari games, Blackjack, Gridworld environments, internet advertising, Mountain Car, and Flappy Bird, will keep you interested until you reach your goal.

By the end of this book, you will have mastered the implementation of popular reinforcement learning algorithms and learned the best practices of applying reinforcement learning techniques to solve other real-world problems.

Who this book is for

Machine learning engineers, data scientists, and AI researchers looking for quick solutions to different problems in reinforcement learning will find this book useful. Prior exposure to machine learning concepts is required, while previous experience with PyTorch will be a bonus.

What this book covers

Chapter 1, *Getting Started with Reinforcement Learning and PyTorch*, is the starting point for readers who are looking forward to beginning this book's step-by-step guide to reinforcement learning with PyTorch. We will set up the working environment and OpenAI Gym and get familiar with reinforcement learning environments using the Atari and CartPole playgrounds. The chapter will also cover the implementation of several basic reinforcement learning algorithms, including random search, hill-climbing, and policy gradient. At the end, readers will also have a chance to review the essentials of PyTorch and get ready for the upcoming learning examples and projects.

Chapter 2, *Markov Decision Process and Dynamic Programming*, starts with the creation of a Markov chain and a Markov Decision Process, which is the core of most reinforcement learning algorithms. It will then move on to two approaches to solve a Markov Decision Process (MDP), value iteration and policy iteration. We will get more familiar with MDP and the Bellman equation by practicing policy evaluation. We will also demonstrate how to solve the interesting coin flipping gamble problem step by step. At the end, we will learn how to perform dynamic programming to scale up the learning.

Chapter 3, *Monte Carlo Methods for Making Numerical Estimations*, is focused on Monte Carlo methods. We will start by estimating the value of pi with Monte Carlo. Moving on, we will learn how to use the Monte Carlo method to predict state values and state-action values. We will demonstrate training an agent to win at Blackjack using Monte Carlo. Also, we will explore on-policy, first-visit Monte Carlo control and off-policy Monte Carlo control by developing various algorithms. Monte Carlo Control with an epsilon-greedy policy and weighted importance sampling will also be covered.

Chapter 4, *Temporal Difference and Q-Learning*, starts by setting up the CliffWalking and Windy Gridworld environment playground, which will be used in temporal difference and Q-Learning. Through our step-by-step guide, readers will explore Temporal Difference for prediction, and will gain practical experience with Q-Learning for off-policy control, and SARSA for on-policy control. We will also work on an interesting project, the taxi problem, and demonstrate how to solve it using the Q-Learning and SARSA algorithms. Finally, we will cover the Double Q-learning algorithm as a bonus section.

Chapter 5, *Solving Multi-Armed Bandit Problems*, covers the multi-armed bandit algorithm, which is probably one of the most popular algorithms in reinforcement learning. This will start with the creation of a multi-armed bandit problem. We will see how to solve the multi-armed bandit problem using four strategies, these being the epsilon-greedy policy, softmax exploration, the upper confidence bound algorithm, and the Thompson sampling algorithm. We will also work on a billion-dollar problem, online advertising, and demonstrate how to solve it using the multi-armed bandit algorithm. Finally, we will develop a more complex algorithm, the contextual bandit algorithm, and use it to optimize display advertising.

Chapter 6, *Scaling Up Learning with Function Approximation*, is focused on function approximation and will start with setting up the Mountain Car environment playground. Through our step-by-step guide, we will cover the motivation for function approximation over Table Lookup, and gain experience in incorporating function approximation into existing algorithms such as Q-Learning and SARSA. We will also cover an advanced technique, batching using experience replay. Finally, we will cover how to solve the CartPole problem using what we have learned in the chapter as a whole.

Chapter 7, *Deep Q-Networks in Action*, covers Deep Q-Learning, or **Deep Q Network (DQN)**, which is considered the most modern reinforcement learning technique. We will develop a DQN model step by step and understand the importance of Experience Replay and a target network in making Deep Q-Learning work in practice. To help readers solve Atari games, we will demonstrate how to incorporate convolutional neural networks into DQNs. We will also cover two DQN variants, Double DQNs and Dueling DQNs. We will cover how to fine-tune a Q-Learning algorithm using Double DQNs as an example.

Chapter 8, *Implementing Policy Gradients and Policy Optimization*, focuses on policy gradients and optimization and starts by implementing the REINFORCE algorithm. We will then develop the REINFORCE algorithm with the baseline for CliffWalking. We will also implement the actor-critic algorithm and apply it to solve the CliffWalking problem. To scale up the deterministic policy gradient algorithm, we apply tricks from DQN and develop the Deep Deterministic Policy Gradients. As a bit of fun, we train an agent based on the cross-entropy method to play the CartPole game. Finally, we will talk about how to scale up policy gradient methods using the asynchronous actor-critic method and neural networks.

Chapter 9, *Capstone Project – Playing Flappy Bird with DQN*, takes us through a capstone project – playing Flappy Bird using reinforcement learning. We will apply what we have learned throughout this book to build an intelligent bot. We will focus on building a DQN, fine-tuning model parameters, and deploying the model. Let's see how long the bird can fly in the air.

To get the most out of this book

Data scientists, machine learning engineers, and AI researchers looking for quick solutions to different problems in reinforcement learning will find this book useful. Prior exposure to machine learning concepts is required, while previous experience with PyTorch is not required but will be a bonus.

Download the example code files

You can download the example code files for this book from your account at www.packt.com. If you purchased this book elsewhere, you can visit www.packtpub.com/support and register to have the files emailed directly to you.

You can download the code files by following these steps:

1. Log in or register at www.packt.com.
2. Select the **Support** tab.
3. Click on **Code Downloads**.
4. Enter the name of the book in the **Search** box and follow the onscreen instructions.

Once the file is downloaded, please make sure that you unzip or extract the folder using the latest version of:

- WinRAR/7-Zip for Windows
- Zipeg/iZip/UnRarX for Mac
- 7-Zip/PeaZip for Linux

The code bundle for the book is also hosted on GitHub at https://github.com/PacktPublishing/PyTorch-1.x-Reinforcement-Learning-Cookbook. In case there's an update to the code, it will be updated on the existing GitHub repository.

We also have other code bundles from our rich catalog of books and videos available at https://github.com/PacktPublishing/. Check them out!

Download the color images

We also provide a PDF file that has color images of the screenshots/diagrams used in this book. You can download it here: https://static.packt-cdn.com/downloads/9781838551964_ColorImages.pdf.

Conventions used

There are a number of text conventions used throughout this book.

`CodeInText`: Indicates code words in text, database table names, folder names, filenames, file extensions, pathnames, dummy URLs, user input, and Twitter handles. Here is an example: "By saying `empty`, it doesn't mean all elements have a value of `Null`."

A block of code is set as follows:

```
>>> def random_policy():
...     action = torch.multinomial(torch.ones(n_action), 1).item()
...     return action
```

Any command-line input or output is written as follows:

```
conda install pytorch torchvision -c pytorch
```

Bold: Indicates a new term, an important word, or words that you see onscreen. For example, words in menus or dialog boxes appear in the text like this. Here is an example: "This approach is called **random search**, since the weight is randomly picked in each trial with the hope that the best weight will be found with a large number of trials."

Warnings or important notes appear like this.

Tips and tricks appear like this.

Sections

In this book, you will find several headings that appear frequently (*Getting ready*, *How to do it...*, *How it works...*, *There's more...*, and *See also*).

To give clear instructions on how to complete a recipe, use these sections as follows:

Getting ready

This section tells you what to expect in the recipe and describes how to set up any software or any preliminary settings required for the recipe.

How to do it...

This section contains the steps required to follow the recipe.

How it works...

This section usually consists of a detailed explanation of what happened in the previous section.

There's more...

This section consists of additional information about the recipe in order to make you more knowledgeable about the recipe.

See also

This section provides helpful links to other useful information for the recipe.

Get in touch

Feedback from our readers is always welcome.

General feedback: If you have questions about any aspect of this book, mention the book title in the subject of your message and email us at `customercare@packtpub.com`.

Errata: Although we have taken every care to ensure the accuracy of our content, mistakes do happen. If you have found a mistake in this book, we would be grateful if you would report this to us. Please visit www.packtpub.com/support/errata, selecting your book, clicking on the Errata Submission Form link, and entering the details.

Piracy: If you come across any illegal copies of our works in any form on the Internet, we would be grateful if you would provide us with the location address or website name. Please contact us at copyright@packt.com with a link to the material.

If you are interested in becoming an author: If there is a topic that you have expertise in and you are interested in either writing or contributing to a book, please visit authors.packtpub.com.

Reviews

Please leave a review. Once you have read and used this book, why not leave a review on the site that you purchased it from? Potential readers can then see and use your unbiased opinion to make purchase decisions, we at Packt can understand what you think about our products, and our authors can see your feedback on their book. Thank you!

For more information about Packt, please visit packt.com.

1
Getting Started with Reinforcement Learning and PyTorch

We kick off our journey of practical reinforcement learning and PyTorch with the basic, yet important, reinforcement learning algorithms, including random search, hill climbing, and policy gradient. We will start by setting up the working environment and OpenAI Gym, and you will become familiar with reinforcement learning environments through the Atari and CartPole playgrounds. We will also demonstrate how to develop algorithms to solve the CartPole problem step by step. Also, we will review the essentials of PyTorch and prepare for the upcoming learning examples and projects.

This chapter contains the following recipes:

- Setting up the working environment
- Installing OpenAI Gym
- Simulating Atari environments
- Simulating the CartPole environment
- Reviewing the fundamentals of PyTorch
- Implementing and evaluating a random search policy
- Developing the hill-climbing algorithm
- Developing a policy gradient algorithm

Setting up the working environment

Let's get started with setting up the working environment, including the correct versions of Python and Anaconda, and PyTorch as the main framework that is used throughout the book.

Python is the language we use to implement all reinforcement learning algorithms and techniques throughout the book. In this book, we will be using Python 3, or more specifically, 3.6 or above. If you are a Python 2 user, now is the best time for you to switch to Python 3, as Python 2 will no longer be supported after 2020. The transition is very smooth, though, so don't panic.

Anaconda is an open source Python distribution (`www.anaconda.com/distribution/`) for data science and machine learning. We will be using Anaconda's package manager, `conda`, to install Python packages, along with `pip`.

PyTorch (`https://pytorch.org/`), primarily developed by the Facebook AI Research (FAIR) Group, is a trendy machine learning library based on Torch (`http://torch.ch/`). Tensors in PyTorch replace NumPy's `ndarrays`, which provides more flexibility and compatibility with GPUs. Because of the powerful computational graphs and the simple and friendly interface, the PyTorch community is expanding on a daily basis, and it has seen heavy adoption by more and more tech giants.

Let's see how to properly set up all of these components.

How to do it...

We will begin by installing Anaconda. You can skip this if you already have Anaconda for Python 3.6 or 3.7 running on your system. Otherwise, you can follow the instructions at `https://docs.anaconda.com/anaconda/install/` for your operating system, as follows:

- Installing on Windows
- Installing on macOS
- Installing on Linux

Feel free to play around with PyTorch once the setup is done. To verify that you have the right setup of Anaconda and Python, you can enter the following line in your Terminal in Linux/Mac or Command Prompt in Windows (from now on, we will just call it Terminal):

```
python
```

It will display your Python Anaconda environment. You should see something similar to the following screenshot:

```
Python 3.7.2 (default, Dec 29 2018, 00:00:04)
[Clang 4.0.1 (tags/RELEASE_401/final)] :: Anaconda custom (64-bit) on darwin
Type "help", "copyright", "credits" or "license" for more information.
```

If Anaconda and Python 3.x are not mentioned, please check the system path or the path Python is running from.

The next thing to do is to install PyTorch. First, go to https://pytorch.org/get-started/locally/ and pick the description of your environment from the following table:

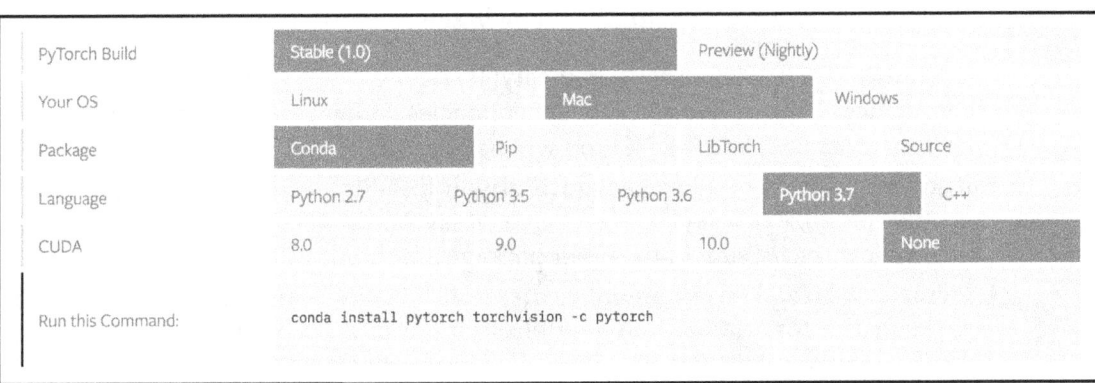

Here, we use **Mac**, **Conda**, **Python 3.7**, and running locally (no CUDA) as an example, and enter the resulting command line in the Terminal:

```
conda install pytorch torchvision -c pytorch
```

To confirm PyTorch is installed correctly, run the following lines of code in Python:

```
>>> import torch
>>> x = torch.empty(3, 4)
>>> print(x)
tensor([[ 0.0000e+00,  2.0000e+00, -1.2750e+16, -2.0005e+00],
        [ 9.8742e-37,  1.4013e-45,  9.9222e-37,  1.4013e-45],
        [ 9.9220e-37,  1.4013e-45,  9.9225e-37,  2.7551e-40]])
```

If a 3 x 4 matrix is displayed, that means PyTorch is installed correctly.

Now we have successfully set up the working environment.

How it works...

We have just created a tensor of size 3 x 4 in PyTorch. It is an empty matrix. By saying `empty`, this doesn't mean all elements are of the value `Null`. Instead, they are a bunch of meaningless floats that are considered placeholders. Users are required to set all the values later. This is very similar to NumPy's empty array.

There's more...

Some of you may question the necessity of installing Anaconda and using `conda` to manage packages since it is easy to install packages with `pip`. In fact, `conda` is a better packaging tool than `pip`. We mainly use `conda` for the following four reasons:

- **It handles library dependencies nicely**: Installing a package with `conda` will automatically download all of its dependencies. However, doing so with `pip` will lead to a warning, and installation will be aborted.
- **It solves conflicts of packages gracefully**: If installing a package requires another package of a specific version (let's say 2.3 or after, for example), `conda` will update the version of the other package automatically.
- **It creates a virtual environment easily**: A virtual environment is a self-contained package directory tree. Different applications or projects can use different virtual environments. All virtual environments are isolated from each other. It is recommended to use virtual environments so that whatever we do for one application doesn't affect our system environment or any other environment.
- **It is also compatible with pip**: We can still use `pip` in `conda` with the following command:

```
conda install pip
```

See also

If you are interested in learning more about `conda`, feel free to check out the following resources:

- **Conda user guide**: https://conda.io/projects/conda/en/latest/user-guide/index.html
- **Creating and managing virtual environments with conda**: https://conda.io/projects/conda/en/latest/user-guide/tasks/manage-environments.html

If you want to get more familiar with PyTorch, you can go through the *Getting Started* section in the official tutorial at `https://pytorch.org/tutorials/#getting-started`. We recommend you at least finish the following:

- **What is PyTorch**: `https://pytorch.org/tutorials/beginner/blitz/tensor_tutorial.html#sphx-glr-beginner-blitz-tensor-tutorial-py`
- **Learning PyTorch with examples**: `https://pytorch.org/tutorials/beginner/pytorch_with_examples.html`

Installing OpenAI Gym

After setting up the working environment, we can now install OpenAI Gym. You can't work on reinforcement learning without using OpenAI Gym, which gives you a variety of environments in which to develop your learning algorithms.

OpenAI (`https://openai.com/`) is a non-profit research company that is focused on building safe **artificial general intelligence (AGI)** and ensuring that it benefits humans. **OpenAI Gym** is a powerful and open source toolkit for developing and comparing reinforcement learning algorithms. It provides an interface to varieties of reinforcement learning simulations and tasks, from walking to moon landing, from car racing to playing Atari games. See `https://gym.openai.com/envs/` for the full list of environments.We can write **agents** to interact with OpenAI Gym environments using any numerical computation library, such as PyTorch, TensorFlow, or Keras.

How to do it...

There are two ways to install Gym. The first one is to use `pip`, as follows:

```
pip install gym
```

For `conda` users, remember to install `pip` first in `conda` using the following command before installing Gym using `pip`:

```
conda install pip
```

This is because Gym is not officially available in `conda` as of early 2019.

Another approach is to build from source:

1. First, clone the package directly from its Git repository:

    ```
    git clone https://github.com/openai/gym
    ```

2. Go to the downloaded folder and install Gym from there:

    ```
    cd gym
    pip install -e .
    ```

    And now you are good to go. Feel free to play around with gym.

3. You can also check the available gym environment by typing the following lines of code:

    ```
    >>> from gym import envs
    >>> print(envs.registry.all())
    dict_values([EnvSpec(Copy-v0), EnvSpec(RepeatCopy-v0),
    EnvSpec(ReversedAddition-v0), EnvSpec(ReversedAddition3-v0),
    EnvSpec(DuplicatedInput-v0), EnvSpec(Reverse-v0), EnvSpec(CartPole-
    v0), EnvSpec(CartPole-v1), EnvSpec(MountainCar-v0),
    EnvSpec(MountainCarContinuous-v0), EnvSpec(Pendulum-v0),
    EnvSpec(Acrobot-v1), EnvSpec(LunarLander-v2),
    EnvSpec(LunarLanderContinuous-v2), EnvSpec(BipedalWalker-v2),
    EnvSpec(BipedalWalkerHardcore-v2), EnvSpec(CarRacing-v0),
    EnvSpec(Blackjack-v0)
    ...
    ...
    ```

This will give you a long list of environments if you installed Gym properly. We will play around with some of them in the next recipe, *Simulating Atari environments*.

How it works...

Compared to the simple pip approach for installing Gym, the second approach provides more flexibility if you want to add new environments and modify Gym itself.

There's more...

You may wonder why we need to test reinforcement learning algorithms on Gym's environments since the actual environments we work in can be a lot different. You will recall that reinforcement learning doesn't make many assumptions about the environment, but it gets to know more about the environment by interacting with it. Also, when comparing the performance of different algorithms, we need to apply them to standardized environments. Gym is a perfect benchmark, covering many versatile and easy-to-use environments. This is similar to the datasets that we often use as benchmarks in supervised and unsupervised learning, such as MNIST, Imagenet, MovieLens, and Thomson Reuters News.

See also

Take a look at the official Gym documentation at `https://gym.openai.com/docs/`.

Simulating Atari environments

To get started with Gym, let's play some Atari games with it.

The Atari environments (`https://gym.openai.com/envs/#atari`) are a variety of **Atari 2600** video games, such as Alien, AirRaid, Pong, and Space Race. If you have ever played Atari games, this recipe should be fun for you, as you will play an Atari game, Space Invaders. However, an agent will act on your behalf.

How to do it...

Let's simulate the Atari environments by following these steps:

1. To run any `atari` environment for the first time, we need to install the `atari` dependencies by running this command in the Terminal:

```
pip install gym[atari]
```

Alternatively, if you used the second approach in the previous recipe to `install gym`, you can run the following command instead:

```
pip install -e '.[atari]'
```

2. After installing the Atari dependencies, we import the `gym` library in Python:

```
>>> import gym
```

3. Create an instance of the `SpaceInvaders` environment:

```
>>> env = gym.make('SpaceInvaders-v0')
```

4. Reset the environment:

```
>>> env.reset()
 array([[[ 0,  0, 0],
         [ 0, 0,  0],
         [ 0, 0,  0],
         ...,
         ...,
         [80, 89, 22],
         [80, 89, 22],
         [80, 89, 22]]], dtype=uint8)
```

As you can see, this also returns the initial state of the environment.

5. Render the environment:

```
>>> env.render()
True
```

You will see a small window popping up, as follows:

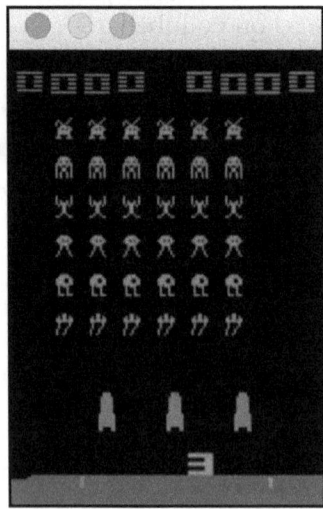

As you can see from the game window, the spaceship starts with three lives (the red spaceships).

6. Randomly pick one possible move and execute the action:

```
>>> action = env.action_space.sample()
>>> new_state, reward, is_done, info = env.step(action)
```

The `step()` method returns what happens after an action is taken, including the following:

- **New state**: The new observation.
- **Reward**: The reward associated with that action in that state.
- **Is done**: A flag indicating whether the game ends. In a `SpaceInvaders` environment, this will be `True` if the spaceship has no more lives left or all the aliens are gone; otherwise, it will remain `False`.
- **Info**: Extra information pertaining to the environment. This is about the number of lives left in this case. This is useful for debugging.

Let's take a look at the `is_done` flag and `info`:

```
>>> print(is_done)
False
>>> print(info)
{'ale.lives': 3}
```

Now we render the environment:

```
>>> env.render()
 True
```

The game window becomes the following:

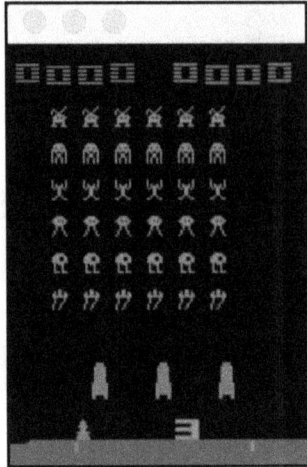

You won't notice much difference in the game window, because the spaceship just made a move.

7. Now, let's make a `while` loop and let the agent perform as many actions as it can:

```
>>> is_done = False
>>> while not is_done:
...       action = env.action_space.sample()
...       new_state, reward, is_done, info = env.step(action)
...       print(info)
...       env.render()
{'ale.lives': 3}
True
{'ale.lives': 3}
True
......
......
{'ale.lives': 2}
True
{'ale.lives': 2}
True
......
......
{'ale.lives': 1}
True
{'ale.lives': 1}
True
```

Meanwhile, you will see that the game is running, and the spaceship keeps moving and shooting, and so do the aliens. And it is pretty fun to watch, too. At the end, when the game ends, the window looks like the following:

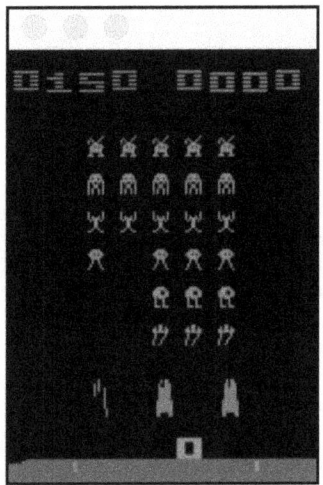

As you can see, we scored 150 points in this game. You may get a higher or lower score than this because the actions the agent performs are all randomly selected.

We also confirm that no lives are left with the last piece of info:

```
>>> print(info)
{'ale.lives': 0}
```

How it works...

Using Gym, we can easily create an environment instance by calling the `make()` method with the name of the environment as the parameter.

As you may have noticed, the actions that the agent performs are randomly chosen using the `sample()` method.

Note that, normally, we would have a more sophisticated agent guided by reinforcement learning algorithms. Here, we just demonstrated how to simulate an environment, and how an agent takes actions regardless of the outcome.

Run this a few times and see what we get:

```
>>> env.action_space.sample()
0
>>> env.action_space.sample()
3
>>> env.action_space.sample()
0
>>> env.action_space.sample()
4
>>> env.action_space.sample()
2
>>> env.action_space.sample()
1
>>> env.action_space.sample()
4
>>> env.action_space.sample()
5
>>> env.action_space.sample()
1
>>> env.action_space.sample()
0
```

There are six possible actions in total. We can also see this by running the following command:

```
>>> env.action_space
Discrete(6)
```

Actions from 0 to 5 stand for No Operation, Fire, Up, Right, Left, and Down, respectively, which are all the moves the spaceship in the game can do.

The `step()` method will let the agent take the action that is specified as its parameter. The `render()` method will update the display window based on the latest observation of the environment.

The observation of the environment, `new_state`, is represented by a 210 x 160 x 3 matrix, as follows:

```
>>> print(new_state.shape)
(210, 160, 3)
```

This means that each frame of the display screen is an RGB image of size 210 x 160.

There's more...

You may wonder why we need to install Atari dependencies. In fact, there are a few more environments that do not accompany the installation of gym, such as Box2d, Classic control, MuJoCo, and Robotics.

Take the Box2d environments, for example; we need to install the Box2d dependencies before we first run the environments. Again, two installation approaches are as follows:

```
pip install gym[box2d]
pip install -e '.[box2d]'
```

After that, we can play around with the LunarLander environment, as follows:

```
>>> env = gym.make('LunarLander-v2')
>>> env.reset()
array([-5.0468446e-04,  1.4135642e+00, -5.1140346e-02,  1.1751971e-01,
        5.9164839e-04,  1.1584054e-02, 0.0000000e+00,  0.0000000e+00],
      dtype=float32)
>>> env.render()
```

A game window will pop up:

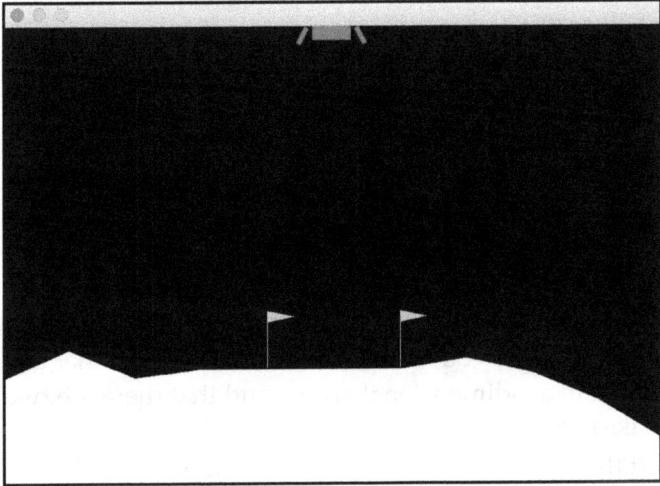

See also

If you are looking to simulate an environment but are not sure of the name you should use in the make() method, you can find it in the table of environments at https://github.com/openai/gym/wiki/Table-of-environments. Besides the name used to call an environment, the table also shows the size of the observation matrix and the number of possible actions. Have fun playing around with the environments.

Simulating the CartPole environment

In this recipe, we will work on simulating one more environment in order to get more familiar with Gym. The CartPole environment is a classic one in reinforcement learning research.

CartPole is a traditional reinforcement learning task in which a pole is placed upright on top of a cart. The agent moves the cart either to the left or to the right by 1 unit in a timestep. The goal is to balance the pole and prevent it from falling over. The pole is considered to have fallen if it is more than 12 degrees from the vertical, or the cart moves 2.4 units away from the origin. An episode terminates when any of the following occurs:

- The pole falls over
- The number of timesteps reaches 200

How to do it...

Let's simulate the CartPole environment by following these steps:

1. To run the CartPole environment, let's first search for its name in the table of environments at https://github.com/openai/gym/wiki/Table-of-environments. We get 'CartPole-v0' and also learn that the observation space is represented in a 4-dimensional array, and that there are two possible actions (which makes sense).

2. We import the Gym library and create an instance of the CartPole environment:

```
>>> import gym
>>> env = gym.make('CartPole-v0')
```

3. Reset the environment:

```
>>> env.reset()
array([-0.00153354,  0.01961605, -0.03912845, -0.01850426])
```

As you can see, this also returns the initial state represented by an array of four floats.

4. Render the environment:

```
>>> env.render()
True
```

You will see a small window popping up, as follows:

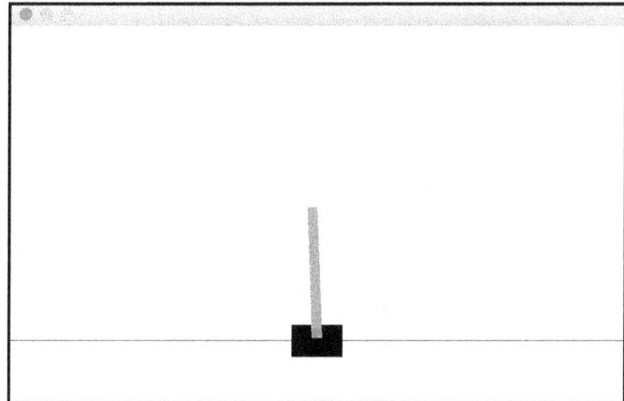

5. Now, let's make a `while` loop and let the agent perform as many random actions as it can:

```
>>> is_done = False
>>> while not is_done:
...         action = env.action_space.sample()
...         new_state, reward, is_done, info = env.step(action)
...         print(new_state)
...         env.render()
...
[-0.00114122 -0.17492355 -0.03949854  0.26158095]
True
[-0.00463969 -0.36946006 -0.03426692  0.54154857]
True
......
......
[-0.11973207 -0.41075106  0.19355244 1.11780626]
```

```
True
[-0.12794709 -0.21862176  0.21590856 0.89154351]
True
```

Meanwhile, you will see that the cart and pole are moving. At the end, you will see they both stop. The window looks like the following:

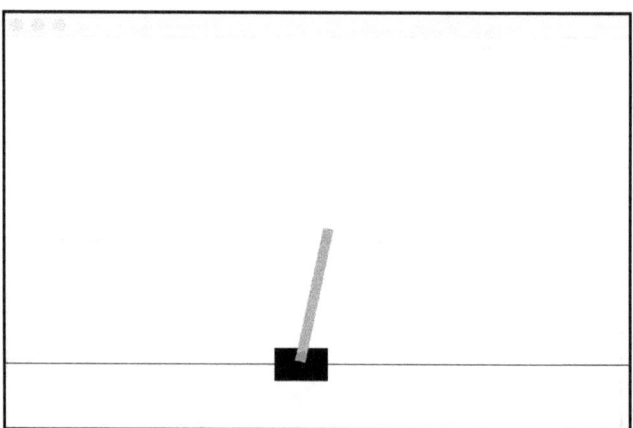

The episode only lasts several steps because the left or right actions are chosen randomly. Can we record the whole process so we can replay it afterward? We can do so with just two lines of code in Gym, as shown in *Step 7*. If you are using a Mac or Linux system, you need to complete *Step 6* first; otherwise, you can jump to *Step 7*.

6. To record video, we need to install the ffmpeg package. For Mac, it can be installed via the following command:

```
brew install ffmpeg
```

For Linux, the following command should do it:

```
sudo apt-get install ffmpeg
```

7. After creating the CartPole instance, add these two lines:

```
>>> video_dir = './cartpole_video/'
>>> env = gym.wrappers.Monitor(env, video_dir)
```

This will record what is displayed in the window and store it in the specified directory.

Now re-run the codes from *Step 3* to *Step 5*. After an episode terminates, we can see that an `.mp4` file is created in the `video_dir` folder. The video is quite short; it may last 1 second or so.

How it works...

In this recipe, we print out the state array for every step. But what does each float in the array mean? We can find more information about CartPole on Gym's GitHub wiki page: `https://github.com/openai/gym/wiki/CartPole-v0`. It turns out that those four floats represent the following:

- Cart position: This ranges from -2.4 to 2.4, and any position beyond this range will trigger episode termination.
- Cart velocity.
- Pole angle: Any value less than -0.209 (-12 degrees) or greater than 0.209 (12 degrees) will trigger episode termination.
- Pole velocity at the tip.

In terms of the action, it is either 0 or 1, which corresponds to pushing the cart to the left and to the right, respectively.

The **reward** in this environment is +1 for every timestep before the episode terminates. We can also verify this by printing out the reward for every step. And the total reward is simply the number of timesteps.

There's more...

So far, we've run only one episode. In order to assess how well the agent performs, we can simulate many episodes and then average the total rewards for an individual episode. The average total reward will tell us about the performance of the agent that takes random actions.

Let's set 10,000 episodes:

```
>>> n_episode = 10000
```

In each episode, we compute the total reward by accumulating the reward in every step:

```
>>> total_rewards = []
>>> for episode in range(n_episode):
...        state = env.reset()
...        total_reward = 0
...        is_done = False
...        while not is_done:
...            action = env.action_space.sample()
...            state, reward, is_done, _ = env.step(action)
...            total_reward += reward
...        total_rewards.append(total_reward)
```

Finally, we calculate the average total reward:

```
>>> print('Average total reward over {} episodes: {}'.format(
...        n_episode, sum(total_rewards) / n_episode))
Average total reward over 10000 episodes: 22.2473
```

On average, taking a random action scores 22.25.

We all know that taking random actions is not sophisticated enough, and we will implement an advanced policy in upcoming recipes. But for the next recipe, let's take a break and review the basics of PyTorch.

Reviewing the fundamentals of PyTorch

As we've already mentioned, PyTorch is the numerical computation library we use to implement reinforcement learning algorithms in this book.

PyTorch is a trendy scientific computing and machine learning (including deep learning) library developed by Facebook. Tensor is the core data structure in PyTorch, which is similar to NumPy's ndarrays. PyTorch and NumPy are comparable in scientific computing. However, PyTorch is faster than NumPy in array operations and array traversing. This is mainly due to the fact that array element access is faster in PyTorch. Hence, more and more people believe PyTorch will replace NumPy.

How to do it...

Let's do a quick review of the basic programming in PyTorch to get more familiar with it:

1. We created an uninitialized matrix in an earlier recipe. How about a randomly initialized one? See the following commands:

```
>>> import torch
>>> x = torch.rand(3, 4)
>>> print(x)
tensor([[0.8052, 0.3370, 0.7676, 0.2442],
        [0.7073, 0.4468, 0.1277, 0.6842],
        [0.6688, 0.2107, 0.0527, 0.4391]])
```

Random floats from a uniform distribution in the interval (0, 1) are generated.

2. We can specify the desired data type of the returned tensor. For example, a tensor of the double type (float64) is returned as follows:

```
>>> x = torch.rand(3, 4, dtype=torch.double)
>>> print(x)
tensor([[0.6848, 0.3155, 0.8413, 0.5387],
        [0.9517, 0.1657, 0.6056, 0.5794],
        [0.0351, 0.3801, 0.7837, 0.4883]], dtype=torch.float64)
```

By default, float is the returned data type.

3. Next, let's create a matrix full of zeros and a matrix full of ones:

```
>>> x = torch.zeros(3, 4)
>>> print(x)
tensor([[0., 0., 0., 0.],
        [0., 0., 0., 0.],
        [0., 0., 0., 0.]])
>>> x = torch.ones(3, 4)
>>> print(x)
tensor([[1., 1., 1., 1.],
        [1., 1., 1., 1.],
        [1., 1., 1., 1.]])
```

4. To get the size of a tensor, use this code:

```
>>> print(x.size())
torch.Size([3, 4])
```

torch.Size is actually a tuple.

5. To reshape a tensor, we can use the `view()` method:

```
>>> x_reshaped = x.view(2, 6)
>>> print(x_reshaped)
tensor([[1., 1., 1., 1., 1., 1.],
        [1., 1., 1., 1., 1., 1.]])
```

6. We can create a tensor directly from data, including a single value, a list, and a nested list:

```
>>> x1 = torch.tensor(3)
>>> print(x1)
tensor(3)
>>> x2 = torch.tensor([14.2, 3, 4])
>>> print(x2)
tensor([14.2000,  3.0000, 4.0000])
>>> x3 = torch.tensor([[3, 4, 6], [2, 1.0, 5]])
>>> print(x3)
tensor([[3., 4., 6.],
        [2., 1., 5.]])
```

7. To access the elements in a tensor of more than one element, we can use indexing in a similar way to NumPy:

```
>>> print(x2[1])
tensor(3.)
>>> print(x3[1, 0])
tensor(2.)
>>> print(x3[:, 1])
tensor([4., 1.])
>>> print(x3[:, 1:])
tensor([[4., 6.],
        [1., 5.]])
```

As with a one-element tensor, we do so by using the `item()` method:

```
>>> print(x1.item())
3
```

8. Tensor and NumPy arrays are mutually convertible. Convert a tensor to a NumPy array using the `numpy()` method:

```
>>> x3.numpy()
array([[3., 4., 6.],
       [2., 1., 5.]], dtype=float32)
```

Convert a NumPy array to a tensor with `from_numpy()`:

```
>>> import numpy as np
>>> x_np = np.ones(3)
>>> x_torch = torch.from_numpy(x_np)
>>> print(x_torch)
tensor([1., 1., 1.], dtype=torch.float64)
```

 Note that if the input NumPy array is of the float data type, the output tensor will be of the double type. Typecasting may occasionally be needed.

Take a look at the following example, where a tensor of the double type is converted to a `float`:

```
>>> print(x_torch.float())
tensor([1., 1., 1.])
```

9. Operations in PyTorch are similar to NumPy as well. Take addition as an example; we can simply do the following:

```
>>> x4 = torch.tensor([[1, 0, 0], [0, 1.0, 0]])
>>> print(x3 + x4)
tensor([[4., 4., 6.],
        [2., 2., 5.]])
```

Or we can use the `add()` method as follows:

```
>>> print(torch.add(x3, x4))
tensor([[4., 4., 6.],
        [2., 2., 5.]])
```

10. PyTorch supports in-place operations, which mutate the tensor object. For example, let's run this command:

```
>>> x3.add_(x4)
tensor([[4., 4., 6.],
        [2., 2., 5.]])
```

You will see that x3 is changed to the result of the original x3 plus x4:

```
>>> print(x3)
tensor([[4., 4., 6.],
        [2., 2., 5.]])
```

There's more...

Any method with _ indicates that it is an in-place operation, which updates the tensor with the resulting value.

See also

For the full list of tensor operations in PyTorch, please go to the official docs at `https://pytorch.org/docs/stable/torch.html`. This is the best place to search for information if you get stuck on a PyTorch programming problem.

Implementing and evaluating a random search policy

After some practice with PyTorch programming, starting from this recipe, we will be working on more sophisticated policies to solve the CartPole problem than purely random actions. We start with the random search policy in this recipe.

A simple, yet effective, approach is to map an observation to a vector of two numbers representing two actions. The action with the higher value will be picked. The linear mapping is depicted by a weight matrix whose size is 4 x 2 since the observations are 4-dimensional in this case. In each episode, the weight is randomly generated and is used to compute the action for every step in this episode. The total reward is then calculated. This process repeats for many episodes and, in the end, the weight that enables the highest total reward will become the learned policy. This approach is called **random search** because the weight is randomly picked in each trial with the hope that the best weight will be found with a large number of trials.

How to do it...

Let's go ahead and implement a random search algorithm with PyTorch:

1. Import the Gym and PyTorch packages and create an environment instance:

```
>>> import gym
>>> import torch
>>> env = gym.make('CartPole-v0')
```

2. Obtain the dimensions of the observation and action space:

```
>>> n_state = env.observation_space.shape[0]
>>> n_state
 4
>>> n_action = env.action_space.n
>>> n_action
 2
```

These will be used when we define the tensor for the weight matrix, which is size 4 x 2 in size.

3. Define a function that simulates an episode given the input weight and returns the total reward:

```
>>> def run_episode(env, weight):
...         state = env.reset()
...         total_reward = 0
...         is_done = False
...         while not is_done:
...             state = torch.from_numpy(state).float()
...             action = torch.argmax(torch.matmul(state, weight))
...             state, reward, is_done, _ = env.step(action.item())
...             total_reward += reward
...         return total_reward
```

Here, we convert the state array to a tensor of the float type because we need to compute the multiplication of the state and weight tensor, `torch.matmul(state, weight)`, for linear mapping. The action with the higher value is selected using the `torch.argmax()` operation. And don't forget to take the value of the resulting action tensor using `.item()` because it is a one-element tensor.

4. Specify the number of episodes:

```
>>> n_episode = 1000
```

5. We need to keep track of the best total reward on the fly, as well as the corresponding weight. So, we specify their starting values:

```
>>> best_total_reward = 0
>>> best_weight = None
```

We will also record the total reward for every episode:

```
>>> total_rewards = []
```

6. Now, we can run `n_episode`. For each episode, we do the following:

- Randomly pick the weight
- Let the agent take actions according to the linear mapping
- An episode terminates and returns the total reward
- Update the best total reward and the best weight if necessary
- Also, keep a record of the total reward

Put this into code as follows:

```
>>> for episode in range(n_episode):
...     weight = torch.rand(n_state, n_action)
...     total_reward = run_episode(env, weight)
...     print('Episode {}: {}'.format(episode+1, total_reward))
...     if total_reward > best_total_reward:
...         best_weight = weight
...         best_total_reward =  total_reward
...     total_rewards.append(total_reward)
...
Episode 1: 10.0
Episode 2: 73.0
Episode 3: 86.0
Episode 4: 10.0
Episode 5: 11.0
......
......
Episode 996: 200.0
Episode 997: 11.0
Episode 998: 200.0
Episode 999: 200.0
Episode 1000: 9.0
```

We have obtained the best policy through 1,000 random searches. The best policy is parameterized by `best_weight`.

7. Before we test out the best policy in the testing episodes, we can calculate the average total reward achieved by random linear mapping:

```
>>> print('Average total reward over {} episode: {}'.format(
...         n_episode, sum(total_rewards) / n_episode))
Average total reward over 1000 episode: 47.197
```

This is more than twice what we got from the random action policy (22.25).

8. Now, let's see how the learned policy performs on 100 new episodes:

```
>>> n_episode_eval = 100
>>> total_rewards_eval = []
>>> for episode in range(n_episode_eval):
...     total_reward = run_episode(env, best_weight)
...     print('Episode {}: {}'.format(episode+1, total_reward))
...     total_rewards_eval.append(total_reward)
...
Episode 1: 200.0
Episode 2: 200.0
Episode 3: 200.0
Episode 4: 200.0
Episode 5: 200.0
......
......
Episode 96: 200.0
Episode 97: 188.0
Episode 98: 200.0
Episode 99: 200.0
Episode 100: 200.0
>>> print('Average total reward over {} episode: {}'.format(
            n_episode, sum(total_rewards_eval) / n_episode_eval))
Average total reward over 1000 episode: 196.72
```

Surprisingly, the average reward for the testing episodes is close to the maximum of 200 steps with the learned policy. Be aware that this value may vary a lot. It could be anywhere from 160 to 200.

How it works...

The random search algorithm works so well mainly because of the simplicity of our CartPole environment. Its observation state is composed of only four variables. You will recall that the observation in the Atari Space Invaders game is more than 100,000 (which is 210 * 160 * 3) . The number of dimensions of the action state in CartPole is a third of that in Space Invaders. In general, simple algorithms work well for simple problems. In our case, we simply search for the best linear mapping from the observation to the action from a random pool.

Another interesting thing we've noticed is that before we select and deploy the best policy (the best linear mapping), random search also outperforms random action. This is because random linear mapping does take the observations into consideration. With more information from the environment, the decisions made in the random search policy are more intelligent than completely random ones.

There's more...

We can also plot the total reward for every episode in the training phase:

```
>>> import matplotlib.pyplot as plt
>>> plt.plot(total_rewards)
>>> plt.xlabel('Episode')
>>> plt.ylabel('Reward')
>>> plt.show()
```

This will generate the following plot:

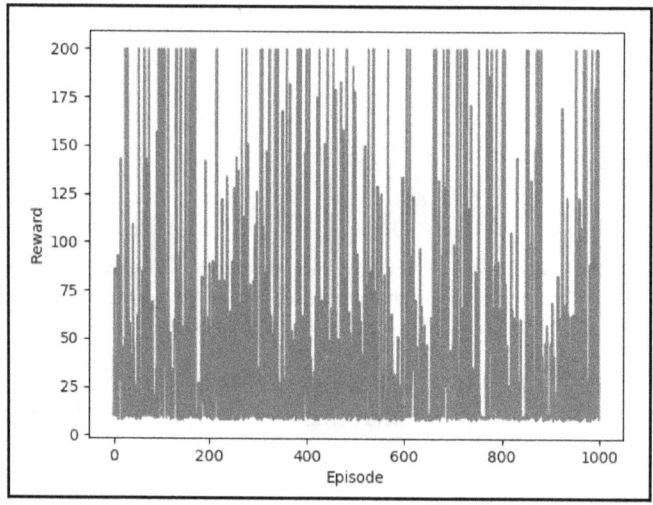

If you have not installed matplotlib, you can do so via the following command:

```
conda install matplotlib
```

We can see that the reward for each episode is pretty random, and that there is no trend of improvement as we go through the episodes. This is basically what we expected.

In the plot of reward versus episodes, we can see that there are some episodes in which the reward reaches 200. We can end the training phase whenever this occurs since there is no room to improve. Incorporating this change, we now have the following for the training phase:

```
>>> n_episode = 1000
>>> best_total_reward = 0
>>> best_weight = None
>>> total_rewards = []
>>> for episode in range(n_episode):
```

```
...        weight = torch.rand(n_state, n_action)
...        total_reward = run_episode(env, weight)
...        print('Episode {}: {}'.format(episode+1, total_reward))
...        if total_reward > best_total_reward:
...            best_weight = weight
...            best_total_reward = total_reward
...        total_rewards.append(total_reward)
...        if best_total_reward == 200:
...            break
Episode 1: 9.0
Episode 2: 8.0
Episode 3: 10.0
Episode 4: 10.0
Episode 5: 10.0
Episode 6: 9.0
Episode 7: 17.0
Episode 8: 10.0
Episode 9: 43.0
Episode 10: 10.0
Episode 11: 10.0
Episode 12: 106.0
Episode 13: 8.0
Episode 14: 32.0
Episode 15: 98.0
Episode 16: 10.0
Episode 17: 200.0
```

The policy achieving the maximal reward is found in episode 17. Again, this may vary a lot because the weights are generated randomly for each episode. To compute the expectation of training episodes needed, we can repeat the preceding training process 1,000 times and take the average of the training episodes:

```
>>> n_training = 1000
>>> n_episode_training = []
>>> for _ in range(n_training):
...        for episode in range(n_episode):
...            weight = torch.rand(n_state, n_action)
...            total_reward = run_episode(env, weight)
...            if total_reward == 200:
...                n_episode_training.append(episode+1)
...                break
>>> print('Expectation of training episodes needed: ',
...        sum(n_episode_training) / n_training)
Expectation of training episodes needed:  13.442
```

On average, we expect that it takes around 13 episodes to find the best policy.

Developing the hill-climbing algorithm

As we can see in the random search policy, each episode is independent. In fact, all episodes in random search can be run in parallel, and the weight that achieves the best performance will eventually be selected. We've also verified this with the plot of reward versus episode, where there is no upward trend. In this recipe, we will develop a different algorithm, a hill-climbing algorithm, to transfer the knowledge acquired in one episode to the next episode.

In the hill-climbing algorithm, we also start with a randomly chosen weight. But here, for every episode, we add some noise to the weight. If the total reward improves, we update the weight with the new one; otherwise, we keep the old weight. In this approach, the weight is gradually improved as we progress through the episodes, instead of jumping around in each episode.

How to do it...

Let's go ahead and implement the hill-climbing algorithm with PyTorch:

1. As before, import the necessary packages, create an environment instance, and obtain the dimensions of the observation and action space:

```
>>> import gym
>>> import torch
>>> env = gym.make('CartPole-v0')
>>> n_state = env.observation_space.shape[0]
>>> n_action = env.action_space.n
```

2. We will reuse the run_episode function we defined in the previous recipe, so we will not repeat it here. Again, given the input weight, it simulates an episode and returns the total reward.

3. Let's make it 1,000 episodes for now:

```
>>> n_episode = 1000
```

4. We need to keep track of the best total reward on the fly, as well as the corresponding weight. So, let's specify their starting values:

```
>>> best_total_reward = 0
>>> best_weight = torch.rand(n_state, n_action)
```

We will also record the total reward for every episode:

```
>>> total_rewards = []
```

5. As we mentioned, we will add some noise to the weight for each episode. In fact, we will apply a scale to the noise so that the noise won't overwhelm the weight. Here, we will choose 0.01 as the noise scale:

```
>>> noise_scale = 0.01
```

6. Now, we can run the n_episode function. After we randomly pick an initial weight, for each episode, we do the following:

- Add random noise to the weight
- Let the agent take actions according to the linear mapping
- An episode terminates and returns the total reward
- If the current reward is greater than the best one obtained so far, update the best reward and the weight
- Otherwise, the best reward and the weight remain unchanged
- Also, keep a record of the total reward

Put this into code as follows:

```
>>> for episode in range(n_episode):
...        weight = best_weight +
                       noise_scale * torch.rand(n_state, n_action)
...        total_reward = run_episode(env, weight)
...        if total_reward >= best_total_reward:
...            best_total_reward = total_reward
...            best_weight = weight
...        total_rewards.append(total_reward)
...        print('Episode {}: {}'.format(episode + 1, total_reward))
...
Episode 1: 56.0
Episode 2: 52.0
Episode 3: 85.0
Episode 4: 106.0
Episode 5: 41.0
......
......
Episode 996: 39.0
Episode 997: 51.0
Episode 998: 49.0
Episode 999: 54.0
Episode 1000: 41.0
```

We also calculate the average total reward achieved by the hill-climbing version of linear mapping:

```
>>> print('Average total reward over {} episode: {}'.format(
           n_episode, sum(total_rewards) / n_episode))
Average total reward over 1000 episode: 50.024
```

7. To assess the training using the hill-climbing algorithm, we repeat the training process multiple times (by running the code from *Step 4* to *Step 6* multiple times). We observe that the average total reward fluctuates a lot. The following are the results we got when running it 10 times:

```
Average total reward over 1000 episode: 9.261
Average total reward over 1000 episode: 88.565
Average total reward over 1000 episode: 51.796
Average total reward over 1000 episode: 9.41
Average total reward over 1000 episode: 109.758
Average total reward over 1000 episode: 55.787
Average total reward over 1000 episode: 189.251
Average total reward over 1000 episode: 177.624
Average total reward over 1000 episode: 9.146
Average total reward over 1000 episode: 102.311
```

What could cause such variance? It turns out that if the initial weight is bad, adding noise at a small scale will have little effect on improving the performance. This will cause poor convergence. On the other hand, if the initial weight is good, adding noise at a big scale might move the weight away from the optimal weight and jeopardize the performance. How can we make the training of the hill-climbing model more stable and reliable? We can actually make the noise scale adaptive to the performance, just like the adaptive learning rate in gradient descent. Let's see *Step 8* for more details.

8. To make the noise adaptive, we do the following:

- Specify a starting noise scale.
- If the performance in an episode improves, decrease the noise scale. In our case, we take half of the scale, but set 0.0001 as the lower bound.
- If the performance in an episode drops, increase the noise scale. In our case, we double the scale, but set 2 as the upper bound.

Put this into code:

```
>>> noise_scale = 0.01
>>> best_total_reward = 0
>>> total_rewards = []
>>> for episode in range(n_episode):
...     weight = best_weight +
                        noise_scale * torch.rand(n_state, n_action)
...     total_reward = run_episode(env, weight)
...     if total_reward >= best_total_reward:
...         best_total_reward = total_reward
...         best_weight = weight
...         noise_scale = max(noise_scale / 2, 1e-4)
...     else:
...         noise_scale = min(noise_scale * 2, 2)
...     print('Episode {}: {}'.format(episode + 1, total_reward))
...     total_rewards.append(total_reward)
...
Episode 1: 9.0
Episode 2: 9.0
Episode 3: 9.0
Episode 4: 10.0
Episode 5: 10.0
......
......
Episode 996: 200.0
Episode 997: 200.0
Episode 998: 200.0
Episode 999: 200.0
Episode 1000: 200.0
```

The reward is increasing as the episodes progress. It reaches the maximum of 200 within the first 100 episodes and stays there. The average total reward also looks promising:

```
>>> print('Average total reward over {} episode: {}'.format(
        n_episode, sum(total_rewards) / n_episode))
Average total reward over 1000 episode: 186.11
```

We also plot the total reward for every episode as follows:

```
>>> import matplotlib.pyplot as plt
>>> plt.plot(total_rewards)
>>> plt.xlabel('Episode')
>>> plt.ylabel('Reward')
>>> plt.show()
```

In the resulting plot, we can see a clear upward trend before it plateaus at the maximum value:

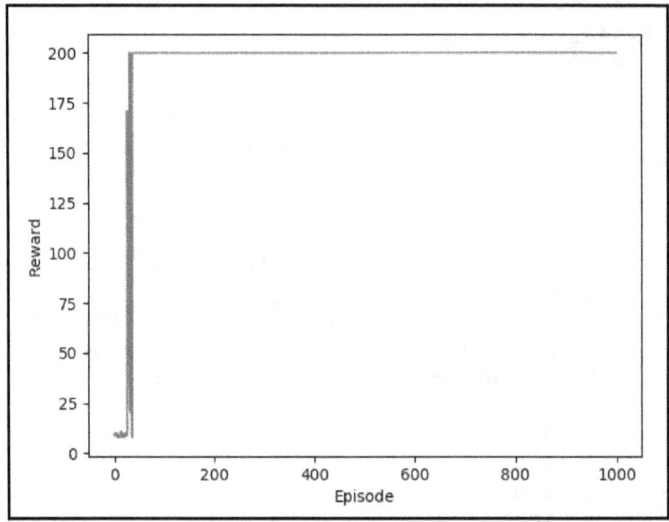

Feel free to run the new training process a few times. The results are very stable compared to learning with a constant noise scale.

9. Now, let's see how the learned policy performs on 100 new episodes:

```
>>> n_episode_eval = 100
>>> total_rewards_eval = []
>>> for episode in range(n_episode_eval):
...         total_reward = run_episode(env, best_weight)
...         print('Episode {}: {}'.format(episode+1, total_reward))
...         total_rewards_eval.append(total_reward)
...
Episode 1: 200.0
Episode 2: 200.0
Episode 3: 200.0
Episode 4: 200.0
Episode 5: 200.0
......
......
Episode 96: 200.0
Episode 97: 200.0
Episode 98: 200.0
Episode 99: 200.0
Episode 100: 200.0
```

Let's see the average performance:

```
>>> print('Average total reward over {} episode: {}'.format(n_episode,
sum(total_rewards) / n_episode))
 Average total reward over 1000 episode: 199.94
```

The average reward for the testing episodes is close to the maximum of 200 that we obtained with the learned policy. You can re-run the evaluation multiple times. The results are pretty consistent.

How it works...

We are able to achieve much better performance with the hill-climbing algorithm than with random search by simply adding adaptive noise to each episode. We can think of it as a special kind of gradient descent without a target variable. The additional noise is the gradient, albeit in a random way. The noise scale is the learning rate, and it is adaptive to the reward from the previous episode. The target variable in hill climbing becomes achieving the highest reward. In summary, rather than isolating each episode, the agent in the hill-climbing algorithm makes use of the knowledge learned from each episode and performs a more reliable action in the next episode. As the name hill climbing implies, the reward moves upwards through the episodes as the weight gradually moves towards the optimum value.

There's more...

We can observe that the reward can reach the maximum value within the first 100 episodes. Can we just stop training when the reward reaches 200, as we did with the random search policy? That might not be a good idea. Remember that the agent is making continuous improvements in hill climbing. Even if it finds a weight that generates the maximum reward, it can still search around this weight for the optimal point. Here, we define the optimal policy as the one that can solve the CartPole problem. According to the following wiki page, https://github.com/openai/gym/wiki/CartPole-v0, "solved" means the average reward over 100 consecutive episodes is no less than 195.

We refine the stopping criterion accordingly:

```
>>> noise_scale = 0.01
>>> best_total_reward = 0
>>> total_rewards = []
>>> for episode in range(n_episode):
...         weight = best_weight + noise_scale * torch.rand(n_state, n_action)
...         total_reward = run_episode(env, weight)
```

```
...         if total_reward >= best_total_reward:
...             best_total_reward = total_reward
...             best_weight = weight
...             noise_scale = max(noise_scale / 2, 1e-4)
...         else:
...             noise_scale = min(noise_scale * 2, 2)
...         print('Episode {}: {}'.format(episode + 1, total_reward))
...         total_rewards.append(total_reward)
...         if episode >= 99 and sum(total_rewards[-100:]) >= 19500:
...             break
...
Episode 1: 9.0
Episode 2: 9.0
Episode 3: 10.0
Episode 4: 10.0
Episode 5: 9.0
......
......
Episode 133: 200.0
Episode 134: 200.0
Episode 135: 200.0
Episode 136: 200.0
Episode 137: 200.0
```

At episode 137, the problem is considered solved.

See also

If you are interested in learning more about the hill-climbing algorithm, the following resources are useful:

- https://en.wikipedia.org/wiki/Hill_climbing
- https://www.geeksforgeeks.org/introduction-hill-climbing-artificial-intelligence/

Developing a policy gradient algorithm

The last recipe of the first chapter is about solving the CartPole environment with a policy gradient algorithm. This may be more complicated than we need for this simple problem, in which the random search and hill-climbing algorithms suffice. However, it is a great algorithm to learn, and we will use it in more complicated environments later in the book.

In the policy gradient algorithm, the model weight moves in the direction of the gradient at the end of each episode. We will explain the computation of gradients in the next section. Also, in each step, it **samples** an action from the policy based on the probabilities computed using the state and weight. It no longer takes an action with certainty, in contrast with random search and hill climbing (by taking the action achieving the higher score). Hence, the policy switches from deterministic to **stochastic**.

How to do it...

Now, it is time to implement the policy gradient algorithm with PyTorch:

1. As before, import the necessary packages, create an environment instance, and obtain the dimensions of the observation and action space:

```
>>> import gym
>>> import torch
>>> env = gym.make('CartPole-v0')
>>> n_state = env.observation_space.shape[0]
>>> n_action = env.action_space.n
```

2. We define the `run_episode` function, which simulates an episode given the input weight and returns the total reward and the gradients computed. More specifically, it does the following tasks in each step:

- Calculates the probabilities, `probs`, for both actions based on the current state and input weight
- Samples an action, `action`, based on the resulting probabilities
- Computes the derivatives, `d_softmax`, of the `softmax` function with the probabilities as input
- Divides the resulting derivatives, `d_softmax`, by the probabilities, probs, to get the derivatives, `d_log`, of the log term with respect to the policy
- Applies the chain rule to compute the gradient, `grad`, of the weights
- Records the resulting gradient, grad
- Performs the action, accumulates the reward, and updates the state

Putting all of this into code, we have the following:

```
>>> def run_episode(env, weight):
...        state = env.reset()
...        grads = []
...        total_reward = 0
...        is_done = False
```

```
...        while not is_done:
...            state = torch.from_numpy(state).float()
...            z = torch.matmul(state, weight)
...            probs = torch.nn.Softmax()(z)
...            action = int(torch.bernoulli(probs[1]).item())
...            d_softmax = torch.diag(probs) -
                            probs.view(-1, 1) * probs
...            d_log = d_softmax[action] / probs[action]
...            grad = state.view(-1, 1) * d_log
...            grads.append(grad)
...            state, reward, is_done, _ = env.step(action)
...            total_reward += reward
...            if is_done:
...                break
...        return total_reward, grads
```

After an episode finishes, it returns the total reward obtained in this episode and the gradients computed for the individual steps. These two outputs will be used to update the weight.

3. Let's make it 1,000 episodes for now:

    ```
    >>> n_episode = 1000
    ```

    This means we will run run_episode and n_episodetimes.

4. Initiate the weight:

    ```
    >>> weight = torch.rand(n_state, n_action)
    ```

    We will also record the total reward for every episode:

    ```
    >>> total_rewards = []
    ```

5. At the end of each episode, we need to update the weight using the computed gradients. For every step of the episode, the weight moves by *learning rate * gradient* calculated in this *step * total* reward in the remaining steps. Here, we choose 0.001 as the learning rate:

    ```
    >>> learning_rate = 0.001
    ```

Now, we can run `n_episode` episodes:

```
>>> for episode in range(n_episode):
...     total_reward, gradients = run_episode(env, weight)
...     print('Episode {}: {}'.format(episode + 1, total_reward))
...     for i, gradient in enumerate(gradients):
...         weight += learning_rate * gradient * (total_reward -
i)
...     total_rewards.append(total_reward)
......
......
Episode 101: 200.0
Episode 102: 200.0
Episode 103: 200.0
Episode 104: 190.0
Episode 105: 133.0
......
......
Episode 996: 200.0
Episode 997: 200.0
Episode 998: 200.0
Episode 999: 200.0
Episode 1000: 200.0
```

6. Now, we calculate the average total reward achieved by the policy gradient algorithm:

```
>>> print('Average total reward over {} episode: {}'.format(
...         n_episode, sum(total_rewards) / n_episode))
Average total reward over 1000 episode: 179.728
```

7. We also plot the total reward for every episode as follows:

```
>>> import matplotlib.pyplot as plt
>>> plt.plot(total_rewards)
>>> plt.xlabel('Episode')
>>> plt.ylabel('Reward')
>>> plt.show()
```

In the resulting plot, we can see a clear upward trend before it stays at the maximum value:

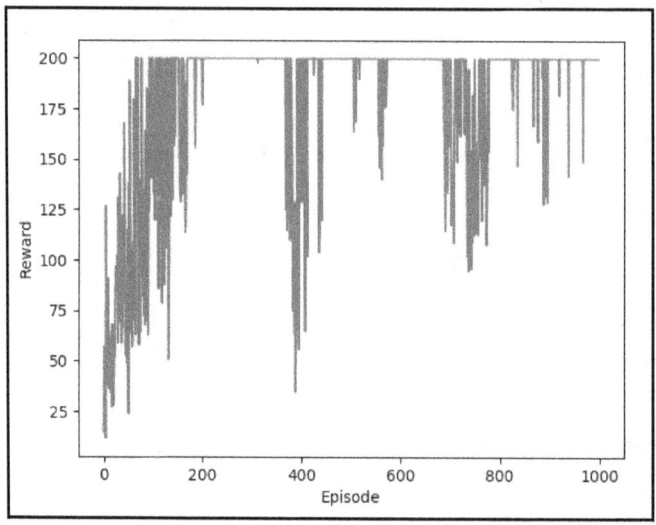

We can also see that the rewards oscillate even after it converges. This is because the policy gradient algorithm is a stochastic policy.

8. Now, let's see how the learned policy performs on 100 new episodes:

```
>>> n_episode_eval = 100
>>> total_rewards_eval = []
>>> for episode in range(n_episode_eval):
...     total_reward, _ = run_episode(env, weight)
...     print('Episode {}: {}'.format(episode+1, total_reward))
...     total_rewards_eval.append(total_reward)
...
Episode 1: 200.0
Episode 2: 200.0
Episode 3: 200.0
Episode 4: 200.0
Episode 5: 200.0
......
......
Episode 96: 200.0
Episode 97: 200.0
Episode 98: 200.0
Episode 99: 200.0
Episode 100: 200.0
```

Let's see the average performance:

```
>>> print('Average total reward over {} episode:
{}'.format(n_episode, sum(total_rewards) / n_episode))
 Average total reward over 1000 episode: 199.78
```

The average reward for the testing episodes is close to the maximum value of 200 for the learned policy. You can re-run the evaluation multiple times. The results are pretty consistent.

How it works...

The policy gradient algorithm trains an agent by taking small steps and updating the weight based on the rewards associated with those steps at the end of an episode. The technique of having the agent run through an entire episode and then updating the policy based on the rewards obtained is called **Monte Carlo** policy gradient.

The action is selected based on the probability distribution computed based on the current state and the model's weight. For example, if the probabilities for the left and right actions are [0.6, 0.4], this means the left action is selected 60% of the time; it doesn't mean the left action is chosen, as in the random search and hill-climbing algorithms.

We know that the reward is 1 for each step before an episode terminates. Hence, the future reward we use to calculate the policy gradient at each step is the number of steps remaining. After each episode, we feed the gradient history multiplied by the future rewards to update the weight using the stochastic gradient ascent method. In this way, the longer an episode is, the bigger the update of the weight. This will eventually increase the chance of getting a larger total reward.

As we mentioned at the start of this section, the policy gradient algorithm might be overkill for a simple environment such as CartPole, but it should get us ready for more complicated problems.

There's more...

If we examine the reward/episode plot, it seems that we can also stop early during training when it has been solved – the average reward over 100 consecutive episodes is no less than 195. We just add the following lines of code to the training session:

```
>>> if episode >= 99 and sum(total_rewards[-100:]) >= 19500:
...         break
```

Re-run the training session. You should get something similar to the following, which stops after several hundred episodes:

```
Episode 1: 10.0
Episode 2: 27.0
Episode 3: 28.0
Episode 4: 15.0
Episode 5: 12.0
......
......
Episode 549: 200.0
Episode 550: 200.0
Episode 551: 200.0
Episode 552: 200.0
Episode 553: 200.0
```

See also

Check out http://www.scholarpedia.org/article/Policy_gradient_methods for more information about policy gradient methods.

2
Markov Decision Processes and Dynamic Programming

In this chapter, we will continue our practical reinforcement learning journey with PyTorch by looking at **Markov decision processes (MDPs)** and dynamic programming. This chapter will start with the creation of a Markov chain and an MDP, which is the core of most reinforcement learning algorithms. You will also become more familiar with Bellman equations by practicing policy evaluation. We will then move on and apply two approaches to solving an MDP: value iteration and policy iteration. We will use the FrozenLake environment as an example. At the end of the chapter, we will demonstrate how to solve the interesting coin-flipping gamble problem with dynamic programming step by step.

The following recipes will be covered in this chapter:

- Creating a Markov chain
- Creating an MDP
- Performing policy evaluation
- Simulating the FrozenLake environment
- Solving an MDP with a value iteration algorithm
- Solving an MDP with a policy iteration algorithm
- Solving the coin-flipping gamble problem

Technical requirements

You will need the following programs installed on your system to successfully execute the recipes in this chapter:

- Python 3.6, 3.7, or above
- Anaconda
- PyTorch 1.0 or above
- OpenAI Gym

Creating a Markov chain

Let's get started by creating a Markov chain, on which the MDP is developed.

A Markov chain describes a sequence of events that comply with the **Markov property**. It is defined by a set of possible states, $S = \{s0, s1, ... , sm\}$, and a transition matrix, $T(s, s')$, consisting of the probabilities of state s transitioning to state s'. With the Markov property, the future state of the process, given the present state, is conditionally independent of past states. In other words, the state of the process at $t+1$ is dependent only on the state at t. Here, we use a process of study and sleep as an example and create a Markov chain based on two states, $s0$ (study) and $s1$ (sleep). Let's say we have the following transition matrix:

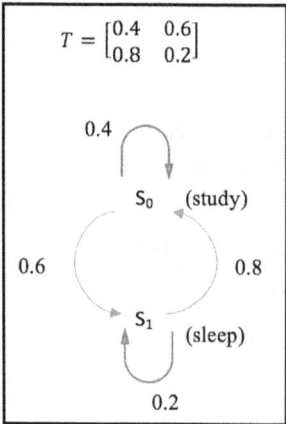

In the next section, we will compute the transition matrix after k steps, and the probabilities of being in each state given an initial distribution of states, such as *[0.7, 0.3]*, meaning there is a 70% chance that the process starts with study and a 30% chance that it starts with sleep.

How to do it...

To create a Markov chain for the study - and - sleep process and conduct some analysis on it, perform the following steps:

1. Import the library and define the transition matrix:

```
>>> import torch
>>> T = torch.tensor([[0.4, 0.6],
...                    [0.8, 0.2]])
```

2. Calculate the transition probability after k steps. Here, we use k = 2, 5, 10, 15, and 20 as examples:

```
>>> T_2 = torch.matrix_power(T, 2)
>>> T_5 = torch.matrix_power(T, 5)
>>> T_10 = torch.matrix_power(T, 10)
>>> T_15 = torch.matrix_power(T, 15)
>>> T_20 = torch.matrix_power(T, 20)
```

3. Define the initial distribution of two states:

```
>>> v = torch.tensor([[0.7, 0.3]])
```

4. Calculate the state distribution after k = 1, 2, 5, 10, 15, and 20 steps:

```
>>> v_1 = torch.mm(v, T)
>>> v_2 = torch.mm(v, T_2)
>>> v_5 = torch.mm(v, T_5)
>>> v_10 = torch.mm(v, T_10)
>>> v_15 = torch.mm(v, T_15)
>>> v_20 = torch.mm(v, T_20)
```

How it works...

In *Step 2*, we calculated the transition probability after k steps, which is the kth power of the transition matrix. You will see the following output:

```
>>> print("Transition probability after 2 steps:\n{}".format(T_2))
Transition probability after 2 steps:
tensor([[0.6400, 0.3600],
        [0.4800, 0.5200]])
>>> print("Transition probability after 5 steps:\n{}".format(T_5))
Transition probability after 5 steps:
tensor([[0.5670, 0.4330],
        [0.5773, 0.4227]])
```

```
>>> print(
"Transition probability after 10 steps:\n{}".format(T_10))
Transition probability after 10 steps:
tensor([[0.5715, 0.4285],
        [0.5714, 0.4286]])
>>> print(
"Transition probability after 15 steps:\n{}".format(T_15))
Transition probability after 15 steps:
tensor([[0.5714, 0.4286],
        [0.5714, 0.4286]])
>>> print(
"Transition probability after 20 steps:\n{}".format(T_20))
Transition probability after 20 steps:
tensor([[0.5714, 0.4286],
        [0.5714, 0.4286]])
```

We can see that, after 10 to 15 steps, the transition probability converges. This means that, no matter what state the process is in, it has the same probability of transitioning to s0 (57.14%) and s1 (42.86%).

In *Step 4*, we calculated the state distribution after k = 1, 2, 5, 10, 15, and 20 steps, which is the multiplication of the initial state distribution and the transition probability. You can see the results here:

```
>>> print("Distribution of states after 1 step:\n{}".format(v_1))
Distribution of states after 1 step:
tensor([[0.5200, 0.4800]])
>>> print("Distribution of states after 2 steps:\n{}".format(v_2))
Distribution of states after 2 steps:
tensor([[0.5920, 0.4080]])
>>> print("Distribution of states after 5 steps:\n{}".format(v_5))
Distribution of states after 5 steps:
tensor([[0.5701, 0.4299]])
>>> print(
    "Distribution of states after 10 steps:\n{}".format(v_10))
Distribution of states after 10 steps:
tensor([[0.5714, 0.4286]])
>>> print(
    "Distribution of states after 15 steps:\n{}".format(v_15))
Distribution of states after 15 steps:
tensor([[0.5714, 0.4286]])
>>> print(
    "Distribution of states after 20 steps:\n{}".format(v_20))
Distribution of states after 20 steps:
tensor([[0.5714, 0.4286]])
```

We can see that, after 10 steps, the state distribution converges. The probability of being in s0 (57.14%) and the probability of being in s1 (42.86%) remain unchanged in the long run.

Starting with [0.7, 0.3], the state distribution after one iteration becomes [0.52, 0.48]. Details of its calculation are illustrated in the following diagram:

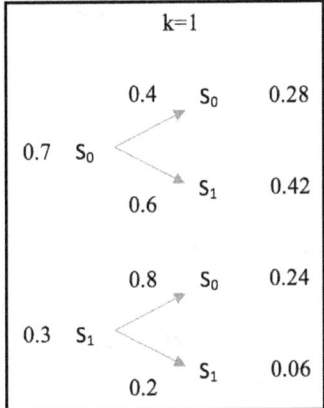

After another iteration, the state distribution becomes [0.592, 0.408] as calculated in the following diagram:

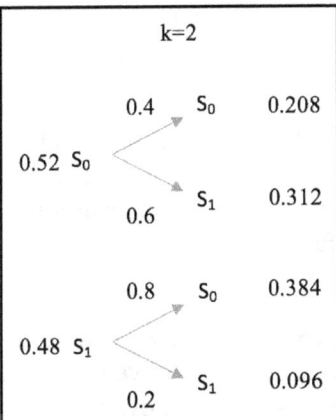

As time progresses, the state distribution reaches equilibrium.

There's more...

In fact, irrespective of the initial state the process was in, the state distribution will always converge to [0.5714, 0.4286]. You could test with other initial distributions, such as [0.2, 0.8] and [1, 0]. The distribution will remain [0.5714, 0.4286] after 10 steps.

A Markov chain does not necessarily converge, especially when it contains transient or current states. But if it does converge, it will reach the same equilibrium regardless of the starting distribution.

See also

If you want to read more about Markov chains, the following are globally two great blog articles with nice visualizations:

- https://brilliant.org/wiki/markov-chains/
- http://setosa.io/ev/markov-chains/

Creating an MDP

Developed upon the Markov chain, an MDP involves an agent and a decision-making process. Let's go ahead with developing an MDP and calculating the value function under the optimal policy.

Besides a set of possible states, $S = \{s0, s1, ... , sm\}$, an MDP is defined by a set of actions, $A = \{a0, a1, ... , an\}$; a transition model, $T(s, a, s')$; a reward function, $R(s)$; and a discount factor, γ. The transition matrix, $T(s, a, s')$, contains the probabilities of taking action a from state s then landing in s'. The discount factor, γ, controls the tradeoff between future rewards and immediate ones.

To make our MDP slightly more complicated, we extend the study and sleep process with one more state, s2 play games. Let's say we have two actions, a0 work and a1 slack. The 3 * 2 * 3 transition matrix $T(s, a, s')$ is as follows:

$$T = \begin{cases} \begin{bmatrix} 0.8 & 0.1 & 0.1 \\ 0.1 & 0.6 & 0.3 \end{bmatrix} \\ \begin{bmatrix} 0.7 & 0.2 & 0.1 \\ 0.1 & 0.8 & 0.1 \end{bmatrix} \\ \begin{bmatrix} 0.6 & 0.2 & 0.2 \\ 0.1 & 0.4 & 0.5 \end{bmatrix} \end{cases}$$

This means, for example, that when taking the a1 slack action from state s0 study, there is a 60% chance that it will become s1 sleep (maybe getting tired) and a 30% chance that it will become s2 play games (maybe wanting to relax), and that there is a 10% chance of keeping on studying (maybe a true workaholic). We define the reward function as [+1, 0, -1] for three states, to compensate for the hard work. Obviously, the **optimal policy**, in this case, is choosing a0 work for each step (keep on studying – no pain no gain, right?). Also, we choose 0.5 as the discount factor, to begin with. In the next section, we will compute the **state-value function** (also called the **value function**, just the **value** for short, or **expected utility**) under the optimal policy.

How to do it...

Creating an MDP can be done via the following steps:

1. Import PyTorch and define the transition matrix:

```
>>> import torch
>>> T = torch.tensor([[[0.8, 0.1, 0.1],
                       [0.1, 0.6, 0.3]],
...                   [[0.7, 0.2, 0.1],
...                    [0.1, 0.8, 0.1]],
...                   [[0.6, 0.2, 0.2],
...                    [0.1, 0.4, 0.5]]]
...                  )
```

2. Define the reward function and the discount factor:

```
>>> R = torch.tensor([1., 0, -1.])
>>> gamma = 0.5
```

3. The optimal policy in this case is selecting action a0 in all circumstances:

```
>>> action = 0
```

4. We calculate the value, V, of the optimal policy using the **matrix inversion** method in the following function:

```
>>> def cal_value_matrix_inversion(gamma, trans_matrix, rewards):
...     inv = torch.inverse(torch.eye(rewards.shape[0])
                                     - gamma *
trans_matrix)
...     V = torch.mm(inv, rewards.reshape(-1, 1))
...     return V
```

We will demonstrate how to derive the value in the next section.

5. We feed all variables we have to the function, including the transition probabilities associated with action a0:

```
>>> trans_matrix = T[:, action]
>>> V = cal_value_matrix_inversion(gamma, trans_matrix, R)
>>> print("The value function under the optimal
            policy is:\n{}".format(V))
The value function under the optimal policy is:
tensor([[ 1.6787],
        [ 0.6260],
        [-0.4820]])
```

How it works...

In this oversimplified study-sleep-game process, the optimal policy, that is, the policy that achieves the highest total reward, is choosing action a0 in all steps. However, it won't be that straightforward in most cases. Also, the actions taken in individual steps won't necessarily be the same. They are usually dependent on states. So, we will have to solve an MDP by finding the optimal policy in real-world cases.

The value function of a policy measures how good it is for an agent to be in each state, given the policy being followed. The greater the value, the better the state.

In *Step 4*, we calculated the value, V, of the optimal policy using **matrix inversion**. According to the **Bellman Equation**, the relationship between the value at step *t+1* and that at step *t* can be expressed as follows:

$$V_{t+1} = R + \gamma * T * V_t$$

When the value converges, which means *Vt+1 = Vt*, we can derive the value, V, as follows:

$$V = R + \gamma * T * V$$
$$V = (I - \gamma * T)^{-1} * R$$

Here, *I* is the identity matrix with 1s on the main diagonal.

One advantage of solving an MDP with matrix inversion is that you always get an exact answer. But the downside is its scalability. As we need to compute the inversion of an m * m matrix (where *m* is the number of possible states), the computation will become costly if there is a large number of states.

There's more...

We decide to experiment with different values for the discount factor. Let's start with 0, which means we only care about the immediate reward:

```
>>> gamma = 0
>>> V = cal_value_matrix_inversion(gamma, trans_matrix, R)
>>> print("The value function under the optimal policy is:\n{}".format(V))
The value function under the optimal policy is:
tensor([[ 1.],
        [ 0.],
        [-1.]])
```

This is consistent with the reward function as we only look at the reward received in the next move.

As the discount factor increases toward 1, future rewards are considered. Let's take a look at **γ**=0.99:

```
>>> gamma = 0.99
>>> V = cal_value_matrix_inversion(gamma, trans_matrix, R)
>>> print("The value function under the optimal policy is:\n{}".format(V))
The value function under the optimal policy is:
tensor([[65.8293],
        [64.7194],
        [63.4876]])
```

See also

This cheatsheet, `https://cs-cheatsheet.readthedocs.io/en/latest/subjects/ai/mdp.html`, serves as a quick reference for MDPs.

Performing policy evaluation

We have just developed an MDP and computed the value function of the optimal policy using matrix inversion. We also mentioned the limitation of inverting an m * m matrix with a large m value (let's say 1,000, 10,000, or 100,000). In this recipe, we will talk about a simpler approach called **policy evaluation**.

Policy evaluation is an iterative algorithm. It starts with arbitrary policy values and then iteratively updates the values based on the **Bellman expectation equation** until they converge. In each iteration, the value of a policy, π, for a state, s, is updated as follows:

$$V(s) := \sum_a \pi(s, a)[R(s, a) + \gamma \sum_{s'} T(s, a, s')V(s')]$$

Here, $\pi(s, a)$ denotes the probability of taking action a in state s under policy π. $T(s, a, s')$ is the transition probability from state s to state s' by taking action a, and $R(s, a)$ is the reward received in state s by taking action a.

There are two ways to terminate an iterative updating process. One is by setting a fixed number of iterations, such as 1,000 and 10,000, which might be difficult to control sometimes. Another one involves specifying a threshold (usually 0.0001, 0.00001, or something similar) and terminating the process only if the values of all states change to an extent that is lower than the threshold specified.

In the next section, we will perform policy evaluation on the study-sleep-game process under the optimal policy and a random policy.

How to do it...

Let's develop a policy evaluation algorithm and apply it to our study-sleep-game process as follows:

1. Import PyTorch and define the transition matrix:

```
>>> import torch
>>> T = torch.tensor([[[0.8, 0.1, 0.1],
...                     [0.1, 0.6, 0.3]],
...                    [[0.7, 0.2, 0.1],
...                     [0.1, 0.8, 0.1]],
...                    [[0.6, 0.2, 0.2],
...                     [0.1, 0.4, 0.5]]]
...                   )
```

2. Define the reward function and the discount factor (let's use 0.5 for now):

```
>>> R = torch.tensor([1., 0, -1.])
>>> gamma = 0.5
```

3. Define the threshold used to determine when to stop the evaluation process:

```
>>> threshold = 0.0001
```

4. Define the optimal policy where action a0 is chosen under all circumstances:

```
>>> policy_optimal = torch.tensor([[1.0, 0.0],
...                                 [1.0, 0.0],
...                                 [1.0, 0.0]])
```

5. Develop a policy evaluation function that takes in a policy, transition matrix, rewards, discount factor, and a threshold and computes the `value` function:

```
>>> def policy_evaluation(
                    policy, trans_matrix, rewards, gamma, threshold):
...         """
...         Perform policy evaluation
...         @param policy: policy matrix containing actions and their
...                         probability in each state
...         @param trans_matrix: transformation matrix
...         @param rewards: rewards for each state
...         @param gamma: discount factor
...         @param threshold: the evaluation will stop once values
...                         for all states are less than the threshold
...         @return: values of the given policy for all possible states
...         """
...         n_state = policy.shape[0]
...         V = torch.zeros(n_state)
...         while True:
...             V_temp = torch.zeros(n_state)
...             for state, actions in enumerate(policy):
...                 for action, action_prob in enumerate(actions):
...                     V_temp[state] += action_prob * (R[state] +
...                                 gamma * torch.dot(
...                                 trans_matrix[state, action], V))
...             max_delta = torch.max(torch.abs(V - V_temp))
...             V = V_temp.clone()
...             if max_delta <= threshold:
...                 break
...         return V
```

6. Now let's plug in the optimal policy and all other variables:

```
>>> V = policy_evaluation(policy_optimal, T, R, gamma, threshold)
>>> print(
    "The value function under the optimal policy is:\n{}".format(V))
The value function under the optimal policy is:
tensor([ 1.6786,  0.6260, -0.4821])
```

This is almost the same as what we got using matrix inversion.

7. We now experiment with another policy, a random policy where actions are picked with the same probabilities:

```
>>> policy_random = torch.tensor([[0.5, 0.5],
...                               [0.5, 0.5],
...                               [0.5, 0.5]])
```

8. Plug in the random policy and all other variables:

```
>>> V = policy_evaluation(policy_random, T, R, gamma, threshold)
>>> print(
        "The value function under the random policy
is:\n{}".format(V))
The value function under the random policy is:
tensor([ 1.2348,  0.2691, -0.9013])
```

How it works...

We have just seen how effective it is to compute the value of a policy using policy evaluation. It is a simple convergent iterative approach, in the **dynamic programming family**, or to be more specific, **approximate dynamic programming**. It starts with random guesses as to the values and then iteratively updates them according to the Bellman expectation equation until they converge.

In Step 5, the policy evaluation function does the following tasks:

- Initializes the policy values as all zeros.
- Updates the values based on the Bellman expectation equation.
- Computes the maximal change of the values across all states.
- If the maximal change is greater than the threshold, it keeps updating the values. Otherwise, it terminates the evaluation process and returns the latest values.

Since policy evaluation uses iterative approximation, its result might not be exactly the same as the result of the matrix inversion method, which uses exact computation. In fact, we don't really need the value function to be that precise. Also, it can solve the **curses of dimensionality** problem, which can result in scaling up the computation to thousands of millions of states. Therefore, we usually prefer policy evaluation over the other.

One more thing to remember is that policy evaluation is used to **predict** how great a we will get from a given policy; it is not used for **control** problems.

There's more...

To take a closer look, we also plot the policy values over the whole evaluation process.

We first need to record the value for each iteration in the `policy_evaluation` function:

```
>>> def policy_evaluation_history(
                policy, trans_matrix, rewards, gamma, threshold):
...     n_state = policy.shape[0]
...     V = torch.zeros(n_state)
...     V_his = [V]
...     i = 0
...     while True:
...         V_temp = torch.zeros(n_state)
...         i += 1
...         for state, actions in enumerate(policy):
...             for action, action_prob in enumerate(actions):
...                 V_temp[state] += action_prob * (R[state] + gamma *
                            torch.dot(trans_matrix[state, action], V))
...         max_delta = torch.max(torch.abs(V - V_temp))
...         V = V_temp.clone()
...         V_his.append(V)
...         if max_delta <= threshold:
...             break
...     return V, V_his
```

Now we feed the `policy_evaluation_history` function with the optimal policy, a discount factor of 0.5, and other variables:

```
>>> V, V_history = policy_evaluation_history(
                    policy_optimal, T, R, gamma, threshold)
```

We then plot the resulting history of values using the following lines of code:

```
>>> import matplotlib.pyplot as plt
>>> s0, = plt.plot([v[0] for v in V_history])
>>> s1, = plt.plot([v[1] for v in V_history])
>>> s2, = plt.plot([v[2] for v in V_history])
>>> plt.title('Optimal policy with gamma = {}'.format(str(gamma)))
>>> plt.xlabel('Iteration')
>>> plt.ylabel('Policy values')
>>> plt.legend([s0, s1, s2],
...             ["State s0",
...              "State s1",
...              "State s2"], loc="upper left")
>>> plt.show()
```

We see the following result:

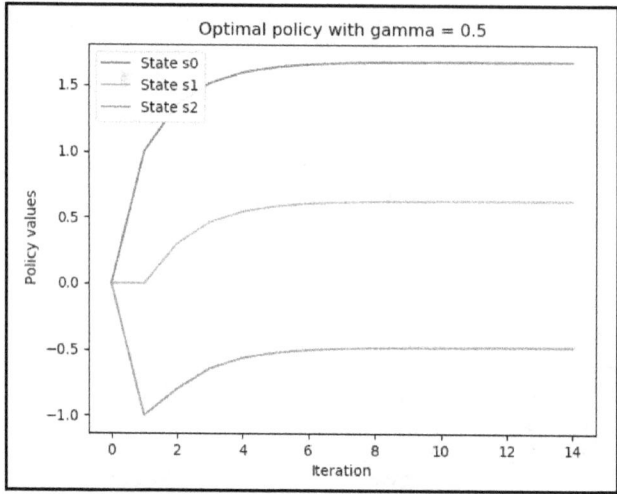

It is interesting to see the stabilization between iterations 10 to 14 during the convergence.

Next, we run the same code but with two different discount factors, 0.2 and 0.99. We get the following plot with the discount factor at 0.2:

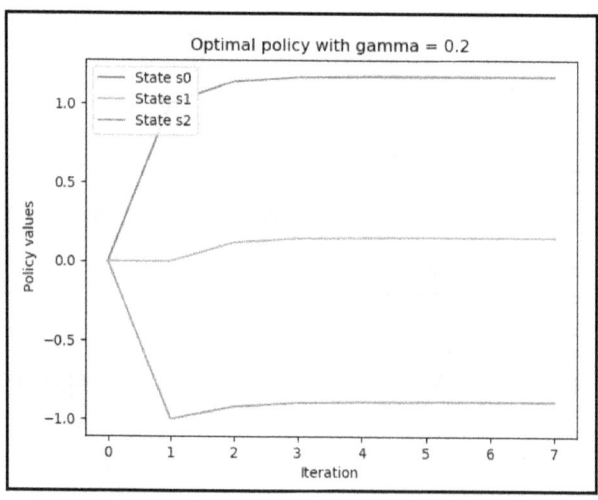

Comparing the plot with a discount factor of 0.5 with this one, we can see that the smaller the factor, the faster the policy values converge.

We also get the following plot with a discount factor of 0.99:

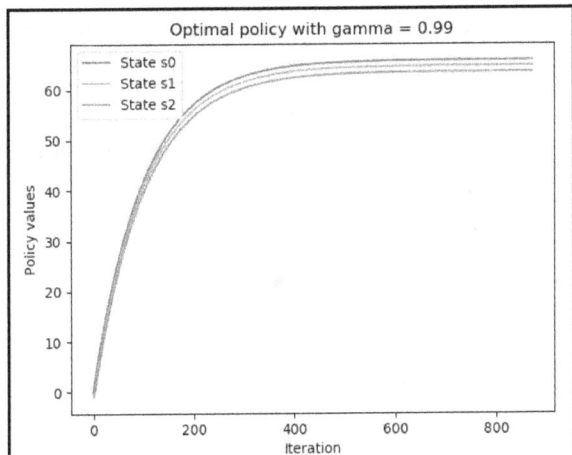

By comparing the plot with a discount factor of 0.5 to the plot with a discount factor of 0.99, we can see that the larger the factor, the longer it takes for policy values to converge. The discount factor is a tradeoff between rewards now and rewards in the future.

Simulating the FrozenLake environment

The optimal policies for the MDPs we have dealt with so far are pretty intuitive. However, it won't be that straightforward in most cases, such as the FrozenLake environment. In this recipe, let's play around with the FrozenLake environment and get ready for upcoming recipes where we will find its optimal policy.

FrozenLake is a typical Gym environment with a **discrete** state space. It is about moving an agent from the starting location to the goal location in a grid world, and at the same time avoiding traps. The grid is either four by four (`https://gym.openai.com/envs/FrozenLake-v0/`) or eight by eigh.

t (`https://gym.openai.com/envs/FrozenLake8x8-v0/`). The grid is made up of the following four types of tiles:

- **S**: The starting location
- **G**: The goal location, which terminates an episode
- **F**: The frozen tile, which is a walkable location
- **H**: The hole location, which terminates an episode

There are four actions, obviously: moving left (0), moving down (1), moving right (2), and moving up (3). The reward is +1 if the agent successfully reaches the goal location, and 0 otherwise. Also, the observation space is represented in a 16-dimensional integer array, and there are 4 possible actions (which makes sense).

What is tricky in this environment is that, as the ice surface is slippery, the agent won't always move in the direction it intends. For example, it may move to the left or to the right when it intends to move down.

Getting ready

To run the FrozenLake environment, let's first search for it in the table of environments here: `https://github.com/openai/gym/wiki/Table-of-environments`. The search gives us `FrozenLake-v0`.

How to do it...

Let's simulate the four-by-four FrozenLake environment in the following steps:

1. We import the `gym` library and create an instance of the FrozenLake environment:

```
>>> import gym
>>> import torch
>>> env = gym.make("FrozenLake-v0")
>>> n_state = env.observation_space.n
>>> print(n_state)
16
>>> n_action = env.action_space.n
>>> print(n_action)
4
```

2. Reset the environment:

```
>>> env.reset()
0
```

The agent starts with state 0.

3. Render the environment:

```
>>> env.render()
```

4. Let's make a down movement since it is walkable:

```
>>> new_state, reward, is_done, info = env.step(1)
>>> env.render()
```

6. Print out all the returning information to confirm that the agent lands in state 4 with a probability of 33.33%:

```
>>> print(new_state)
4
>>> print(reward)
0.0
>>> print(is_done)
False
>>> print(info)
{'prob': 0.3333333333333333}
```

You get 0 as a reward, since it has not reached the goal and the episode is not done yet. Again, you might see the agent landing in state 1, or staying in state 0 because of the slippery surface.

7. To demonstrate how difficult it is to walk on the frozen lake, implement a random policy and calculate the average total reward over 1,000 episodes. First, define a function that simulates a FrozenLake episode given a policy and returns the total reward (we know it is either 0 or 1):

```
>>> def run_episode(env, policy):
...     state = env.reset()
...     total_reward = 0
...     is_done = False
...     while not is_done:
...         action = policy[state].item()
...         state, reward, is_done, info = env.step(action)
...         total_reward += reward
...         if is_done:
...             break
...     return total_reward
```

8. Now run 1000 episodes, and a policy will be randomly generated and will be used in each episode:

```
>>> n_episode = 1000
>>> total_rewards = []
>>> for episode in range(n_episode):
...     random_policy = torch.randint(
...                     high=n_action, size=(n_state,))
...     total_reward = run_episode(env, random_policy)
```

```
...         total_rewards.append(total_reward)
...
>>> print('Average total reward under random policy: {}'.format(
            sum(total_rewards) / n_episode))
Average total reward under random policy: 0.014
```

This basically means there is only a 1.4% chance on average that the agent can reach the goal if we randomize the actions.

9. Next, we experiment with a random search policy. In the training phase, we randomly generate a bunch of policies and record the first one that reaches the goal:

```
>>> while True:
...         random_policy = torch.randint(
                            high=n_action, size=(n_state,))
...         total_reward = run_episode(env, random_policy)
...         if total_reward == 1:
...             best_policy = random_policy
...             break
```

10. Take a look at the best policy:

```
>>> print(best_policy)
tensor([0, 3, 2, 2, 0, 2, 1, 1, 3, 1, 3, 0, 0, 1, 1, 1])
```

11. Now run 1,000 episodes with the policy we just cherry-picked:

```
>>> total_rewards = []
>>> for episode in range(n_episode):
...         total_reward = run_episode(env, best_policy)
...         total_rewards.append(total_reward)
...
>>> print('Average total reward under random search
        policy: {}'.format(sum(total_rewards) / n_episode))
Average total reward under random search policy: 0.208
```

Using the random search algorithm, the goal will be reached 20.8% of the time on average.

Note that this result could vary a lot, as the policy we picked might happen to reach the goal because of the slippery ice and might not be the optimal one.

How it works...

In this recipe, we randomly generated a policy that was composed of 16 actions for the 16 states. Keep in mind that in FrozenLake, the movement direction is only partially dependent on the chosen action. This increases the uncertainty of control.

After running the code in *Step 4*, you will see a 4 * 4 matrix as follows, representing the frozen lake and the tile (state 0) where the agent stands:

After running the lines of code in *Step 5*, you will see the resulting grid as follows, where the agent moves down to state 4:

An episode will terminate if either of the following two conditions is met:

- Moving to an H tile (state 5, 7, 11, 12). This will generate a total reward of 0.
- Moving to the G tile (state 15). This will generate a total reward of +1.

There's more...

We can look into the details of the FrozenLake environment, including the transformation matrix and rewards for each state and action, by using the P attribute. For example, for state 6, we can do the following:

```
>>> print(env.env.P[6])
{0: [(0.3333333333333333, 2, 0.0, False), (0.3333333333333333, 5, 0.0,
True), (0.3333333333333333, 10, 0.0, False)], 1: [(0.3333333333333333, 5,
0.0, True), (0.3333333333333333, 10, 0.0, False), (0.3333333333333333, 7,
0.0, True)], 2: [(0.3333333333333333, 10, 0.0, False), (0.3333333333333333,
```

```
7, 0.0, True), (0.3333333333333333, 2, 0.0, False)], 3:
[(0.3333333333333333, 7, 0.0, True), (0.3333333333333333, 2, 0.0, False),
(0.3333333333333333, 5, 0.0, True)]}
```

This returns a dictionary with keys 0, 1, 2, and 3, representing four possible actions. The value is a list of movements after taking an action. The movement list is in the following format: (transformation probability, new state, reward received, is done). For instance, if the agent resides in state 6 and intends to take action 1 (down), there is a 33.33% chance that it will land in state 5, receiving a reward of 0 and terminating the episode; there is a 33.33% chance that it will land in state 10 and receive a reward of 0; and there is a 33.33% chance that it will land in state 7, receiving a reward of 0 and terminating the episode.

For state 11, we can do the following:

```
>>> print(env.env.P[11])
{0: [(1.0, 11, 0, True)], 1: [(1.0, 11, 0, True)], 2: [(1.0, 11, 0, True)],
3: [(1.0, 11, 0, True)]}
```

As stepping on a hole will terminate an episode, it won't make any movement afterward.

Feel free to check out the other states.

Solving an MDP with a value iteration algorithm

An MDP is considered solved if its optimal policy is found. In this recipe, we will figure out the optimal policy for the FrozenLake environment using a **value iteration** algorithm.

The idea behind value iteration is quite similar to that of policy evaluation. It is also an iterative algorithm. It starts with arbitrary policy values and then iteratively updates the values based on the **Bellman optimality equation** until they converge. So in each iteration, instead of taking the expectation (average) of values across all actions, it picks the action that achieves the maximal policy values:

$$V^*(s) := max_a[R(s,a) + \gamma \sum_{s'} T(s,a,s')V^*(s')]$$

Here, V*(s) denotes the optimal value, which is the value of the optimal policy; T(s, a, s') is the transition probability from state s to state s' by taking action a; and R(s, a) is the reward received in state s by taking action a.

Once the optimal values are computed, we can easily obtain the optimal policy accordingly:

$$\pi^*(s) := argmax_a \sum_{s'} T(s, a, s')[R(s, a, s') + \gamma V^*(s')]$$

How to do it...

Let's solve the FrozenLake environment using a value iteration algorithm as follows:

1. We import the necessary libraries and create an instance of the FrozenLake environment:

```
>>> import torch
>>> import gym
>>> env = gym.make('FrozenLake-v0')
```

2. Set 0.99 as the discount factor for now, and 0.0001 as the convergence threshold:

```
>>> gamma = 0.99
>>> threshold = 0.0001
```

3. Now define the function that computes optimal values based on the value iteration algorithm:

```
>>> def value_iteration(env, gamma, threshold):
...     """
...     Solve a given environment with value iteration algorithm
...     @param env: OpenAI Gym environment
...     @param gamma: discount factor
...     @param threshold: the evaluation will stop once values for
...                       all states are less than the threshold
...     @return: values of the optimal policy for the given
...              environment
...     """
...     n_state = env.observation_space.n
...     n_action = env.action_space.n
...     V = torch.zeros(n_state)
...     while True:
...         V_temp = torch.empty(n_state)
...         for state in range(n_state):
...             v_actions = torch.zeros(n_action)
...             for action in range(n_action):
...                 for trans_prob, new_state, reward, _ in
...                                     env.env.P[state][action]:
```

```
...                         v_actions[action] += trans_prob * (reward
...                                            + gamma * V[new_state])
...                 V_temp[state] = torch.max(v_actions)
...             max_delta = torch.max(torch.abs(V - V_temp))
...             V = V_temp.clone()
...             if max_delta <= threshold:
...                 break
...         return V
```

4. Plug in the environment, discount factor, and convergence threshold, then print the optimal values:

```
>>> V_optimal = value_iteration(env, gamma, threshold)
>>> print('Optimal values:\n{}'.format(V_optimal))
Optimal values:
tensor([0.5404, 0.4966, 0.4681, 0.4541, 0.5569, 0.0000, 0.3572,
0.0000, 0.5905,
        0.6421, 0.6144, 0.0000, 0.0000, 0.7410, 0.8625, 0.0000])
```

5. Now that we have the optimal values, we develop the function that extracts the optimal policy out of them:

```
>>> def extract_optimal_policy(env, V_optimal, gamma):
...         """
...         Obtain the optimal policy based on the optimal values
...         @param env: OpenAI Gym environment
...         @param V_optimal: optimal values
...         @param gamma: discount factor
...         @return: optimal policy
...         """
...         n_state = env.observation_space.n
...         n_action = env.action_space.n
...         optimal_policy = torch.zeros(n_state)
...         for state in range(n_state):
...             v_actions = torch.zeros(n_action)
...             for action in range(n_action):
...                 for trans_prob, new_state, reward, _ in
...                                 env.env.P[state][action]:
...                     v_actions[action] += trans_prob * (reward
...                             + gamma * V_optimal[new_state])
...             optimal_policy[state] = torch.argmax(v_actions)
...         return optimal_policy
```

6. Plug in the environment, discount factor, and optimal values, then print the optimal policy:

```
>>> optimal_policy = extract_optimal_policy(env, V_optimal, gamma)
>>> print('Optimal policy:\n{}'.format(optimal_policy))
Optimal policy:
tensor([0., 3., 3., 3., 0., 3., 2., 3., 3., 1., 0., 3., 3., 2., 1.,
3.])
```

7. We want to gauge how good the optimal policy is. So, let's run 1,000 episodes with the optimal policy and check the average reward. Here, we will reuse the `run_episode` function we defined in the previous recipe:

```
>>> n_episode = 1000
>>> total_rewards = []
>>> for episode in range(n_episode):
...         total_reward = run_episode(env, optimal_policy)
...         total_rewards.append(total_reward)
>>> print('Average total reward under the optimal
            policy: {}'.format(sum(total_rewards) / n_episode))
Average total reward under the optimal policy: 0.75
```

Under the optimal policy, the agent will reach the goal 75% of the time, on average. This is the best we are able to get since the ice is slippery.

How it works...

In a value iteration algorithm, we get the optimal value function by iteratively applying the Bellman optimality equation.

The following is another version of the Bellman optimality equation, which can deal with environments where rewards are partially dependent on the new state:

$$V^*(s) := max_a \sum_{s'} T(s, a, s')[R(s, a, s') + \gamma V^*(s')]$$

Here, R(s, a, s') is the reward received as a result of moving to state s' from state s by taking action a. As this version is more compatible, we developed our `value_iteration` function according to it. As you saw in *Step 3*, we perform the following tasks:

- Initialize the policy values as all zeros.
- Update the values based on the Bellman optimality equation.
- Compute the maximal change of the values across all states.
- If the maximal change is greater than the threshold, we keep updating the values. Otherwise, we terminate the evaluation process and return the latest values as the optimal values.

There's more...

We obtained a success rate of 75% with a discount factor of 0.99. How does the discount factor affect the performance? Let's do some experiments with different factors, including `0`, `0.2`, `0.4`, `0.6`, `0.8`, `0.99`, and `1.`:

```
>>> gammas = [0, 0.2, 0.4, 0.6, 0.8, .99, 1.]
```

For each discount factor, we compute the average success rate over 10,000 episodes:

```
>>> avg_reward_gamma = []
>>> for gamma in gammas:
...     V_optimal = value_iteration(env, gamma, threshold)
...     optimal_policy = extract_optimal_policy(env, V_optimal, gamma)
...     total_rewards = []
...     for episode in range(n_episode):
...         total_reward = run_episode(env, optimal_policy)
...         total_rewards.append(total_reward)
...     avg_reward_gamma.append(sum(total_rewards) / n_episode)
```

We draw a plot of the average success rate versus the discount factor:

```
>>> import matplotlib.pyplot as plt
>>> plt.plot(gammas, avg_reward_gamma)
>>> plt.title('Success rate vs discount factor')
>>> plt.xlabel('Discount factor')
>>> plt.ylabel('Average success rate')
>>> plt.show()
```

We get the following plot:

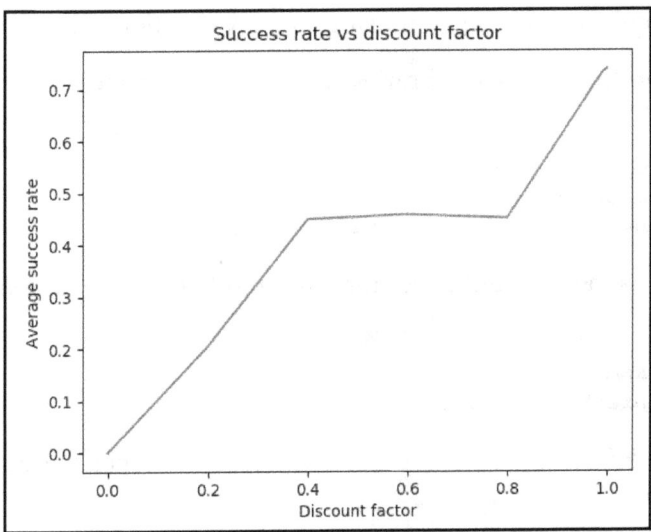

The result shows that the performance improves when there is an increase in the discount factor. This verifies the fact that a small discount factor values the reward now and a large discount factor values a better reward in the future.

Solving an MDP with a policy iteration algorithm

Another approach to solving an MDP is by using a **policy iteration** algorithm, which we will discuss in this recipe.

A policy iteration algorithm can be subdivided into two components: policy evaluation and policy improvement. It starts with an arbitrary policy. And in each iteration, it first computes the policy values given the latest policy, based on the Bellman expectation equation; it then extracts an improved policy out of the resulting policy values, based on the Bellman optimality equation. It iteratively evaluates the policy and generates an improved version until the policy doesn't change any more.

Let's develop a policy iteration algorithm and use it to solve the FrozenLake environment. After that, we will explain how it works.

How to do it...

Let's solve the FrozenLake environment using a policy iteration algorithm as follows:

1. We import the necessary libraries and create an instance of the FrozenLake environment:

```
>>> import torch
>>> import gym
>>> env = gym.make('FrozenLake-v0')
```

2. Set `0.99` as the discount factor for now, and `0.0001` as the convergence threshold:

```
>>> gamma = 0.99
>>> threshold = 0.0001
```

3. Now we define the `policy_evaluation` function that computes the values given a policy:

```
>>> def policy_evaluation(env, policy, gamma, threshold):
...     """
...     Perform policy evaluation
...     @param env: OpenAI Gym environment
...     @param policy: policy matrix containing actions and
...                            their probability in each state
...     @param gamma: discount factor
...     @param threshold: the evaluation will stop once values
...                 for all states are less than the threshold
...     @return: values of the given policy
...     """
...     n_state = policy.shape[0]
...     V = torch.zeros(n_state)
...     while True:
...         V_temp = torch.zeros(n_state)
...         for state in range(n_state):
...             action = policy[state].item()
...             for trans_prob, new_state, reward, _ in
...                                 env.env.P[state][action]:
...                 V_temp[state] += trans_prob * (reward
...                                 + gamma * V[new_state])
...         max_delta = torch.max(torch.abs(V - V_temp))
...         V = V_temp.clone()
...         if max_delta <= threshold:
...             break
...     return V
```

This is similar to what we did in the *Performing policy evaluation* recipe, but with the Gym environment as an input.

4. Next, we develop the second main component of the policy iteration algorithm, the policy improvement part:

```
>>> def policy_improvement(env, V, gamma):
...     """
...     Obtain an improved policy based on the values
...     @param env: OpenAI Gym environment
...     @param V: policy values
...     @param gamma: discount factor
...     @return: the policy
...     """
...     n_state = env.observation_space.n
...     n_action = env.action_space.n
...     policy = torch.zeros(n_state)
...     for state in range(n_state):
...         v_actions = torch.zeros(n_action)
...         for action in range(n_action):
...             for trans_prob, new_state, reward, _ in
                                    env.env.P[state][action]:
...                 v_actions[action] += trans_prob * (reward
                                        + gamma * V[new_state])
...         policy[state] = torch.argmax(v_actions)
...     return policy
```

This extracts an improved policy from the given policy values, based on the Bellman optimality equation.

5. Now that we have both components ready, we develop the policy iteration algorithm as follows:

```
>>> def policy_iteration(env, gamma, threshold):
...     """
...     Solve a given environment with policy iteration algorithm
...     @param env: OpenAI Gym environment
...     @param gamma: discount factor
...     @param threshold: the evaluation will stop once values
                        for all states are less than the threshold
...     @return: optimal values and the optimal policy for the
given
                    environment
...     """
...     n_state = env.observation_space.n
...     n_action = env.action_space.n
...     policy = torch.randint(high=n_action,
```

```
            size=(n_state,)).float()
...            while True:
...                V = policy_evaluation(env, policy, gamma, threshold)
...                policy_improved = policy_improvement(env, V, gamma)
...                if torch.equal(policy_improved, policy):
...                    return V, policy_improved
...                policy = policy_improved
```

6. Plug in the environment, discount factor, and convergence threshold:

```
>>> V_optimal, optimal_policy =
                policy_iteration(env, gamma, threshold)
```

7. We've obtained the optimal values and optimal policy. Let's take a look at them:

```
>>> print('Optimal values:\n{}'.format(V_optimal))
Optimal values:
tensor([0.5404, 0.4966, 0.4681, 0.4541, 0.5569, 0.0000, 0.3572,
0.0000, 0.5905,
        0.6421, 0.6144, 0.0000, 0.0000, 0.7410, 0.8625, 0.0000])
>>> print('Optimal policy:\n{}'.format(optimal_policy))
Optimal policy:
tensor([0., 3., 3., 3., 0., 3., 2., 3., 3., 1., 0., 3., 3., 2., 1.,
3.])
```

They are exactly the same as what we got using the value iteration algorithm.

How it works...

Policy iteration combines policy evaluation and policy improvement in each iteration. In policy evaluation, the values for a given policy (not the optimal one) are calculated based on the Bellman expectation equation until they converge:

$$V(s) := \sum_{s'} T(s, a, s')[R(s, a, s') + \gamma V(s')]$$

Here, a = π(s), which is the action taken under policy π in state s.

In policy improvement, the policy is updated using the resulting converged policy values, V(s), based on the Bellman optimality equation:

$$\pi(s) := argmax_a \sum_{s'} T(s, a, s')[R(s, a, s') + \gamma V(s')]$$

This repeats the policy evaluation and policy improvement steps until the policy converges. At convergence, the latest policy and its value function are the optimal policy and the optimal value function. Hence, in Step 5, the `policy_iteration` function does the following tasks:

- Initializes a random policy.
- Computes the values of the policy with the policy evaluation algorithm.
- Obtains an improved policy based on the policy values.
- If the new policy is different from the old one, it updates the policy and runs another iteration. Otherwise, it terminates the iteration process and returns the policy values and the policy.

There's more...

We have just solved the FrozenLake environment with a policy iteration algorithm. So, you may wonder when it is better to use policy iteration over value iteration and vice versa. There are basically three scenarios where one has the edge over the other:

- If there is a large number of actions, use policy iteration, as it can converge faster.
- If there is a small number of actions, use value iteration.
- If there is already a viable policy (obtained either by intuition or domain knowledge), use policy iteration.

Outside those scenarios, policy iteration and value iteration are generally comparable.

In the next recipe, we will apply each algorithm to solve the coin-flipping-gamble problem. We will see which algorithm converges faster.

See also

Feel free to use what we've learned in these two recipes to solve a bigger ice grid, the `FrozenLake8x8-v0` environment (`https://gym.openai.com/envs/FrozenLake8x8-v0/`).

Solving the coin-flipping gamble problem

Gambling on coin flipping should sound familiar to everyone. In each round of the game, the gambler can make a bet on whether a coin flip will show heads. If it turns out heads, the gambler will win the same amount they bet; otherwise, they will lose this amount. The game continues until the gambler loses (ends up with nothing) or wins (wins more than 100 dollars, let's say). Let's say the coin is unfair and it lands on heads 40% of the time. In order to maximize the chance of winning, how much should the gambler bet based on their current capital in each round? This will definitely be an interesting problem to solve.

If the coin lands on heads more than 50% of the time, there is nothing to discuss. The gambler can just keep betting one dollar each round and should win the game most of the time. If it is a fair coin, the gambler could bet one dollar each round and end up winning around 50% of the time. It gets tricky when the probability of heads is lower than 50%; the safe-bet strategy wouldn't work anymore. Nor would a random strategy, either. We need to resort to the reinforcement learning techniques we've learned in this chapter to make smart bets.

Let's get started by formulating the coin-flipping gamble problem as an MDP. It is basically an undiscounted, episodic, and finite MDP with the following properties:

- The state is the gambler's capital in dollars. There are 101 states: 0, 1, 2, ..., 98, 99, and 100+.
- The reward is 1 if the state 100+ is reached; otherwise, the reward is 0.
- The action is the possible amount the gambler bets in a round. Given state s, the possible actions include 1, 2, ..., and min(s, 100 - s). For example, when the gambler has 60 dollars, they can bet any amount from 1 to 40. Any amount above 40 doesn't make any sense as it increases the loss and doesn't increase the chance of winning.
- The next state after taking an action depends on the probability of the coin coming up heads. Let's say it is 40%. So, the next state of state s after taking action *a* will be *s+a* by 40%, *s-a* by 60%.
- The process terminates at state 0 and state 100+.

How to do it...

We first solve the coin-flipping gamble problem by using a value iteration algorithm and performing the following steps:

1. Import PyTorch:

```
>>> import torch
```

2. Specify the discount factor and convergence threshold:

```
>>> gamma = 1
>>> threshold = 1e-10
```

Here, we set 1 as the discount factor as the MDP is an undiscounted process; we set a small threshold as we expect small policy values since all rewards are 0 except the last state.

3. Define the following environment variables.

There are 101 states in total:

```
>>> capital_max = 100
>>> n_state = capital_max + 1
```

The corresponding reward is displayed as follows:

```
>>> rewards = torch.zeros(n_state)
>>> rewards[-1] = 1
>>> print(rewards)
tensor([0., 0., 0., 0., 0., 0., 0., 0., 0., 0., 0., 0., 0., 0., 0.,
0., 0., 0.,
        0., 0., 0., 0., 0., 0., 0., 0., 0., 0., 0., 0., 0., 0., 0.,
0., 0., 0.,
        0., 0., 0., 0., 0., 0., 0., 0., 0., 0., 0., 0., 0., 0., 0.,
0., 0., 0.,
        0., 0., 0., 0., 0., 0., 0., 0., 0., 0., 0., 0., 0., 0., 0.,
0., 0., 0.,
        0., 0., 0., 0., 0., 0., 0., 0., 0., 0., 0., 0., 0., 0., 0.,
0., 0., 0.,
        0., 0., 0., 0., 0., 0., 0., 0., 0., 0., 1.])
```

Let's say the probability of getting heads is 40%:

```
>>> head_prob = 0.4
```

Put these variables into a dictionary:

```
>>> env = {'capital_max': capital_max,
...        'head_prob': head_prob,
...        'rewards': rewards,
...        'n_state': n_state}
```

4. Now we develop a function that computes optimal values based on the value iteration algorithm:

```
>>> def value_iteration(env, gamma, threshold):
...     """
...     Solve the coin flipping gamble problem with
...             value iteration algorithm
...     @param env: the coin flipping gamble environment
...     @param gamma: discount factor
...     @param threshold: the evaluation will stop once values
...             for all states are less than the threshold
...     @return: values of the optimal policy for the given
...             environment
...     """
...     head_prob = env['head_prob']
...     n_state = env['n_state']
...     capital_max = env['capital_max']
...     V = torch.zeros(n_state)
...     while True:
...         V_temp = torch.zeros(n_state)
...         for state in range(1, capital_max):
...             v_actions = torch.zeros(
...                     min(state, capital_max - state) + 1)
...             for action in range(
...                     1, min(state, capital_max - state) + 1):
...                 v_actions[action] += head_prob * (
...                         rewards[state + action] +
...                         gamma * V[state + action])
...                 v_actions[action] += (1 - head_prob) * (
...                         rewards[state - action] +
...                         gamma * V[state - action])
...             V_temp[state] = torch.max(v_actions)
...         max_delta = torch.max(torch.abs(V - V_temp))
...         V = V_temp.clone()
...         if max_delta <= threshold:
...             break
...     return V
```

We only need to compute the values for states 1 to 99, as the values for state 0 and state 100+ are 0. And given state *s*, the possible actions can be anything from 1 up to *min(s, 100 - s)*. We should keep this in mind while computing the Bellman optimality equation.

5. Next, we develop a function that extracts the optimal policy based on the optimal values:

```
>>> def extract_optimal_policy(env, V_optimal, gamma):
...     """
...     Obtain the optimal policy based on the optimal values
...     @param env: the coin flipping gamble environment
...     @param V_optimal: optimal values
...     @param gamma: discount factor
...     @return: optimal policy
...     """
...     head_prob = env['head_prob']
...     n_state = env['n_state']
...     capital_max = env['capital_max']
...     optimal_policy = torch.zeros(capital_max).int()
...     for state in range(1, capital_max):
...         v_actions = torch.zeros(n_state)
...         for action in range(1,
...                 min(state, capital_max - state) + 1):
...             v_actions[action] += head_prob * (
...                         rewards[state + action] +
...                         gamma * V_optimal[state + action])
...             v_actions[action] += (1 - head_prob) * (
...                         rewards[state - action] +
...                         gamma * V_optimal[state - action])
...         optimal_policy[state] = torch.argmax(v_actions)
...     return optimal_policy
```

6. Finally, we can plug in the environment, discount factor, and convergence threshold to compute the optimal values and optimal policy after . Also, we time how long it takes to solve the gamble MDP with value iteration; we will compare this with the time it takes for policy iteration to complete:

```
>>> import time
>>> start_time = time.time()
>>> V_optimal = value_iteration(env, gamma, threshold)
>>> optimal_policy = extract_optimal_policy(env, V_optimal, gamma)
>>> print("It takes {:.3f}s to solve with value
        iteration".format(time.time() - start_time))
It takes 4.717s to solve with value iteration
```

We solved the gamble problem with value iteration in 4.717 seconds.

7. Take a look at the optimal policy values and the optimal policy we got:

```
>>> print('Optimal values:\n{}'.format(V_optimal))
>>> print('Optimal policy:\n{}'.format(optimal_policy))
```

8. We can plot the policy value versus state as follows:

```
>>> import matplotlib.pyplot as plt
>>> plt.plot(V_optimal[:100].numpy())
>>> plt.title('Optimal policy values')
>>> plt.xlabel('Capital')
>>> plt.ylabel('Policy value')
>>> plt.show()
```

Now that we've solved the gamble problem with value iteration, how about policy iteration? Let's see.

9. We start by developing the `policy_evaluation` function that computes the values given a policy:

```
>>> def policy_evaluation(env, policy, gamma, threshold):
...     """
...     Perform policy evaluation
...     @param env: the coin flipping gamble environment
...     @param policy: policy tensor containing actions taken
...                     for individual state
...     @param gamma: discount factor
...     @param threshold: the evaluation will stop once values
...                 for all states are less than the threshold
...     @return: values of the given policy
...     """
...     head_prob = env['head_prob']
...     n_state = env['n_state']
...     capital_max = env['capital_max']
...     V = torch.zeros(n_state)
...     while True:
...         V_temp = torch.zeros(n_state)
...         for state in range(1, capital_max):
...             action = policy[state].item()
...             V_temp[state] += head_prob * (
...                             rewards[state + action] +
...                             gamma * V[state + action])
...             V_temp[state] += (1 - head_prob) * (
...                             rewards[state - action] +
...                             gamma * V[state - action])
...         max_delta = torch.max(torch.abs(V - V_temp))
```

```
...             V = V_temp.clone()
...             if max_delta <= threshold:
...                 break
...     return V
```

10. Next, we develop another main component of the policy iteration algorithm, the policy improvement part:

```
>>> def policy_improvement(env, V, gamma):
...     """
...     Obtain an improved policy based on the values
...     @param env: the coin flipping gamble environment
...     @param V: policy values
...     @param gamma: discount factor
...     @return: the policy
...     """
...     head_prob = env['head_prob']
...     n_state = env['n_state']
...     capital_max = env['capital_max']
...     policy = torch.zeros(n_state).int()
...     for state in range(1, capital_max):
...         v_actions = torch.zeros(
...                     min(state, capital_max - state) + 1)
...         for action in range(
...                     1, min(state, capital_max - state) + 1):
...             v_actions[action] += head_prob * (
...                             rewards[state + action] +
...                             gamma * V[state + action])
...             v_actions[action] += (1 - head_prob) * (
...                             rewards[state - action] +
...                             gamma * V[state - action])
...         policy[state] = torch.argmax(v_actions)
...     return policy
```

11. With both components ready, we can develop the main entry to the policy iteration algorithm as follows:

```
>>> def policy_iteration(env, gamma, threshold):
...     """
...     Solve the coin flipping gamble problem with policy
...             iteration algorithm
...     @param env: the coin flipping gamble environment
...     @param gamma: discount factor
...     @param threshold: the evaluation will stop once values
...             for all states are less than the threshold
...     @return: optimal values and the optimal policy for the
...             given environment
...     """
```

```
...        n_state = env['n_state']
...        policy = torch.zeros(n_state).int()
...        while True:
...            V = policy_evaluation(env, policy, gamma, threshold)
...            policy_improved = policy_improvement(env, V, gamma)
...            if torch.equal(policy_improved, policy):
...                return V, policy_improved
...            policy = policy_improved
```

12. Finally, we plug in the environment, discount factor, and convergence threshold to compute the optimal values and the optimal policy. We record the time spent solving the MDP as well:

```
>>> start_time = time.time()
>>> V_optimal, optimal_policy
                 = policy_iteration(env, gamma, threshold)
>>> print("It takes {:.3f}s to solve with policy
              iteration".format(time.time() - start_time))
It takes 2.002s to solve with policy iteration
```

13. Check out the optimal values and optimal policy we just obtained:

```
>>> print('Optimal values:\n{}'.format(V_optimal))
>>> print('Optimal policy:\n{}'.format(optimal_policy))
```

How it works...

After executing the lines of code in *Step 7*, you will see the optimal policy values:

```
Optimal values:
tensor([0.0000, 0.0021, 0.0052, 0.0092, 0.0129, 0.0174, 0.0231, 0.0278,
0.0323,
        0.0377, 0.0435, 0.0504, 0.0577, 0.0652, 0.0695, 0.0744, 0.0807,
0.0866,
        0.0942, 0.1031, 0.1087, 0.1160, 0.1259, 0.1336, 0.1441, 0.1600,
0.1631,
        0.1677, 0.1738, 0.1794, 0.1861, 0.1946, 0.2017, 0.2084, 0.2165,
0.2252,
        0.2355, 0.2465, 0.2579, 0.2643, 0.2716, 0.2810, 0.2899, 0.3013,
0.3147,
        0.3230, 0.3339, 0.3488, 0.3604, 0.3762, 0.4000, 0.4031, 0.4077,
0.4138,
        0.4194, 0.4261, 0.4346, 0.4417, 0.4484, 0.4565, 0.4652, 0.4755,
0.4865,
        0.4979, 0.5043, 0.5116, 0.5210, 0.5299, 0.5413, 0.5547, 0.5630,
0.5740,
```

```
            0.5888,  0.6004,  0.6162,  0.6400,  0.6446,  0.6516,  0.6608,  0.6690,
    0.6791,
            0.6919,  0.7026,  0.7126,  0.7248,  0.7378,  0.7533,  0.7697,  0.7868,
    0.7965,
            0.8075,  0.8215,  0.8349,  0.8520,  0.8721,  0.8845,  0.9009,  0.9232,
    0.9406,
            0.9643,  0.0000])
```

You will also see the optimal policy:

```
Optimal policy:
tensor([ 0,   1,  2,  3,  4,   5,  6,  7,  8,  9, 10, 11, 12, 13, 14, 15, 16, 17,
         18, 19, 20, 21, 22, 23, 24, 25, 26, 27, 22, 29, 30, 31, 32, 33,   9,
    35,
         36, 37, 38, 11, 40,   9, 42, 43, 44,  5,  4,   3,  2,  1, 50,  1,  2, 47,
          4,  5, 44,   7,  8,  9, 10, 11, 38, 12, 36, 35, 34, 17, 32, 19, 30,
    4,
          3,  2, 26, 25, 24, 23, 22, 21, 20, 19, 18, 17, 16, 15, 14, 13, 12,
    11,
         10,  9,  8,   7,  6,  5,  4,   3,  2,  1], dtype=torch.int32)
```

Step 8 generates the following plot for the optimal policy values:

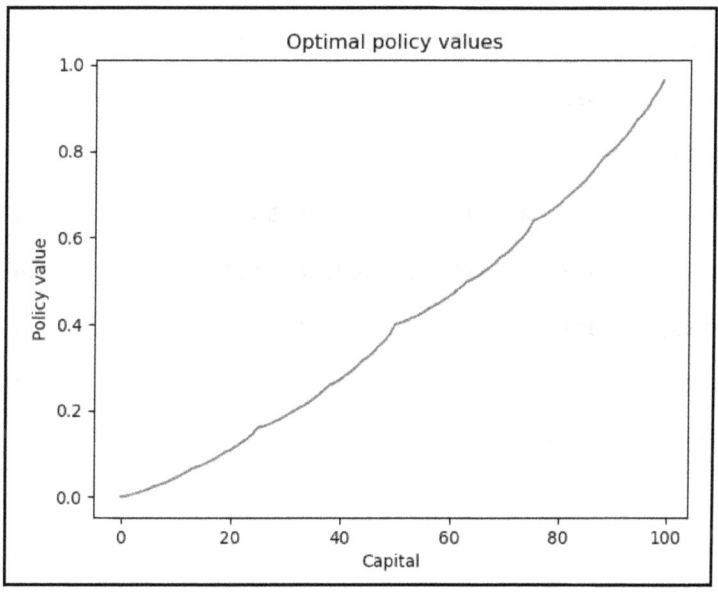

We can see that, as the capital (state) increases, the estimated reward (policy value) also increases, which makes sense.

What we did in *Step 9* is very similar to what we did in the *Solving an MDP with a policy iteration algorithm* recipe, but for the coin-flipping gamble environment this time.

In *Step 10*, the policy improvement function extracts an improved policy out of the given policy values, based on the Bellman optimality equation.

As you can see in *Step 12*, we solved the gamble problem with policy iteration in 2.002 seconds, which is less than half the time it took with value iteration.

The results we got from *Step 13* include the following optimal values:

```
Optimal values:
tensor([0.0000, 0.0021, 0.0052, 0.0092, 0.0129, 0.0174, 0.0231, 0.0278,
0.0323,
        0.0377, 0.0435, 0.0504, 0.0577, 0.0652, 0.0695, 0.0744, 0.0807,
0.0866,
        0.0942, 0.1031, 0.1087, 0.1160, 0.1259, 0.1336, 0.1441, 0.1600,
0.1631,
        0.1677, 0.1738, 0.1794, 0.1861, 0.1946, 0.2017, 0.2084, 0.2165,
0.2252,
        0.2355, 0.2465, 0.2579, 0.2643, 0.2716, 0.2810, 0.2899, 0.3013,
0.3147,
        0.3230, 0.3339, 0.3488, 0.3604, 0.3762, 0.4000, 0.4031, 0.4077,
0.4138,
        0.4194, 0.4261, 0.4346, 0.4417, 0.4484, 0.4565, 0.4652, 0.4755,
0.4865,
        0.4979, 0.5043, 0.5116, 0.5210, 0.5299, 0.5413, 0.5547, 0.5630,
0.5740,
        0.5888, 0.6004, 0.6162, 0.6400, 0.6446, 0.6516, 0.6608, 0.6690,
0.6791,
        0.6919, 0.7026, 0.7126, 0.7248, 0.7378, 0.7533, 0.7697, 0.7868,
0.7965,
        0.8075, 0.8215, 0.8349, 0.8520, 0.8721, 0.8845, 0.9009, 0.9232,
0.9406,
        0.9643, 0.0000])
```

They also include the optimal policy:

```
Optimal policy:
tensor([ 0,  1, 2, 3, 4,  5, 6, 7, 8, 9, 10, 11, 12, 13, 14, 15, 16, 17,
        18, 19, 20, 21, 22, 23, 24, 25, 26, 27, 22, 29, 30, 31, 32, 33,  9,
35,
        36, 37, 38, 11, 40,  9, 42, 43, 44, 5, 4,  3, 2, 1, 50, 1, 2, 47,
         4, 5, 44,  7, 8, 9, 10, 11, 38, 12, 36, 35, 34, 17, 32, 19, 30,
4,
         3, 2, 26, 25, 24, 23, 22, 21, 20, 19, 18, 17, 16, 15, 14, 13, 12,
11,
        10, 9, 8,  7, 6, 5, 4,  3, 2, 1, 0], dtype=torch.int32)
```

The results from the two approaches, value iteration and policy iteration, are consistent.

We have solved the gamble problem by using value iteration and policy iteration. To deal with a reinforcement learning problem, one of the trickiest tasks is to formulate the process into an MDP. In our case, the policy is transformed from the current capital (states) to the new capital (new states) by betting certain stakes (actions). The optimal policy maximizes the probability of winning the game (+1 reward), and evaluates the probability of winning under the optimal policy.

Another interesting thing to note is how the transformation probabilities and new states are determined in the Bellman equation in our example. Taking action a in state s (having capital s and making a bet of 1 dollar) will have two possible outcomes:

- Moving to new state s+a, if the coin lands on heads. Hence, the transformation probability is equal to the probability of heads.
- Moving to new state s-a, if the coin lands on tails. Therefore, the transformation probability is equal to the probability of tails.

This is quite similar to the FrozenLake environment, where the agent lands on the intended tile only by a certain probability.

We also verified that policy iteration converges faster than value iteration in this case. This is because there are up to 50 possible actions, which is more than the 4 actions in FrozenLake. For MDPs with a large number of actions, solving with policy iteration is more efficient than doing so with value iteration.

There's more...

You may want to know whether the optimal policy really works. Let's act like smart gamblers and play 10,000 episodes of the game. We are going to compare the optimal policy with two other strategies: conservative (betting one dollar each round) and random (betting a random amount):

1. We start by defining the three aforementioned betting strategies.

    We define the optimal strategy first:

    ```
    >>> def optimal_strategy(capital):
    ...        return optimal_policy[capital].item()
    ```

    Then we define the conservative strategy:

    ```
    >>> def conservative_strategy(capital):
    ...        return 1
    ```

    Finally, we define the random strategy:

    ```
    >>> def random_strategy(capital):
    ...        return torch.randint(1, capital + 1, (1,)).item()
    ```

2. Define a wrapper function that runs one episode with a strategy and returns whether or not the game was won:

    ```
    >>> def run_episode(head_prob, capital, policy):
    ...        while capital > 0:
    ...            bet = policy(capital)
    ...            if torch.rand(1).item() < head_prob:
    ...                capital += bet
    ...                if capital >= 100:
    ...                    return 1
    ...            else:
    ...                capital -= bet
    ...        return 0
    ```

3. Specify a starting capital (let's say 50 dollars) and a number of episodes (10000):

```
>>> capital = 50
>>> n_episode = 10000
```

4. Run 10,000 episodes and keep track of the winning times:

```
>>> n_win_random = 0
>>> n_win_conservative = 0
>>> n_win_optimal = 0
>>> for episode in range(n_episode):
...         n_win_random += run_episode(
                        head_prob, capital, random_strategy)
...         n_win_conservative += run_episode(
                        head_prob, capital, conservative_strategy)
...         n_win_optimal += run_episode(
                        head_prob, capital, optimal_strategy)
```

5. Print out the winning probabilities for the three strategies:

```
>>> print('Average winning probability under the random
            policy: {}'.format(n_win_random/n_episode))
Average winning probability under the random policy: 0.2251
>>> print('Average winning probability under the conservative
            policy: {}'.format(n_win_conservative/n_episode))
Average winning probability under the conservative policy: 0.0
>>> print('Average winning probability under the optimal
            policy: {}'.format(n_win_optimal/n_episode))
Average winning probability under the optimal policy: 0.3947
```

Our optimal policy is clearly the winner!

3
Monte Carlo Methods for Making Numerical Estimations

In the previous chapter, we evaluated and solved a **Markov Decision Process** (**MDP**) using **dynamic programming** (**DP**). Model-based methods such as DP have some drawbacks. They require the environment to be fully known, including the transition matrix and reward matrix. They also have limited scalability, especially for environments with plenty of states.

In this chapter, we will continue our learning journey with a model-free approach, the **Monte Carlo** (**MC**) methods, which have no requirement of prior knowledge of the environment and are much more scalable than DP. We will start by estimating the value of Pi with the Monte Carlo method. Moving on, we will talk about how to use the MC method to predict state values and state-action values in a first-visit and every-visit manner. We will demonstrate training an agent to play the Blackjack card game using Monte Carlo. Also, we will implement on-policy and off-policy MC control to find the optimal policy for Blackjack. Advanced MC control with epsilon-greedy policy and weighted importance sampling will also be covered.

The following recipes will be covered in this chapter:

- Calculating Pi using the Monte Carlo method
- Performing Monte Carlo policy evaluation
- Playing Blackjack with Monte Carlo prediction
- Performing on-policy Monte Carlo control
- Developing Monte Carlo control with epsilon-greedy policy
- Performing off-policy Monte Carlo control
- Developing MC control with weighted importance sampling

Calculating Pi using the Monte Carlo method

Let's get started with a simple project: estimating the value of π using the Monte Carlo method, which is the core of model-free reinforcement learning algorithms.

A **Monte Carlo method** is any method that uses randomness to solve problems. The algorithm repeats suitable **random sampling** and observes the fraction of samples that obey particular properties in order to make numerical estimations.

Let's do a fun exercise where we approximate the value of π using the MC method. We'll place a large number of random points in a square whose width = 2 (-1<x<1, -1<y<1), and count how many points fall within the circle of unit radius. We all know that the area of the square is:

$$C = 2^2 = 4$$

And the area of the circle is:

$$S = \pi * 1^2 = \pi$$

If we divide the area of the circle by the area of the square, we have the following:

$$S/C = \pi/4$$

S/C can be measured by the fraction of points falling within the circle. As a result, the value of π can be estimated as four times *S/C*.

How to do it...

We use the MC method to estimate the value of π as follows:

1. Import the necessary modules, including PyTorch, `math` for the true value of π, and `matplotlib` to plot the random points in the square:

```
>>> import torch
>>> import math
>>> import matplotlib.pyplot as plt
```

2. We randomly generate 1,000 points within the square, with the range of -1<x<1 and -1<y<1:

```
>>> n_point = 1000
>>> points = torch.rand((n_point, 2)) * 2 - 1
```

3. Initialize the number of points falling within the unit circle, and a list storing those points:

```
>>> n_point_circle = 0
>>> points_circle = []
```

4. For each random point, calculate the distance to the origin. A point falls within the circle if the distance is less than 1:

```
>>> for point in points:
...     r = torch.sqrt(point[0] ** 2 + point[1] ** 2)
...     if r <= 1:
...         points_circle.append(point)
...         n_point_circle += 1
```

5. Count the number of points in the circle and keep track of those points:

```
>>> points_circle = torch.stack(points_circle)
```

6. Plot all random points and use a different color for those in the circle:

```
>>> plt.plot(points[:, 0].numpy(), points[:, 1].numpy(), 'y.')
>>> plt.plot(points_circle[:, 0].numpy(), points_circle[:,
1].numpy(), 'c.')
```

7. Draw the circle for better visualization:

```
>>> i = torch.linspace(0, 2 * math.pi)
>>> plt.plot(torch.cos(i).numpy(), torch.sin(i).numpy())
>>> plt.axes().set_aspect('equal')
>>> plt.show()
```

8. Finally, calculate the value of π:

```
>>> pi_estimated = 4 * (n_point_circle / n_point)
>>> print('Estimated value of pi is:', pi_estimated)
```

How it works...

In *Step 5*, you will see the following plot, where dots are randomly placed inside the circle:

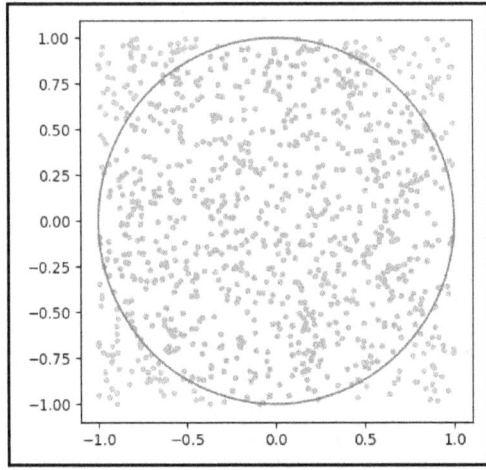

The Monte Carlo method is so powerful thanks to the **Law of Large Numbers** (**LLN**). Under LLN, the average performance of a large number of repeated events or actions will eventually converge to the expected value. In our case, with a large number of random points, `4 * (n_point_circle / n_point)` will eventually converge to the true value of π.

Finally, in *Step 8*, we print the estimated value of pi and get the following result:

```
Estimated value of pi is: 3.156
```

The value of π approximated using the Monte Carlo method is quite close to its true value (3.14159...).

There's more...

We can further improve our estimation with more iterations than 1,000. Here, we'll experiment with 10,000 iterations. In each iteration, we randomly generate a point in the square and see whether it is in the circle; we estimate the value of π on the fly based on the fraction of existing points falling within the circle.

We then plot the estimation history along with the true value of π. Put these into the following function:

```
>>> def estimate_pi_mc(n_iteration):
...     n_point_circle = 0
...     pi_iteration = []
...     for i in range(1, n_iteration+1):
...         point = torch.rand(2) * 2 - 1
...         r = torch.sqrt(point[0] ** 2 + point[1] ** 2)
...         if r <= 1:
...             n_point_circle += 1
...         pi_iteration.append(4 * (n_point_circle / i))
...     plt.plot(pi_iteration)
...     plt.plot([math.pi] * n_iteration, '--')
...     plt.xlabel('Iteration')
...     plt.ylabel('Estimated pi')
...     plt.title('Estimation history')
...     plt.show()
...     print('Estimated value of pi is:', pi_iteration[-1])

The estimated value of pi is: 3.1364
```

And we call this function with 10,000 iterations:

```
>>> estimate_pi_mc(10000)
```

Refer to the following plot for the resulting estimation history:

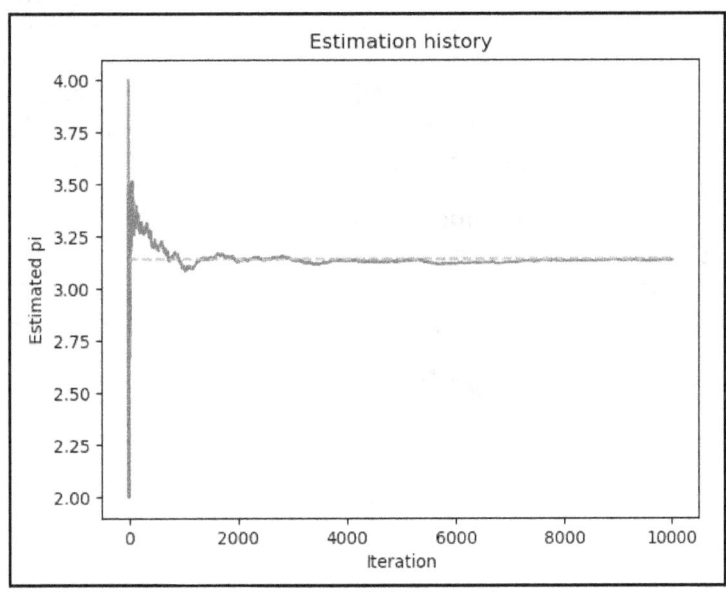

We can see that with more iterations, the estimation of π is getting closer to the true value. There is always some variation in an event or action. More repetitions can help smooth it out.

See also

If you are interested in seeing more applications of the Monte Carlo method, here are some interesting ones:

- *Playing games such as Go, Havannah, and Battleship, with MC tree search, which searches for the best move*: https://en.wikipedia.org/wiki/Monte_Carlo_tree_search
- *Assessing investments and portfolio*: https://en.wikipedia.org/wiki/Monte_Carlo_methods_in_finance
- *Studying biological systems with MC simulations*: https://en.wikipedia.org/wiki/Bayesian_inference_in_phylogeny

Performing Monte Carlo policy evaluation

In `Chapter 2`, *Markov Decision Process and Dynamic Programming*, we applied DP to perform policy evaluation, which is the value (or state-value) function of a policy. It works really well, but has some limitations. Fundamentally, it requires a fully known environment, including the transition matrix and reward matrix. However, the transition matrix in most real-life situations is not known beforehand. A reinforcement learning algorithm that needs a known MDP is categorized as a **model-based** algorithm. On the other hand, one with no requirement of prior knowledge of transitions and rewards is called a **model-free** algorithm. Monte Carlo-based reinforcement learning is a model-free approach.

In this recipe, we will evaluate the value function using the Monte Carlo method. We will use the FrozenLake environment again as an example, assuming we don't have access to both of its transition and reward matrices. You will recall that the **returns** of a process, which are the total rewards over the long run, are as follows:

$$G_t = \sum_k \gamma^k R_{t+k+1}$$

MC policy evaluation uses **empirical mean return** instead of **expected return** (as in DP) to estimate the value function. There are two ways to perform MC policy evaluation. One is **first-visit MC prediction**, which averages the returns **only** for the **first occurrence** of a state, s, in an episode. Another one is **every-visit MC prediction**, which averages the returns for **every occurrence** of a state, s, in an episode. Obviously, first-visit MC prediction has a lot fewer calculations than the every-visit version, hence it is more frequently used.

How to do it...

We perform first-visit MC prediction for the optimal policy of FrozenLake as follows:

1. Import the PyTorch and Gym libraries, and create an instance of the FrozenLake environment:

```
>>> import torch
>>> import gym
>>> env = gym.make("FrozenLake-v0")
```

2. To evaluate a policy using the Monte Carlo method, we first need to define a function that simulates a FrozenLake episode given a policy and returns the reward and state for each step:

```
>>> def run_episode(env, policy):
...         state = env.reset()
...         rewards = []
...         states = [state]
...         is_done = False
...         while not is_done:
...             action = policy[state].item()
...             state, reward, is_done, info = env.step(action)
...             states.append(state)
...             rewards.append(reward)
...             if is_done:
...                 break
...         states = torch.tensor(states)
...         rewards = torch.tensor(rewards)
...         return states, rewards
```

Again, in the Monte Carlo setting, we need to keep track of the states and rewards for all steps, since we don't have access to the full environment, including the transition probabilities and reward matrix.

3. Now, define the function that evaluates the given policy with first-visit MC:

```
>>> def mc_prediction_first_visit(env, policy, gamma, n_episode):
...      n_state = policy.shape[0]
...      V = torch.zeros(n_state)
...      N = torch.zeros(n_state)
...      for episode in range(n_episode):
...          states_t, rewards_t = run_episode(env, policy)
...          return_t = 0
...          first_visit = torch.zeros(n_state)
...          G = torch.zeros(n_state)
...          for state_t, reward_t in zip(reversed(states_t)[1:],
                                          reversed(rewards_t)):
...              return_t = gamma * return_t + reward_t
...              G[state_t] = return_t
...              first_visit[state_t] = 1
...          for state in range(n_state):
...              if first_visit[state] > 0:
...                  V[state] += G[state]
...                  N[state] += 1
...      for state in range(n_state):
...          if N[state] > 0:
...              V[state] = V[state] / N[state]
...      return V
```

4. We specify the discount rate as 1 for easier computation, and simulate 10,000 episodes:

```
>>> gamma = 1
>>> n_episode = 10000
```

5. We use the optimal policy calculated in the previous chapter, *Markov Decision Process and Dynamic Programming*, and feed it to the first-visit MC function, along with other parameters:

```
>>> optimal_policy = torch.tensor([0., 3., 3., 3., 0., 3., 2., 3.,
3., 1., 0., 3., 3., 2., 1., 3.])
>>> value = mc_prediction_first_visit(env, optimal_policy, gamma,
n_episode)
>>> print('The value function calculated by first-visit MC
prediction:\n', value)
The value function calculated by first-visit MC prediction:
tensor([0.7463, 0.5004, 0.4938, 0.4602, 0.7463, 0.0000, 0.3914,
0.0000, 0.7463, 0.7469, 0.6797, 0.0000, 0.0000, 0.8038, 0.8911,
0.0000])
```

We have just solved the value function of the optimal policy using first-visit MC prediction.

How it works...

In *Step 3*, we perform the following tasks in MC prediction:

- We run `n_episode` episodes
- For each episode, we compute the returns for the first visit of each state
- For each state, we obtain the value by averaging its first returns from all episodes

As you can see, in MC-based prediction, it is not necessary to know about the full model of the environment. In fact, in most real-world cases, the transition matrix and reward matrix are not known beforehand, or are extremely difficult to obtain. Imagine how many possible states there are playing chess or Go and the number of possible actions; it is almost impossible to work out the transition matrix and reward matrix. Model-free reinforcement learning is about learning from experience by interacting with the environment.

In our case, we only considered what could be observed, which included the new state and reward in each step, and made predictions using the Monte Carlo method. Note that the more episodes we simulate, the more accurate predictions we can obtain. If you plot the value updated after each episode, you will see how it converges over time, which is similar to what we saw when estimating the value of π.

There's more...

We decide to also perform every-visit MC prediction for the optimal policy of FrozenLake:

1. We define the function that evaluates the given policy with every-visit MC:

```
>>> def mc_prediction_every_visit(env, policy, gamma, n_episode):
...        n_state = policy.shape[0]
...        V = torch.zeros(n_state)
...        N = torch.zeros(n_state)
...        G = torch.zeros(n_state)
...        for episode in range(n_episode):
...            states_t, rewards_t = run_episode(env, policy)
...            return_t = 0
...            for state_t, reward_t in zip(reversed(states_t)[1:],
...                                         reversed(rewards_t)):
...                return_t = gamma * return_t + reward_t
...                G[state_t] += return_t
...                N[state_t] += 1
...        for state in range(n_state):
...            if N[state] > 0:
...                V[state] = G[state] / N[state]
...        return V
```

Similar to first-visit MC, the every-visit function does the following tasks:

- It runs `n_episode` episodes
- For each episode, it computes the returns for each visit of a state
- For each state, it obtains the value by averaging all of its returns from all episodes

2. Compute the value by feeding the policy and other parameters in the function:

```
>>> value = mc_prediction_every_visit(env, optimal_policy, gamma,
n_episode)
```

3. Display the resulting value:

```
>>> print('The value function calculated by every-visit MC
prediction:\n', value)
The value function calculated by every-visit MC prediction:
tensor([0.6221, 0.4322, 0.3903, 0.3578, 0.6246, 0.0000, 0.3520,
0.0000, 0.6428, 0.6759, 0.6323, 0.0000, 0.0000, 0.7624, 0.8801,
0.0000])
```

Playing Blackjack with Monte Carlo prediction

In this recipe, we will play Blackjack (also called 21) and evaluate a policy we think might work well. You will get more familiar with Monte Carlo prediction with the Blackjack example, and get ready to search for the optimal policy using Monte Carlo control in the upcoming recipes.

Blackjack is a popular card game where the goal is to have the sum of cards as close to 21 as possible without exceeding it. The J, K, and Q cards have a points value of 10, and cards from 2 to 10 have values from 2 to 10. The ace card can be either 1 or 11 points; when the latter value is chosen, it is called a **usable** ace. The player competes against a dealer. At the beginning, both parties are given two random cards, but only one of the dealer's cards is revealed to the player. The player can request additional cards (called **hit**) or stop receiving any more cards (called **stick**). After the player sticks, the dealer keeps drawing cards until the sum of cards is greater than or equal to 17. Before the player calls **stick**, if the sum of their cards exceeds 21 (called going **bust**), the player loses. Otherwise, if the sum of the dealer's cards exceeds 21, the player wins.

If neither of the two parties goes bust, the one with the highest score will win or it may be a draw. The Blackjack environment in Gym is formulated as follows:

- An episode of the Blackjack finite MDP starts with two cards for each party, and only one of the dealer's cards is observed.
- An episode ends with either party winning or the parties drawing. The final reward of an episode is +1 if the player wins, -1 if they lose, or 0 if a draw occurs.
- In each round, two actions can be taken by the player, hit (1) and stick (0), meaning requesting another card and requesting to not receive any further cards.

We'll first experiment with a simple policy where we keep adding new cards as long as the total number of points is less than 18 (or 19 or 20 if you prefer).

How to do it...

Let's start by simulating the Blackjack environment and exploring its states and actions:

1. Import PyTorch and Gym, and create a `Blackjack` instance:

```
>>> import torch
>>> import gym
>>> env = gym.make('Blackjack-v0')
```

2. Reset the environment:

```
>>> env.reset()
>>> env.reset()
(20, 5, False)
```

It returns three state variables:

- The player's points (`20` in this example)
- The dealer's points (`5` in this example)
- Whether the player has a usable ace (`False` in this example)

A usable ace means the player has an ace that can be counted as 11 without them going bust. If the player doesn't have an ace, or has an ace but it makes them bust, the state parameter will become `False`.

Take a look at the following episode :

```
>>> env.reset()
(18, 6, True)
```

The 18 points and `True` means that the player has an ace and a 7, and the ace is counted as 11.

3. Let's take some actions and see how the Blackjack environment works. First, we take a hit (requesting an additional card) since we have a usable ace, which offers some flexibility:

```
>>> env.step(1)
((20, 6, True), 0, False, {})
```

This returns three state variables `(20, 6, True)`, a reward (0 for now), and whether the episode ends or not (`False` for now).

We then stop drawing cards:

```
>>> env.step(0)
((20, 6, True), 1, True, {})
```

We just won in this episode, hence the reward is 1, and now the episode ends. Again, once the player calls **stick**, the dealer will take their actions.

4. Sometimes we lose; for example:

```
>>> env.reset()
(15, 10, False)
>>> env.step(1)
((25, 10, False), -1, True, {})
```

Next, we'll predict the value for a simple policy where we stop adding new cards when the score reaches 18:

5. As always, we first need to define a function that simulates a Blackjack episode under a simple policy:

```
>>> def run_episode(env, hold_score):
...         state = env.reset()
...         rewards = []
...         states = [state]
...         is_done = False
...         while not is_done:
...             action = 1 if state[0] < hold_score else 0
...             state, reward, is_done, info = env.step(action)
...             states.append(state)
...             rewards.append(reward)
...             if is_done:
...                 break
...         return states, rewards
```

6. Now, we define a function that evaluates a simple Blackjack policy with a first-visit MC:

```
>>> from collections import defaultdict
>>> def mc_prediction_first_visit(env, hold_score, gamma,
                                                n_episode):
...         V = defaultdict(float)
...         N = defaultdict(int)
...         for episode in range(n_episode):
...             states_t, rewards_t = run_episode(env, hold_score)
...             return_t = 0
...             G = {}
...             for state_t, reward_t in zip(states_t[1::-1],
                                                rewards_t[::-1]):
...                 return_t = gamma * return_t + reward_t
...                 G[state_t] = return_t
...             for state, return_t in G.items():
...                 if state[0] <= 21:
...                     V[state] += return_t
...                     N[state] += 1
...         for state in V:
...             V[state] = V[state] / N[state]
...         return V
```

7. We specify `hold_score` as 18, the discount rate as 1, and simulate 500,000 episodes:

```
>>> hold_score = 18
>>> gamma = 1
>>> n_episode = 500000
```

8. Now, let's perform MC prediction by plugging in all the variables:

```
>>> value = mc_prediction_first_visit(env, hold_score, gamma,
n_episode)
```

We try to print the resulting value function:

```
>>> print('The value function calculated by first-visit MC
prediction:\n', value)
```

We have just computed the values for all possible states:

```
>>> print('Number of states:', len(value))
Number of states: 280
```

And there are 280 states in total.

How it works...

As you can see, in *Step 4*, our points exceed 21, so we lose. Again, the state in Blackjack is actually a three-element tuple. The first element is the player's score; the second element is the revealed card from the dealer's deck, whose value can be from 1 to 10; and the third element is about having a reusable ace or not.

It is worth noting that in *Step 5*, in each round of an episode, the agent takes a hit or sticks based on the current score, sticking if it is less than `hold_score`, and taking a hit otherwise. Again, in the Monte Carlo setting, we keep track of the states and rewards for all steps.

Executing the lines of code in *Step 8*, you will see the following result:

```
The value function calculated by first-visit MC prediction:
defaultdict(<class 'float'>, {(20, 6, False): 0.6923485653560042, (17, 5,
False): -0.24390243902439024, (16, 5, False): -0.19118165784832453, (20,
10, False): 0.4326379146490474, (20, 7, False): 0.7686220540168588, (16, 6,
False): -0.19249478804725503,
......
......
(5, 9, False): -0.20612244897959184, (12, 7, True): 0.058823529411764705,
(6, 4, False): -0.26582278481012656, (4, 8, False): -0.14937759336099585,
(4, 3, False): -0.1680327868852459, (4, 9, False): -0.20276497695852536,
(4, 4, False): -0.3201754385964912, (12, 8, True): 0.11057692307692307})
```

We have just experienced how effective it is to compute the value function of 280 states in the Blackjack environment using MC prediction. In the MC prediction function in *Step 2*, we performed the following tasks:

- We ran `n_episode` episodes under the simple Blackjack policy
- For each episode, we computed the returns for the first visit of each state
- For each state, we obtained the value by averaging its first returns from all episodes

Note that we ignore states where the player's sum is greater than 21 since we know they are all going to be -1.

The model of the Blackjack environment, including the transition matrix and reward matrix, is not known beforehand. Moreover, obtaining the transition probabilities between two states is extremely costly. In fact, the transition matrix would be of size 280 * 280 * 2, which would require a lot of computation. In the MC-based solution, we just need to simulate sufficient episodes, and, for each episode, compute the returns and update the value function accordingly.

Next time you play Blackjack with the simple policy (stick if the sum reaches a certain level), it would be interesting to use the predicted values to decide how much to bid in each game.

There's more...

Because there are so many states in this case, it is difficult to read their values one by one. We can actually visualize the value function by making three-dimensional surface plots. The state is three-dimensional, and the third dimension comes with two possible options (having a usable ace or not). We can split our plots into two parts: one for states with a usable ace, and the other for states without a usable ace. In each plot, the x axis is the player's sum, the y axis is the dealer's revealed card, and the z axis is the value.

Let's follow these steps to create the visualization:

1. Import all the necessary modules in matplotlib for visualization:

```
>>> import matplotlib
>>> import matplotlib.pyplot as plt
>>> from mpl_toolkits.mplot3d import Axes3D
```

2. Define a utility function that creates a 3D surface plot:

```
>>> def plot_surface(X, Y, Z, title):
...     fig = plt.figure(figsize=(20, 10))
...     ax = fig.add_subplot(111, projection='3d')
...     surf = ax.plot_surface(X, Y, Z, rstride=1, cstride=1,
...             cmap=matplotlib.cm.coolwarm, vmin=-1.0, vmax=1.0)
...     ax.set_xlabel('Player Sum')
...     ax.set_ylabel('Dealer Showing')
...     ax.set_zlabel('Value')
...     ax.set_title(title)
...     ax.view_init(ax.elev, -120)
...     fig.colorbar(surf)
...     plt.show()
```

3. Next, we define a function that constructs the arrays to be plotted along three dimensions and calls the `plot_surface` to visualize the value with and without a usable ace, respectively:

```
>>> def plot_blackjack_value(V):
...     player_sum_range = range(12, 22)
...     dealer_show_range = range(1, 11)
...     X, Y = torch.meshgrid([torch.tensor(player_sum_range),
...             torch.tensor(dealer_show_range)])
```

```
...      values_to_plot = torch.zeros((len(player_sum_range),
                                   len(dealer_show_range), 2))
...      for i, player in enumerate(player_sum_range):
...          for j, dealer in enumerate(dealer_show_range):
...              for k, ace in enumerate([False, True]):
...                  values_to_plot[i, j, k] =
                                 V[(player, dealer, ace)]
...      plot_surface(X, Y, values_to_plot[:,:,0].numpy(),
               "Blackjack Value Function Without Usable Ace")
...      plot_surface(X, Y, values_to_plot[:,:,1].numpy(),
               "Blackjack Value Function With Usable Ace")
```

We are only interested in looking at states where the player's score is more than 11 and we create a `values_to_plot` tensor to store those values.

4. Finally, we call the `plot_blackjack_value` function:

```
>>> plot_blackjack_value(value)
```

The resulting value plot for states without a usable ace is as follows:

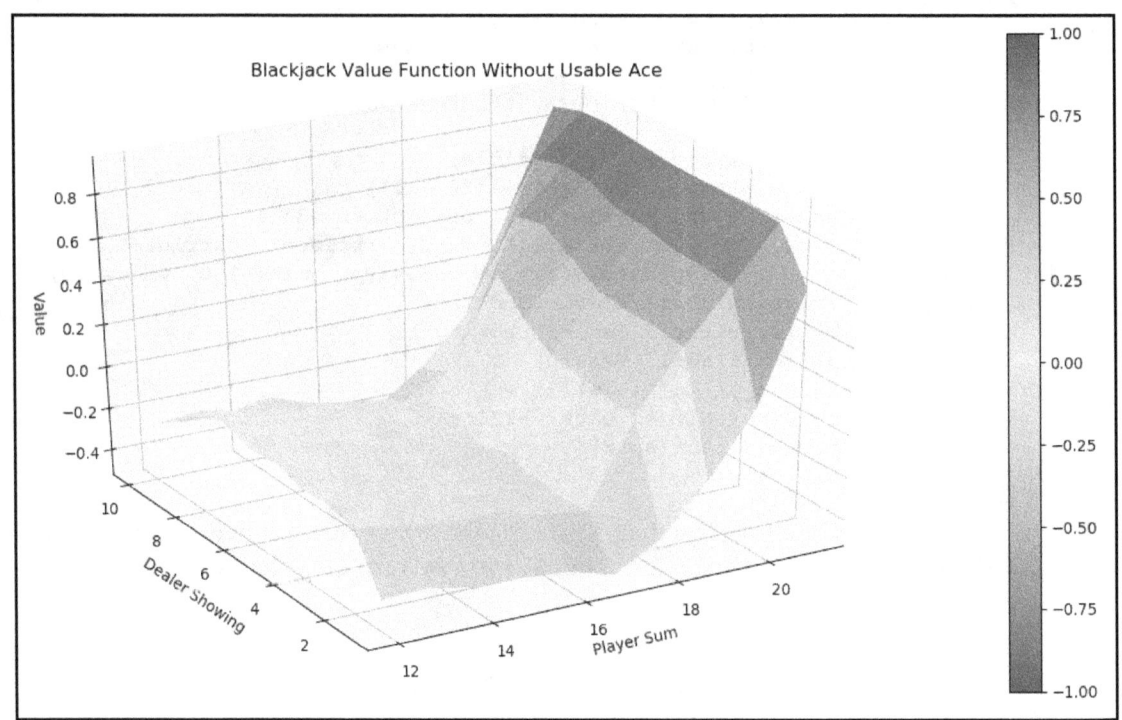

And the value function for states with a usable ace is visualized as follows:

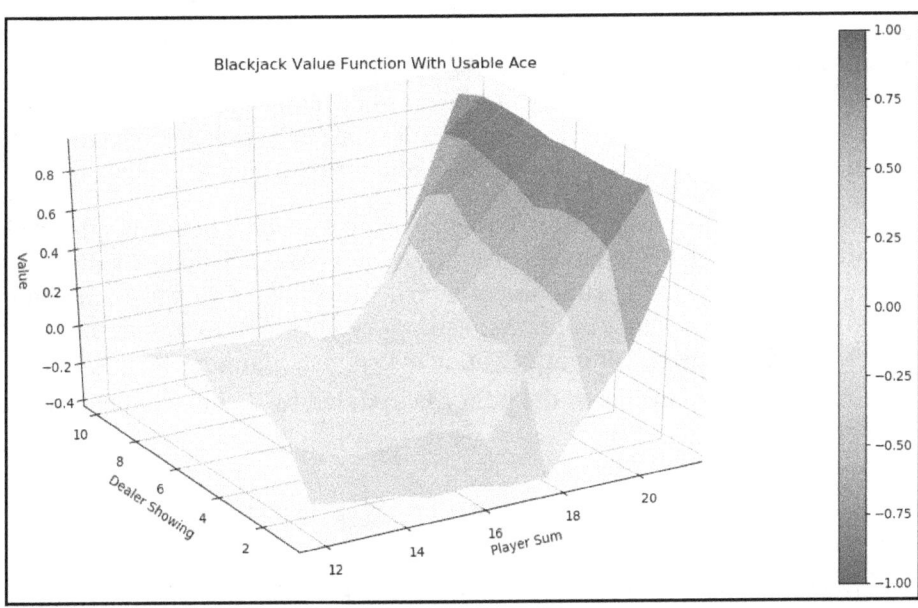

Feel free to play around with the value of `hold_score` and see how it affects the value function.

See also

If the Blackjack environment is new to you, you can learn more about it from the source code at `https://github.com/openai/gym/blob/master/gym/envs/toy_text/blackjack.py`.

Sometimes, it is easier to read code than to read a plain English description.

Performing on-policy Monte Carlo control

In the previous recipe, we predicted the value of a policy where the agent holds if the score gets to 18. This is a simple policy that everyone can easily come up with, although obviously not the optimal one. In this recipe, we will search for the optimal policy to play Blackjack, using on-policy Monte Carlo control.

Monte Carlo prediction is used to evaluate the value for a given policy, while **Monte Carlo control** (**MC control**) is for finding the optimal policy when such a policy is not given. There are basically categories of MC control: on-policy and off-policy. **On-policy** methods learn about the optimal policy by executing the policy and evaluating and improving it, while **off-policy** methods learn about the optimal policy using data generated by another policy. The way on-policy MC control works is quite similar to policy iteration in dynamic programming, which has two phases, evaluation and improvement:

- In the evaluation phase, instead of evaluating the value function (also called the **state value**, or **utility**), it evaluates the action-value. The **action-value** is more frequently called the **Q-function**, which is the utility of a state-action pair *(s, a)* by taking action a in state *s* under a given policy. Again, the evaluation can be conducted in a first-visit manner or an every-visit manner.

- In the improvement phase, the policy is updated by assigning the optimal action to each state:

$$\pi(s) = argmax_a Q(s, a)$$

The optimal policy will be obtained by alternating two phases for a large number of iterations.

How to do it...

Let's search for the optimal Blackjack policy with on-policy MC control by taking the following steps:

1. Import the necessary modules and create a Blackjack instance:

```
>>> import torch
>>> import gym
>>> env = gym.make('Blackjack-v0')
```

2. Next, let's develop a function that runs an episode and takes actions under a Q-function. This is the improvement phase:

```
>>> def run_episode(env, Q, n_action):
...         """
...         Run a episode given a Q-function
...         @param env: OpenAI Gym environment
...         @param Q: Q-function
...         @param n_action: action space
...         @return: resulting states, actions and rewards for the
```

```
entire episode
...         """
...         state = env.reset()
...         rewards = []
...         actions = []
...         states = []
...         is_done = False
...         action = torch.randint(0, n_action, [1]).item()
...         while not is_done:
...             actions.append(action)
...             states.append(state)
...             state, reward, is_done, info = env.step(action)
...             rewards.append(reward)
...             if is_done:
...                 break
...             action = torch.argmax(Q[state]).item()
...         return states, actions, rewards
```

3. Now, we develop the on-policy MC control algorithm:

```
>>> from collections import defaultdict
>>> def mc_control_on_policy(env, gamma, n_episode):
...         """
...         Obtain the optimal policy with on-policy MC control method
...         @param env: OpenAI Gym environment
...         @param gamma: discount factor
...         @param n_episode: number of episodes
...         @return: the optimal Q-function, and the optimal policy
...         """
...         n_action = env.action_space.n
...         G_sum = defaultdict(float)
...         N = defaultdict(int)
...         Q = defaultdict(lambda: torch.empty(env.action_space.n))
...         for episode in range(n_episode):
...             states_t, actions_t, rewards_t = run_episode(env, Q,
                                                             n_action)
...             return_t = 0
...             G = {}
...             for state_t, action_t, reward_t in zip(states_t[::-1],
                     actions_t[::-1], rewards_t[::-1]):
...                 return_t = gamma * return_t + reward_t
...                 G[(state_t, action_t)] = return_t
...             for state_action, return_t in G.items():
...                 state, action = state_action
...                 if state[0] <= 21:
...                     G_sum[state_action] += return_t
...                     N[state_action] += 1
...                     Q[state][action] = G_sum[state_action]
```

```
                                               / N[state_action]
    . . .          policy = {}
    . . .          for state, actions in Q.items():
    . . .              policy[state] = torch.argmax(actions).item()
    . . .          return Q, policy
```

4. We specify the discount rate as 1, and will use 500,000 episodes:

```
>>> gamma = 1
>>> n_episode = 500000
```

5. Perform on-policy MC control to obtain the optimal Q-function and policy:

```
>>> optimal_Q, optimal_policy = mc_control_on_policy(env, gamma,
n_episode)
>>> print(optimal_policy)
```

6. We can also calculate the value function of the optimal policy and print out the optimal value as follows:

```
>>> optimal_value = defaultdict(float)
>>> for state, action_values in optimal_Q.items():
...        optimal_value[state] = torch.max(action_values).item()
>>> print(optimal_value)
```

7. Visualize the value using `plot_blackjack_value` and the `plot_surface` function we developed in the previous recipe, *Playing Blackjack with Monte Carlo prediction*:

```
>>> plot_blackjack_value(optimal_value)
```

How it works...

In this recipe, we solve the Blackjack game with on-policy MC control by exploring starts. This accomplishes our policy optimization goal by alternating between evaluation and improvement with each episode we simulate.

In *Step 2*, we run an episode and take actions under a Q-function by performing the following tasks:

- We initialize an episode.
- We take a random action as an exploring start.
- After the first action, we take actions based on the current Q-function, that is, $a^* = argmax_a Q(s, a)$.

- We record the states, actions, and rewards for all steps in the episode, which will be used in the evaluation phase.

It is important to note that the first action is picked randomly because the MC control algorithm will converge to the optimal solution only in such cases. Starting an episode with a random action in the MC algorithm is called **exploring starts**.

In the exploring starts setting, the first action in an episode is chosen randomly, in order to ensure the policy converges to the optimal solution. Otherwise, some states are never visited, so their state-action values are never optimized, and the policy will become suboptimal in the end.

Step 2 is the improvement phase, and *Step 3* is for MC control, where we perform the following tasks:

- Initialize the Q-function with arbitrary small values.
- Run n_episode episodes.
- For each episode, perform policy improvement and obtain the states, actions, and rewards; and perform policy evaluation using first-visit MC prediction based on the resulting states, actions, and rewards, which updates the Q-function.
- In the end, the optimal Q-function is finalized and the optimal policy is obtained by taking the best action for each state in the optimal Q-function.

In each iteration, we make the policy greedy by taking the optimal action with respect to the current action-value function Q (that is, $\pi(s) = argmax_a Q(s, a)$). As a result, we will be able to obtain an optimal policy, even though we started with an arbitrary policy.

In *Step 5,* you can see the resulting optimal policy, as follows:

```
{(16, 8, True): 1, (11, 2, False): 1, (15, 5, True): 1, (14, 9, False): 1,
(11, 6, False): 1, (20, 3, False): 0, (9, 6, False): 0, (12, 9, False): 0,
(21, 2, True): 0, (16, 10, False): 1, (17, 5, False): 0, (13, 10, False):
1, (12, 10, False): 1, (14, 10, False): 0, (10, 2, False): 1, (20, 4,
False): 0, (11, 4, False): 1, (16, 9, False): 0, (10, 8,
......

......
1, (18, 6, True): 0, (12, 2, True): 1, (8, 3, False): 1, (13, 3, True): 0,
(4, 7, False): 1, (18, 8, True): 0, (6, 5, False): 1, (17, 6, True): 0,
(19, 9, True): 0, (4, 4, False): 0, (14, 5, True): 1, (12, 6, True): 0, (4,
9, False): 1, (13, 4, True): 1, (4, 8, False): 1, (14, 3, True): 1, (12, 4,
True): 1, (4, 6, False): 0, (12, 5, True): 0, (4, 2, False): 1, (4, 3,
False): 1, (5, 4, False): 1, (4, 1, False): 0}
```

In *Step 6,* you can see the resulting values for the optimal policy, as follows:

```
{(21, 8, False): 0.9262458682060242, (11, 8, False): 0.16684606671333313,
(16, 10, False): -0.4662476181983948, (16, 10, True): -0.3643564283847809,
(14, 8, False): -0.2743947207927704, (13, 10, False): -0.3887477219104767,
(12, 9, False): -0.22795115411281586
......
......
(4, 3, False): -0.18421052396297455, (4, 8, False): -0.16806723177433014,
(13, 2, True): 0.05485232174396515, (5, 5, False): -0.09459459781646729,
(5, 8, False): -0.3690987229347229, (20, 2, True): 0.6965699195861816, (17,
2, True): -0.09696969389915466, (12, 2, True): 0.0517241396009922}
```

In *Step 7,* you will see the resulting value plot for states without a usable ace, as follows:

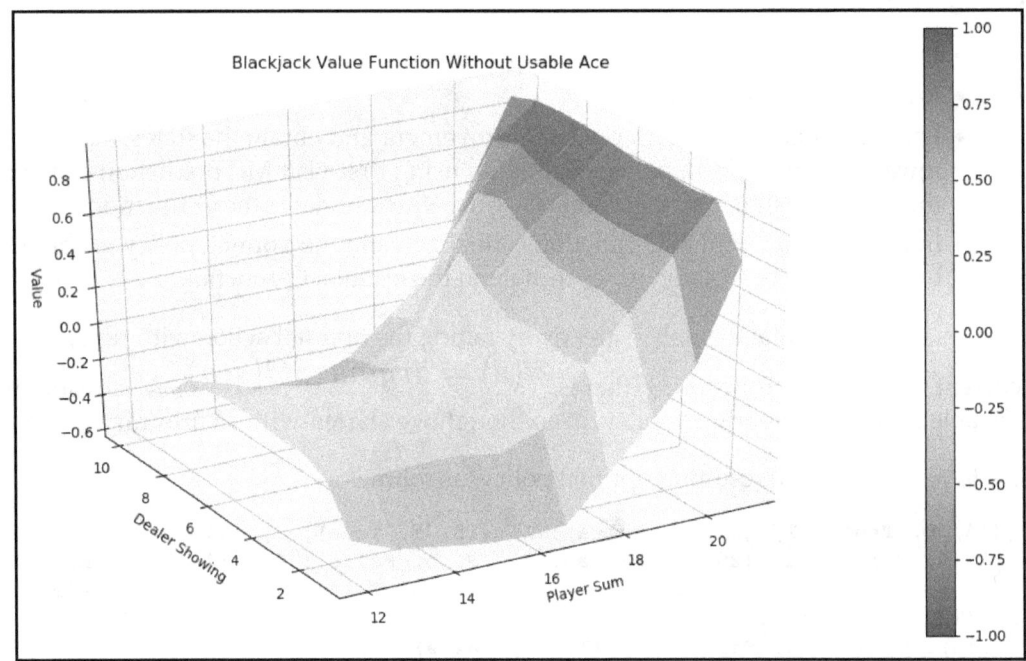

And the value function for states with a usable ace is visualized as follows:

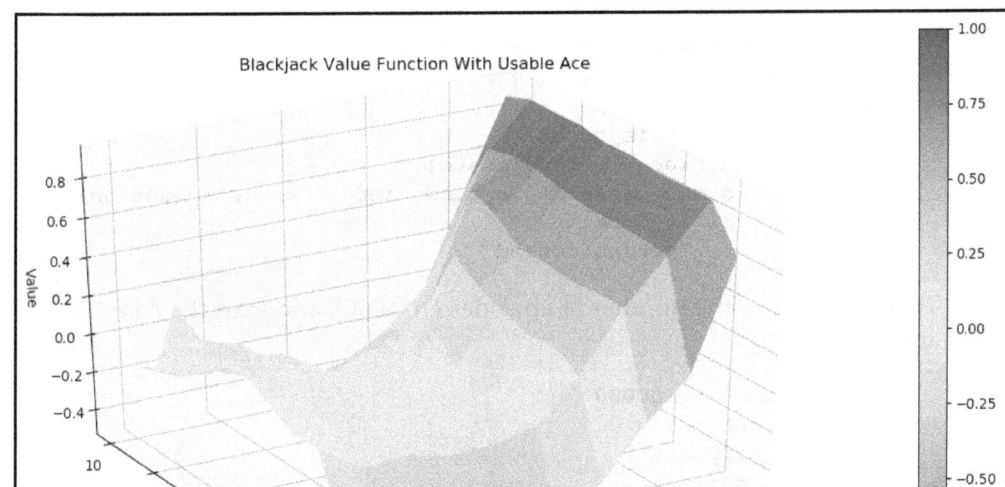

There's more...

You may want to know whether the optimal policy really works better than the simple policy. Let's now simulate 100,000 Blackjack episodes under the optimal policy and the simple policy, respectively. We will compare the chances of winning and losing for both policies:

1. First, we define the simple policy where the **stick** action is taken when the score reaches 18:

```
>>> hold_score = 18
>>> hold_policy = {}
>>> player_sum_range = range(2, 22)
>>> for player in range(2, 22):
...     for dealer in range(1, 11):
...         action = 1 if player < hold_score else 0
...         hold_policy[(player, dealer, False)] = action
...         hold_policy[(player, dealer, True)] = action
```

2. Next, we define a wrapper function that runs one episode under a given policy and returns the final reward:

```
>>> def simulate_episode(env, policy):
...         state = env.reset()
...         is_done = False
...         while not is_done:
...             action = policy[state]
...             state, reward, is_done, info = env.step(action)
...             if is_done:
...                 return reward
```

3. Then, we specify the number of episodes (100,000), and start the count of wins and losses:

```
>>> n_episode = 100000
>>> n_win_optimal = 0
>>> n_win_simple = 0
>>> n_lose_optimal = 0
>>> n_lose_simple = 0
```

4. Then, we run 100,000 episodes and keep track of the wins and losses:

```
>>> for _ in range(n_episode):
...         reward = simulate_episode(env, optimal_policy)
...         if reward == 1:
...             n_win_optimal += 1
...         elif reward == -1:
...             n_lose_optimal += 1
...         reward = simulate_episode(env, hold_policy)
...         if reward == 1:
...             n_win_simple += 1
...         elif reward == -1:
...             n_lose_simple += 1
```

5. Finally, we print out the results we get:

```
>>> print('Winning probability under the simple policy:
{}'.format(n_win_simple/n_episode))
Winning probability under the simple policy: 0.39923
>>> print('Winning probability under the optimal policy:
{}'.format(n_win_optimal/n_episode))
Winning probability under the optimal policy: 0.41281
```

Playing under the optimal policy has a 41.28% chance of winning, while playing under the simple policy has a 39.92% chance. Then, we have the probability of losing:

```
>>> print('Losing probability under the simple policy:
{}'.format(n_lose_simple/n_episode))
Losing probability under the simple policy: 0.51024
>>> print('Losing probability under the optimal policy:
{}'.format(n_lose_optimal/n_episode))
Losing probability under the optimal policy: 0.493
```

On the other hand, playing under the optimal policy has a 49.3% chance of losing, while playing under the simple policy has a 51.02% chance.

Our optimal policy is clearly the winner!

Developing MC control with epsilon-greedy policy

In the previous recipe, we searched for the optimal policy using MC control with greedy search where the action with the highest state-action value was selected. However, the best choice available in early episodes does not guarantee an optimal solution. If we just focus on what is temporarily the best option and ignore the overall problem, we will be stuck in local optima instead of reaching the global optima. The workaround is epsilon-greedy policy.

In MC control with **epsilon-greedy policy**, we no longer exploit the best action all the time, but choose an action randomly under certain probabilities. As the name implies, the algorithm has two folds:

- Epsilon: given a parameter, ε, with a value from *0* to *1*, each action is taken with a probability calculated as follows:

$$\pi(s, a) = \epsilon/|A|$$

Here, |A| is the number of possible actions.

- Greedy: the action with the highest state-action value is favored, and its probability of being chosen is increased by *1-ε*:

$$\pi(s, a) = 1 - \epsilon + \epsilon/|A|$$

Epsilon-greedy policy exploits the best action most of the time and also keeps exploring different actions from time to time.

How to do it...

Let's solve the Blackjack environment using epsilon-greedy policy:

1. Import the necessary modules and create a Blackjack instance:

```
>>> import torch
>>> import gym
>>> env = gym.make('Blackjack-v0')
```

2. Next, let's develop a function that runs an episode and performs epsilon-greedy:

```
>>> def run_episode(env, Q, epsilon, n_action):
...         """
...         Run a episode and performs epsilon-greedy policy
...         @param env: OpenAI Gym environment
...         @param Q: Q-function
...         @param epsilon: the trade-off between exploration and
exploitation
...         @param n_action: action space
...         @return: resulting states, actions and rewards for the
entire episode
...         """
...         state = env.reset()
...         rewards = []
...         actions = []
...         states = []
...         is_done = False
...         while not is_done:
...             probs = torch.ones(n_action) * epsilon / n_action
...             best_action = torch.argmax(Q[state]).item()
...             probs[best_action] += 1.0 - epsilon
...             action = torch.multinomial(probs, 1).item()
...             actions.append(action)
...             states.append(state)
...             state, reward, is_done, info = env.step(action)
...             rewards.append(reward)
```

```
...                    if is_done:
...                            break
...            return states, actions, rewards
```

3. Now, develop the on-policy MC control with epsilon-greedy:

```
>>> from collections import defaultdict
>>> def mc_control_epsilon_greedy(env, gamma, n_episode, epsilon):
...         """
...         Obtain the optimal policy with on-policy MC control with
epsilon_greedy
...         @param env: OpenAI Gym environment
...         @param gamma: discount factor
...         @param n_episode: number of episodes
...         @param epsilon: the trade-off between exploration and
exploitation
...         @return: the optimal Q-function, and the optimal policy
...         """
...         n_action = env.action_space.n
...         G_sum = defaultdict(float)
...         N = defaultdict(int)
...         Q = defaultdict(lambda: torch.empty(n_action))
...         for episode in range(n_episode):
...             states_t, actions_t, rewards_t =
...                     run_episode(env, Q, epsilon, n_action)
...             return_t = 0
...             G = {}
...             for state_t, action_t, reward_t in zip(states_t[::-1],
...                             actions_t[::-1], rewards_t[::-1]):
...                 return_t = gamma * return_t + reward_t
...                 G[(state_t, action_t)] = return_t
...             for state_action, return_t in G.items():
...                 state, action = state_action
...                 if state[0] <= 21:
...                     G_sum[state_action] += return_t
...                     N[state_action] += 1
...                     Q[state][action] =
...                             G_sum[state_action] / N[state_action]
...         policy = {}
...         for state, actions in Q.items():
...             policy[state] = torch.argmax(actions).item()
...         return Q, policy
```

4. We specify the discount rate as 1, ε as 0.1, and will use 500,000 episodes:

```
>>> gamma = 1
>>> n_episode = 500000
>>> epsilon = 0.1
```

5. Perform MC control with epsilon-greedy policy to obtain the optimal Q-function and policy:

```
>>> optimal_Q, optimal_policy = mc_control_epsilon_greedy(env,
gamma, n_episode, epsilon)
```

Feel free to print out the optimal value and visualize it using `plot_blackjack_value` and the `plot_surface` function we developed. We do not repeat the process herein.

6. Finally, we want to know whether the epsilon-greedy method really works better. Again, we simulate 100,000 Blackjack episodes under the optimal policy generated by epsilon-greedy and compute the chances of winning and losing:

```
>>> n_episode = 100000
>>> n_win_optimal = 0
>>> n_lose_optimal = 0
>>> for _ in range(n_episode):
...         reward = simulate_episode(env, optimal_policy)
...         if reward == 1:
...             n_win_optimal += 1
...         elif reward == -1:
...             n_lose_optimal += 1
```

Here, we reuse the `simulate_episode` function from the previous recipe.

How it works...

In this recipe, we solve the Blackjack game with on-policy MC control with epsilon-greedy.

In *Step 2*, we run an episode and perform epsilon-greedy with the following tasks:

- We initialize an episode.
- We compute the probabilities of choosing individual actions: for the best action based on the current Q-function, the probability is $1 - \epsilon + \epsilon/|A|$, otherwise, the probability is $\epsilon/|A|$.
- We record the states, actions, and rewards for all steps in the episode, which will be used in the evaluation phase.

Epsilon-greedy outperforms the greedy search method by exploiting the best action with a probability of $1 - \epsilon + \epsilon/|A|$ and at the same time, allows the exploration of other actions randomly with a probability of $\epsilon/|A|$. The hyperparameter, ϵ, is a trade-off between exploitation and exploration. If its value is 0, the algorithm becomes entirely greedy; if the value is *1*, each action is chosen evenly, so the algorithm just does random exploration.

The value of ϵ needs to be tuned based on the experiment, and there is no universal value that works best for all experiments. With that being said, in general, we can choose 0.1, 0.2, or 0.3 to begin with. Another approach is to start with a slightly larger value (such as 0.5 or 0.7) and gradually reduce it over time (for example, decaying by 0.999 for each episode). In this way, the policy will focus on exploring different actions at the beginning and, over time, it will tend to exploit good actions.

Finally, after performing *Step 6*, averaging the results from 100,000 episodes and printing the winning probability, we now have the following:

```
>>> print('Winning probability under the optimal policy:
{}'.format(n_win_optimal/n_episode))
Winning probability under the optimal policy: 0.42436
```

The optimal policy obtained by the epsilon-greedy method has a 42.44% chance of winning, which is higher than the chance of winning (41.28%) without epsilon-greedy.

Then, we also print the losing probability:

```
>>> print('Losing probability under the optimal policy:
{}'.format(n_lose_optimal/n_episode))
Losing probability under the optimal policy: 0.48048
```

As you can see, the epsilon-greedy method has a lower chance of losing (48.05% versus 49.3% without epsilon-greedy).

Performing off-policy Monte Carlo control

Another MC-based approach to solve an MDP is with **off-policy** control, which we will discuss in this recipe.

The **off-policy** method optimizes the **target policy, π,** using data generated by another policy, called the **behavior policy,** b. The target policy performs exploitation all the time while the behavior policy is for exploration purposes. This means that the target policy is greedy with respect to its current Q-function, and the behavior policy generates behavior so that the target policy has data to learn from. The behavior policy can be anything as long as all actions in all states can be chosen with non-zero probabilities, which guarantees that the behavior policy can explore all possibilities.

Since we are dealing with two different policies in the off-policy method, we can only use the **common** steps in episodes that take place in both policies. This means that we start with the latest step whose action taken under the behavior policy is different from the action taken under the greedy policy. And to learn about the target policy with another policy, we use a technique called **importance sampling,** which is commonly used to estimate the expected value under a distribution, given samples generated from a different distribution. The weighted importance for a state-action pair is calculated as follows:

$$w_t = \sum_{k=t}[\pi(a_k|s_k)/b(a_k|s_k)]$$

Here, π (*ak* | *sk*) is the probability of taking action *ak* in state *sk* under the target policy; b(*ak* | *sk*) is the probability under the behavior policy; and the weight, *wt*, is the multiplication of ratios between those two probabilities from step *t* to the end of the episode. The weight, *wt*, is applied to the return at step *t*.

How to do it...

Let's search for the optimal Blackjack policy with off-policy MC control by using the following steps:

1. Import the necessary modules and create a Blackjack instance:

```
>>> import torch
>>> import gym
>>> env = gym.make('Blackjack-v0')
```

2. We start by defining the behavior policy, which randomly chooses an action with the same probability in our case:

```
>>> def gen_random_policy(n_action):
...     probs = torch.ones(n_action) / n_action
...     def policy_function(state):
...         return probs
```

```
...         return policy_function
>>> random_policy = gen_random_policy(env.action_space.n)
```

The behavior policy can be anything as long as it selects all actions in all states with non-zero probability.

3. Next, let's develop a function that runs an episode and takes actions under the behavior policy:

```
>>> def run_episode(env, behavior_policy):
...         """
...         Run a episode given a behavior policy
...         @param env: OpenAI Gym environment
...         @param behavior_policy: behavior policy
...         @return: resulting states, actions and rewards for the
entire episode
...         """
...         state = env.reset()
...         rewards = []
...         actions = []
...         states = []
...         is_done = False
...         while not is_done:
...             probs = behavior_policy(state)
...             action = torch.multinomial(probs, 1).item()
...             actions.append(action)
...             states.append(state)
...             state, reward, is_done, info = env.step(action)
...             rewards.append(reward)
...             if is_done:
...                 break
...         return states, actions, rewards
```

This records the states, actions, and rewards for all of the steps in the episode, which will be used as learning data for the target policy.

4. Now, we'll develop the off-policy MC control algorithm:

```
>>> from collections import defaultdict
>>> def mc_control_off_policy(env, gamma, n_episode,
behavior_policy):
...         """
...         Obtain the optimal policy with off-policy MC control method
...         @param env: OpenAI Gym environment
...         @param gamma: discount factor
...         @param n_episode: number of episodes
...         @param behavior_policy: behavior policy
...         @return: the optimal Q-function, and the optimal policy
```

```
...         """
...         n_action = env.action_space.n
...         G_sum = defaultdict(float)
...         N = defaultdict(int)
...         Q = defaultdict(lambda: torch.empty(n_action))
...         for episode in range(n_episode):
...             W = {}
...             w = 1
...             states_t, actions_t, rewards_t =
...                     run_episode(env, behavior_policy)
...             return_t = 0
...             G = {}
...             for state_t, action_t, reward_t in zip(states_t[::-1],
...                                 actions_t[::-1], rewards_t[::-1]):
...                 return_t = gamma * return_t + reward_t
...                 G[(state_t, action_t)] = return_t
...                 if action_t != torch.argmax(Q[state_t]).item():
...                     break
...                 w *= 1./ behavior_policy(state_t)[action_t]
...             for state_action, return_t in G.items():
...                 state, action = state_action
...                 if state[0] <= 21:
...                     G_sum[state_action] +=
...                             return_t * W[state_action]
...                     N[state_action] += 1
...                     Q[state][action] =
...                             G_sum[state_action] / N[state_action]
...         policy = {}
...         for state, actions in Q.items():
...             policy[state] = torch.argmax(actions).item()
...         return Q, policy
```

5. We specify the discount rate as 1, and will use 500,000 episodes:

```
>>> gamma = 1
>>> n_episode = 500000
```

6. Perform off-policy MC control with the `random_policy` behavior policy to obtain the optimal Q-function and policy:

```
>>> optimal_Q, optimal_policy = mc_control_off_policy(env, gamma,
n_episode, random_policy)
```

How it works...

In this recipe, we solve the Blackjack game with off-policy MC.

In *Step 4*, the off-policy MC control algorithm does the following tasks:

- It initializes the Q-function with arbitrary small values.
- It runs `n_episode` episodes.
- For each episode, it performs the behavior policy to generate the states, actions, and rewards; it performs policy evaluation on the target policy using first-visit MC prediction based on the **common** steps; and it updates the Q-function based on the weighted return.
- In the end, the optimal Q-function is finalized, and the optimal policy is obtained by taking the best action for each state in the optimal Q-function.

It learns about the target policy by observing another agent and reusing the experience generated from another policy. The target policy is optimized in a greedy way, while the behavior policy keeps exploring different options. It averages the returns from the behavior policy with the importance ratios of their probabilities in the target policy. You may wonder why $\pi\,(ak \mid sk)$ is always equal to 1 in the computation of the importance ratio, wt. Recall that we only consider the common steps taken under the behavior policy and presumably the target policy, and the target policy is always greedy. Hence, $\pi\,(a \mid s) = 1$ is always true.

There's more...

We can actually implement the MC method in an incremental way. In an episode, instead of storing the return and importance ratio for each first-occurring, state-action pair, we can calculate the Q-function on the fly. In a non-incremental way, the Q-function is computed in the end with all stored returns in n episodes:

$$V_n = (\sum_{k=1}^{n} w_k R_k)/n$$

While in the incremental approach, the Q-function is updated in each step of an episode as follows:

$$v_{n+1} = V_n + w_{n+1}(R_{n+1} - V_n)/(n+1)$$

The incremental equivalent is more efficient as it reduces memory consumption and is more scalable. Let's go ahead and implement it:

```
>>> def mc_control_off_policy_incremental(env, gamma, n_episode,
behavior_policy):
...        n_action = env.action_space.n
...        N = defaultdict(int)
...        Q = defaultdict(lambda: torch.empty(n_action))
...        for episode in range(n_episode):
...            W = 1.
...            states_t, actions_t, rewards_t =
                                run_episode(env, behavior_policy)
...            return_t = 0.
...            for state_t, action_t, reward_t in
                        zip(states_t[::-1], actions_t[::-1],
rewards_t[::-1]):
...                return_t = gamma * return_t + reward_t
...                N[(state_t, action_t)] += 1
...                Q[state_t][action_t] += (W / N[(state_t,
action_t)])
                                        * (return_t -
Q[state_t][action_t])
...                if action_t != torch.argmax(Q[state_t]).item():
...                    break
...                W *= 1./ behavior_policy(state_t)[action_t]
...        policy = {}
...        for state, actions in Q.items():
...            policy[state] = torch.argmax(actions).item()
...        return Q, policy
```

We can call this incremental version to obtain the optimal policy:

```
>>> optimal_Q, optimal_policy = mc_control_off_policy_incremental(env,
gamma, n_episode, random_policy)
```

See also

For a detailed explanation of importance sampling, the following is a perfect resource:

```
https://statweb.stanford.edu/~owen/mc/Ch-var-is.pdf
```

Developing MC control with weighted importance sampling

In the previous recipe, we simply averaged the returns from the behavior policy with importance ratios of their probabilities in the target policy. This technique is formally called **ordinary importance sampling**. It is known to have high variance and, therefore, we usually prefer the weighted version of importance sampling, which we will talk about in this recipe.

Weighted importance sampling differs from ordinary importance sampling in the way it averages returns. Instead of simply averaging, it takes the weighted average of the returns:

$$V_n = (\sum_{k=1}^{n} w_k R_k) / \sum_{k=1}^{n} w_k$$

It often has a much lower variance compared to the ordinary version. If you have experimented with ordinary importance sampling for Blackjack, you will find the results vary a lot in each experiment.

How to do it...

Let's solve Blackjack with off-policy MC control with weighted importance sampling by using the following steps:

1. Import the necessary modules and create a Blackjack instance:

```
>>> import torch
>>> import gym
>>> env = gym.make('Blackjack-v0')
```

2. We start by defining the behavior policy, which randomly chooses an action with the same probability in our case:

```
>>> random_policy = gen_random_policy(env.action_space.n)
```

3. Next, we reuse the `run_episode` function, which runs an episode and takes actions under the behavior policy.

3. Now, we develop the off-policy MC control algorithm with weighted importance sampling:

```
>>> from collections import defaultdict
>>> def mc_control_off_policy_weighted(env, gamma, n_episode,
behavior_policy):
...         """
...         Obtain the optimal policy with off-policy MC control method
with weighted importance sampling
...         @param env: OpenAI Gym environment
...         @param gamma: discount factor
...         @param n_episode: number of episodes
...         @param behavior_policy: behavior policy
...         @return: the optimal Q-function, and the optimal policy
...         """
...         n_action = env.action_space.n
...         N = defaultdict(float)
...         Q = defaultdict(lambda: torch.empty(n_action))
...         for episode in range(n_episode):
...             W = 1.
...             states_t, actions_t, rewards_t =
                                run_episode(env, behavior_policy)
...             return_t = 0.
...             for state_t, action_t, reward_t in zip(states_t[::-1],
                                actions_t[::-1], rewards_t[::-1]):
...                 return_t = gamma * return_t + reward_t
...                 N[(state_t, action_t)] += W
...                 Q[state_t][action_t] += (W / N[(state_t,
action_t)])
                                        * (return_t -
Q[state_t][action_t])
...                 if action_t != torch.argmax(Q[state_t]).item():
...                     break
...                 W *= 1./ behavior_policy(state_t)[action_t]
...             policy = {}
...             for state, actions in Q.items():
...                 policy[state] = torch.argmax(actions).item()
...             return Q, policy
```

Note that this is an incremental version of MC control.

5. We specify the discount rate as 1, and will use 500,000 episodes:

```
>>> gamma = 1
>>> n_episode = 500000
```

6. Perform off-policy MC control with the `random_policy` behavior policy to obtain the optimal Q-function and policy:

```
>>> optimal_Q, optimal_policy = mc_control_off_policy_weighted(env,
gamma, n_episode, random_policy)
```

How it works...

We have solved the Blackjack problem using off-policy MC control with weighted importance sampling in this recipe. It is quite similar to ordinary importance sampling, but instead of scaling the returns by the ratios and averaging the results, it scales the returns using the weighted average. And, in practice, weighted importance sampling is of much lower variance than ordinary importance sampling and is therefore strongly preferred.

There's more...

Finally, why don't we simulate some episodes and see what the chances of winning and losing will be under the resulting optimal policy?

We reuse the `simulate_episode` function we developed in the *Performing on-policy Monte Carlo control* recipe and simulate 100,000 episodes:

```
>>> n_episode = 100000
>>> n_win_optimal = 0
>>> n_lose_optimal = 0
>>> for _ in range(n_episode):
...         reward = simulate_episode(env, optimal_policy)
...         if reward == 1:
...             n_win_optimal += 1
...         elif reward == -1:
...             n_lose_optimal += 1
```

Then, we print out the results we get:

```
>>> print('Winning probability under the optimal policy:
{}'.format(n_win_optimal/n_episode))
Winning probability under the optimal policy: 0.43072
>>> print('Losing probability under the optimal policy:
{}'.format(n_lose_optimal/n_episode))
Losing probability under the optimal policy: 0.47756
```

See also

For proof of the fact that weighted importance sampling outperforms ordinary importance sampling, feel free to check out the following:

- *Hesterberg, T. C., Advances in importance sampling, Ph.D. Dissertation, Statistics Department, Stanford University, 1988*
- *Casella, G., Robert, C. P., Post-processing accept-reject samples: recycling and rescaling. Journal of Computational and Graphical Statistics, 7(2):139–157, 1988*
- *Precup, D., Sutton, R. S., Singh, S., Eligibility traces for off-policy policy evaluation. In Proceedings of the 17th International Conference on Machine Learning, pp. 759–766, 2000*

Temporal Difference and Q-Learning 4

In the previous chapter, we solved MDPs by means of the Monte Carlo method, which is a model-free approach that requires no prior knowledge of the environment. However, in MC learning, the value function and Q function are usually updated until the end of an episode. This could be problematic, as some processes are very long or even fail to terminate. We will employ the **temporal difference** (**TD**) method in this chapter to solve this issue. In the TD method, we update the action values in every time step in an episode, which increases learning efficiency significantly.

The chapter will start with setting up the Cliff Walking and Windy Gridworld environment playgrounds, which will be used in TD control methods as the main talking point in this chapter. Through our step-by-step guides, readers will gain practical experience of Q-learning for off-policy control, and SARSA for on-policy control. We will also work on an interesting project, the Taxi problem, and demonstrate how to solve it using Q-learning and the SARSA algorithm, respectively. Finally, we will cover the double Q-learning algorithm by way of a bonus.

We will cover of the following recipes:

- Setting up the Cliff Walking environment playground
- Developing the Q-learning algorithm
- Setting up the Windy Gridworld environment playground
- Developing the SARSA algorithm

- Solving the Taxi problem with Q-learning
- Solving the Taxi problem with SARSA
- Developing the Double Q-learning algorithm

Setting up the Cliff Walking environment playground

In the first recipe, we will start by getting familiar with the Cliff Walking environment, which we will solve with TD methods in upcoming recipes.

Cliff Walking is a typical gym environment, with long episodes without a guarantee of termination. It is a grid problem with a 4 * 12 board. An agent makes a move up, right, down, and left at a step. The bottom-left tile is the starting point for the agent, and the bottom-right is the winning point where an episode will end if it is reached. The remaining tiles in the last row are cliffs where the agent will be reset to the starting position after stepping on any of them, but the episode continues. Each step the agent takes incurs a -1 reward, with the exception of stepping on the cliffs, where a -100 reward is incurred.

Getting ready

To run the Cliff Walking environment, let's first search for its name in the table of environments at https://github.com/openai/gym/wiki/Table-of-environments. We get CliffWalking-v0 and also know that the observation space is represented by an integer ranging from 0 (top-left tile) to 47 (bottom-right goal tile), and that there are four possible actions (up = 0, right = 1, down = 2, and left = 3).

How to do it...

Let's simulate the Cliff Walking environment by performing the following steps:

1. We import the Gym library and create an instance of the Cliff Walking environment:

```
>>> import gym
>>> env = gym.make("CliffWalking-v0")
>>> n_state = env.observation_space.n
>>> print(n_state)
48
```

```
>>> n_action = env.action_space.n
>>> print(n_action)
4
```

2. Then, we reset the environment:

```
>>> env.reset()
0
```

The agent starts with state 36 as the bottom-left tile.

3. Then, we render the environment:

```
>>> env.render()
```

4. Let's now make a down movement regardless, even though it is not walkable:

```
>>> new_state, reward, is_done, info = env.step(2)
>>> env.render()
o  o  o  o  o  o  o  o  o  o  o  o
o  o  o  o  o  o  o  o  o  o  o  o
o  o  o  o  o  o  o  o  o  o  o  o
x  C  C  C  C  C  C  C  C  C  C  T
```

The agent stays still. Now, print out what we have just obtained:

```
>>> print(new_state)
36
>>> print(reward)
-1
```

Again, each movement incurs a -1 reward:

```
>>> print(is_done)
 False
```

The episode is not done as the agent has not yet reached their goal:

```
>>> print(info)
 {'prob': 1.0}
```

This means that the movement is deterministic.

Now, let's perform an up movement since it is walkable:

```
>>> new_state, reward, is_done, info = env.step(0)
>>> env.render()
o  o  o  o  o  o  o  o  o  o  o  o
o  o  o  o  o  o  o  o  o  o  o  o
x  o  o  o  o  o  o  o  o  o  o  o
o  C  C  C  C  C  C  C  C  C  T
```

Print out what we have just obtained:

```
>>> print(new_state)
24
```

The agent moves up:

```
>>> print(reward)
-1
```

This incurs a -1 reward.

5. Now let's try and make a right and a down movement:

```
>>> new_state, reward, is_done, info = env.step(1)
>>> new_state, reward, is_done, info = env.step(2)
>>> env.render()
o  o  o  o  o  o  o  o  o  o  o  o
o  o  o  o  o  o  o  o  o  o  o  o
o  o  o  o  o  o  o  o  o  o  o  o
x  C  C  C  C  C  C  C  C  C  T
```

The agent stepped on the cliff, so was reset to the starting point and received a reward of -100:

```
>>> print(new_state)
36
>>> print(reward)
-100
>>> print(is_done)
False
```

6. Finally, let's try to take the shortest path to reach the goal:

```
>>> new_state, reward, is_done, info = env.step(0)
>>> for _ in range(11):
...        env.step(1)
>>> new_state, reward, is_done, info = env.step(2)
>>> env.render()
o  o  o  o  o  o  o  o  o  o  o  o
```

```
o  o  o  o  o  o  o  o  o  o  o  o
o  o  o  o  o  o  o  o  o  o  o  o
o  c  c  c  c  c  c  c  c  c  c  x
>>> print(new_state)
47
>>> print(reward)
-1
>>> print(is_done)
True
```

How it works...

In *Step 1*, we import the Gym library and create an instance of the Cliff Walking environment. Then, we reset the environment in *Step 2*.

In *Step 3*, we render the environment and you will see a 4 * 12 matrix as follows, representing a grid with the starting tile (x) where the agent is standing, the goal tile (T), 10 cliff tiles (C), and regular tiles (o):

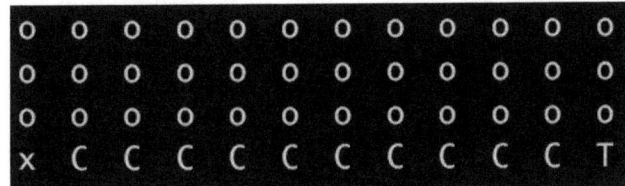

In *Steps 4, 5,* and *6*, we made various moves and saw the various outcomes of these movements and the rewards received.

As you could imagine, a Cliff Walking episode can be very long or even endless, since stepping on a cliff will reset the game. And the earlier the goal is reached the better, because each step will result in a reward of -1 or -100. In the next recipe, we will solve the Cliff Walking problem with the help of a temporal difference method.

Developing the Q-learning algorithm

Temporal difference (TD) learning is also a model-free learning algorithm, just like MC learning. You will recall that Q-function is updated at the end of the entire episode in MC learning (either in first - visit or every - visit mode). The main advantage of TD learning is that it updates the Q-function for every step in an episode.

In this recipe, we will look into a popular TD method called **Q-learning**. Q-learning is an off-policy learning algorithm. It updates the Q-function based on the following equation:

$$Q(s,a) = Q(s,a) + \alpha(r + \gamma max_{a'} Q(s',a') - Q(s,a))$$

Here, s' is the resulting state after taking action, a, in state s; r is the associated reward; α is the learning rate; and γ is the discount factor. Also, $max_{a'} Q(s',a')$ means that the behavior policy is greedy, where the highest Q-value among those in state s' is selected to generate learning data. In Q-learning, actions are taken according to the epsilon-greedy policy.

How to do it...

We perform Q-learning to solve the Cliff Walking environment as follows:

1. Import the PyTorch and Gym libraries and create an instance of the Cliff Walking environment:

```
>>> import torch
>>> import gym
>>> env = gym.make("CliffWalking-v0")
>>> from collections import defaultdict
```

2. Let's start by defining the epsilon-greedy policy:

```
>>> def gen_epsilon_greedy_policy(n_action, epsilon):
...         def policy_function(state, Q):
...             probs = torch.ones(n_action) * epsilon / n_action
...             best_action = torch.argmax(Q[state]).item()
...             probs[best_action] += 1.0 - epsilon
...             action = torch.multinomial(probs, 1).item()
...             return action
...         return policy_function
```

3. Now, define the function that performs Q-learning:

```
>>> def q_learning(env, gamma, n_episode, alpha):
...         """
...         Obtain the optimal policy with off-policy Q-learning
method
...         @param env: OpenAI Gym environment
...         @param gamma: discount factor
...         @param n_episode: number of episodes
...         @return: the optimal Q-function, and the optimal policy
...         """
...         n_action = env.action_space.n
```

```
...         Q = defaultdict(lambda: torch.zeros(n_action))
...         for episode in range(n_episode):
...             state = env.reset()
...             is_done = False
...             while not is_done:
...                 action = epsilon_greedy_policy(state, Q)
...                 next_state, reward, is_done, info =
                                            env.step(action)
...                 td_delta = reward +
                            gamma * torch.max(Q[next_state])
                            - Q[state][action]
...                 Q[state][action] += alpha * td_delta
...                 if is_done:
...                     break
...                 state = next_state
...         policy = {}
...         for state, actions in Q.items():
...             policy[state] = torch.argmax(actions).item()
...         return Q, policy
```

4. We specify the discount rate as 1, the learning rate as 0.4, and epsilon as 0.1; and we simulate 500 episodes:

```
>>> gamma = 1
>>> n_episode = 500
>>> alpha = 0.4
>>> epsilon = 0.1
```

5. Next, we create an instance of the epsilon-greedy policy:

```
>>> epsilon_greedy_policy =
gen_epsilon_greedy_policy(env.action_space.n, epsilon)
```

6. Finally, we perform Q-learning with input parameters defined previously and print out the optimal policy:

```
>>> optimal_Q, optimal_policy = q_learning(env, gamma, n_episode,
alpha)
>>> print('The optimal policy:\n', optimal_policy)
 The optimal policy:
 {36: 0, 24: 1, 25: 1, 13: 1, 12: 2, 0: 3, 1: 1, 14: 2, 2: 1, 26:
1, 15: 1, 27: 1, 28: 1, 16: 2, 4: 2, 3: 1, 29: 1, 17: 1, 5: 0, 30:
1, 18: 1, 6: 1, 19: 1, 7: 1, 31: 1, 32: 1, 20: 2, 8: 1, 33: 1, 21:
1, 9: 1, 34: 1, 22: 2, 10: 2, 23: 2, 11: 2, 35: 2, 47: 3}
```

How it works...

In *Step 2*, the epsilon-greedy policy takes in a parameter, ε, with a value from 0 to 1, and $|A|$, the number of possible actions. Each action is taken with a probability of $\varepsilon/|A|$, and the action with the highest state-action value is chosen with a probability of $1-\varepsilon+\varepsilon/|A|$.

In *Step 3*, we perform Q-learning in the following tasks:

- We initialize the Q-table with all zeros.
- In each episode, we let the agent follow the epsilon-greedy policy to choose what action to take. And we update the Q function for each step.
- We run `n_episode` episodes.
- We obtain the optimal policy based on the optimal Q function.

In *Step 6*, again, up = 0, right = 1, down = 2, and left = 3; thus, following the optimal policy, the agent starts in state 36, then moves up to state 24, and then all the way right to state 35, and finally reaches the goal by moving down:

0	1	2	3	4	5	6	7	8	9	10	11
12	13	14	15	16	17	18	19	20	21	22	23
24	25	26	27	28	29	30	31	32	33	34	35
36	37	38	39	40	41	42	43	44	45	46	47

As you can see in Q-learning , it optimizes the Q function by learning from the experience generated by another policy. This is quite similar to the off-policy MC control method. The difference is that it updates the Q function on the fly, instead of after the entire episode. It is considered advantageous for environments with long episodes where it is inefficient to delay learning until the end of an episode. In every single step in Q-learning (or any other TD method), we gain more information about the environment and use this information to update values right away. In our case, we obtained the optimal policy by running only 500 learning episodes.

There's more...

In fact, the optimal policy was obtained after around 50 episodes. We can plot the length of each episode over time to verify this. The total reward obtained in each episode over time is also an option.

1. We define two lists to store the length and total reward for each episode, respectively:

```
>>> length_episode = [0] * n_episode
>>> total_reward_episode = [0] * n_episode
```

2. We keep track of the length and total reward for each episode during learning. The following is the updated version of q_learning:

```
>>> def q_learning(env, gamma, n_episode, alpha):
...         n_action = env.action_space.n
...         Q = defaultdict(lambda: torch.zeros(n_action))
...         for episode in range(n_episode):
...             state = env.reset()
...             is_done = False
...             while not is_done:
...                 action = epsilon_greedy_policy(state, Q)
...                 next_state, reward, is_done, info =
                                        env.step(action)
...                 td_delta = reward +
                        gamma * torch.max(Q[next_state])
                            - Q[state][action]
...                 Q[state][action] += alpha * td_delta
...                 length_episode[episode] += 1
...                 total_reward_episode[episode] += reward
...                 if is_done:
...                     break
...                 state = next_state
...             policy = {}
...             for state, actions in Q.items():
...                 policy[state] = torch.argmax(actions).item()
...             return Q, policy
```

3. Now, display the plot of episode lengths over time:

```
>>> import matplotlib.pyplot as plt
>>> plt.plot(length_episode)
>>> plt.title('Episode length over time')
>>> plt.xlabel('Episode')
>>> plt.ylabel('Length')
>>> plt.show()
```

This will result in the following plot:

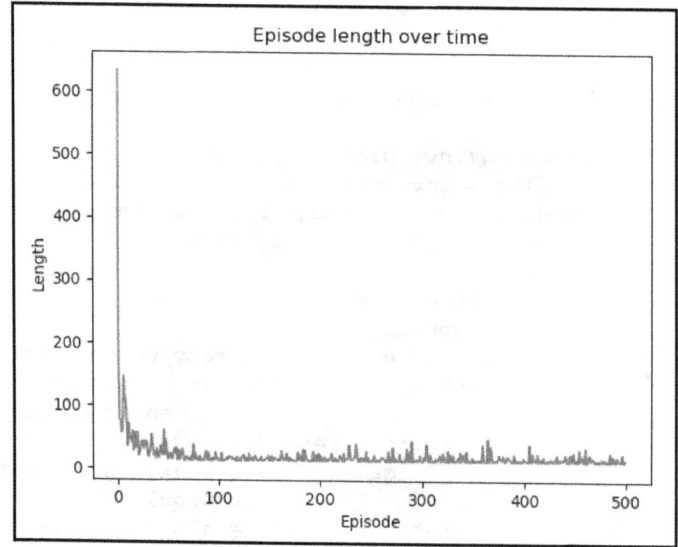

4. Display the plot of episode rewards over time:

```
>>> plt.plot(total_reward_episode)
>>> plt.title('Episode reward over time')
>>> plt.xlabel('Episode')
>>> plt.ylabel('Total reward')
>>> plt.show()
```

This will result in the following plot:

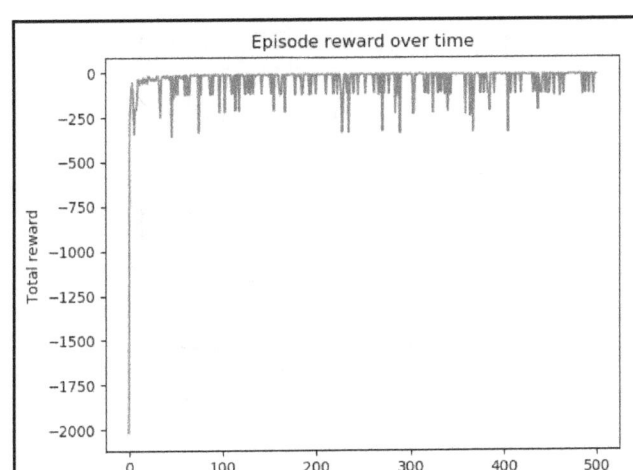

Again, if you reduce the value of epsilon, you will see smaller fluctuations, which are the effects of random exploration in the epsilon-greedy policy.

Setting up the Windy Gridworld environment playground

In the previous recipe, we solved a relatively simple environment where we can easily obtain the optimal policy. In this recipe, let's simulate a more complex grid environment, Windy Gridworld, where an external force moves the agent from certain tiles. This will prepare us to search for the optimal policy using the TD method in the next recipe.

Windy Gridworld is a grid problem with a 7 * 10 board, which is displayed as follows:

0	1	2	3	4	5	6	7	8	9
10	11	12	13	14	15	16	17	18	19
20	21	22	23	24	25	26	27	28	29
30	31	32	33	34	35	36	37	38	39
40	41	42	43	44	45	46	47	48	49
50	51	52	53	54	55	56	57	58	59
60	61	62	63	64	65	66	67	68	69

↑ ↑ ↑ ↑↑↑ ↑

An agent makes a move up, right, down, and left at a step. Tile 30 is the starting point for the agent, and tile 37 is the winning point where an episode will end if it is reached. Each step the agent takes incurs a -1 reward.

The complexity in this environment is that there is extra wind force in columns 4 to 9. Moving from tiles on those columns, the agent will experience an extra push upward. The wind force in the seventh and eighth columns is 1, and the wind force in the fourth, fifth, sixth, and ninth columns is 2. For example, if the agent tries to move right from state 43, they will land in state 34; if the agent tries to move left from state 48, they will land in state 37; if the agent tries to move up from state 67, they will land in state 37 as the agent receives an additional 2-unit force upward; if the agent tries to move down from state 27, they will land in state 17, as the 2 extra force upward offsets 1 downward.

Currently, Windy Gridworld is not included in the Gym environment. We will implement it by taking the Cliff Walking environment as a reference: `https://github.com/openai/gym/blob/master/gym/envs/toy_text/cliffwalking.py`.

How to do it...

Let's develop the Windy Gridworld environment:

1. Import the necessary modules, NumPy, and the `discrete` class, from Gym:

```
>>> import numpy as np
>>> import sys
>>> from gym.envs.toy_text import discrete
```

2. Define four actions:

```
>>> UP = 0
>>> RIGHT = 1
>>> DOWN = 2
>>> LEFT = 3
```

3. Let's start by defining the __init__ method in the `WindyGridworldEnv` class:

```
>>> class WindyGridworldEnv(discrete.DiscreteEnv):
...       def __init__(self):
...           self.shape = (7, 10)
...           nS = self.shape[0] * self.shape[1]
...           nA = 4
...           # Wind locations
...           winds = np.zeros(self.shape)
...           winds[:,[3,4,5,8]] = 1
...           winds[:,[6,7]] = 2
...           self.goal = (3, 7)
...           # Calculate transition probabilities and rewards
...           P = {}
...           for s in range(nS):
...               position = np.unravel_index(s, self.shape)
...               P[s] = {a: [] for a in range(nA)}
...               P[s][UP] = self._calculate_transition_prob(
                                   position, [-1, 0], winds)
...               P[s][RIGHT] = self._calculate_transition_prob(
                                   position, [0, 1], winds)
...               P[s][DOWN] = self._calculate_transition_prob(
                                   position, [1, 0], winds)
...               P[s][LEFT] = self._calculate_transition_prob(
                                   position, [0, -1], winds)
...           # Calculate initial state distribution
...           # We always start in state (3, 0)
...           isd = np.zeros(nS)
...           isd[np.ravel_multi_index((3,0), self.shape)] = 1.0
...           super(WindyGridworldEnv, self).__init__(nS, nA, P,
isd)
```

This defines the observation space, the wind areas and forces, the transition and reward matrices, and the initial state.

4. Next, we define the `_calculate_transition_prob` method to determines the outcome for an action, including the probability (which is 1), the new state, the reward (which is always -1), and whether it is complete:

```
...        def _calculate_transition_prob(self, current,
                                                  delta, winds):
...            """
...            Determine the outcome for an action. Transition
                                               Prob is always 1.0.
...            @param current: (row, col), current position
                                               on the grid
...            @param delta: Change in position for transition
...            @param winds: Wind effect
...            @return: (1.0, new_state, reward, is_done)
...            """
...            new_position = np.array(current) + np.array(delta)
                      + np.array([-1, 0]) * winds[tuple(current)]
...            new_position = self._limit_coordinates(
                                  new_position).astype(int)
...            new_state = np.ravel_multi_index(
                                  tuple(new_position), self.shape)
...            is_done = tuple(new_position) == self.goal
...            return [(1.0, new_state, -1.0, is_done)]
```

This computes the state based on the current state, movement, and wind effect, and ensures that the new position is within the grid. Finally, it checks whether the agent has reached the goal state.

5. Next, we define the `_limit_coordinates` method, which prevents the agent from falling out of the grid world:

```
...        def _limit_coordinates(self, coord):
...            coord[0] = min(coord[0], self.shape[0] - 1)
...            coord[0] = max(coord[0], 0)
...            coord[1] = min(coord[1], self.shape[1] - 1)
...            coord[1] = max(coord[1], 0)
...            return coord
```

6. Finally, we add the `render` method in order to display the agent and the grid environment:

```
...        def render(self):
...            outfile = sys.stdout
...            for s in range(self.nS):
...                position = np.unravel_index(s, self.shape)
...                if self.s == s:
...                    output = " x "
```

```
...                    elif position == self.goal:
...                        output = " T "
...                    else:
...                        output = " o "
...                    if position[1] == 0:
...                        output = output.lstrip()
...                    if position[1] == self.shape[1] - 1:
...                        output = output.rstrip()
...                        output += "\n"
...                    outfile.write(output)
...                outfile.write("\n")
```

X represents the agent's current position, T is the goal tile, and the remaining tiles are denoted as o.

Now, let's simulate the Windy Gridworld environment in the following steps:

1. Create an instance of the Windy Gridworld environment:

    ```
    >>> env = WindyGridworldEnv()
    ```

2. Reset and render the environment:

    ```
    >>> env.reset()
    >>> env.render()
    o  o  o  o  o  o  o  o  o  o
    o  o  o  o  o  o  o  o  o  o
    o  o  o  o  o  o  o  o  o  o
    x  o  o  o  o  o  o  T  o  o
    o  o  o  o  o  o  o  o  o  o
    o  o  o  o  o  o  o  o  o  o
    o  o  o  o  o  o  o  o  o  o
    ```

    The agent starts with state 30.

3. Make a right movement:

    ```
    >>> print(env.step(1))
    >>> env.render()
    (31, -1.0, False, {'prob': 1.0})
    o  o  o  o  o  o  o  o  o  o
    o  o  o  o  o  o  o  o  o  o
    o  o  o  o  o  o  o  o  o  o
    o  x  o  o  o  o  o  T  o  o
    o  o  o  o  o  o  o  o  o  o
    o  o  o  o  o  o  o  o  o  o
    o  o  o  o  o  o  o  o  o  o
    ```

The agent lands in state 31, with a reward of -1.

4. Make two right moves:

```
>>> print(env.step(1))
>>> print(env.step(1))
>>> env.render()
(32, -1.0, False, {'prob': 1.0})
(33, -1.0, False, {'prob': 1.0})
 o  o  o  o  o  o  o  o  o  o
 o  o  o  o  o  o  o  o  o  o
 o  o  o  o  o  o  o  o  o  o
 o  o  o  x  o  o  o  T  o  o
 o  o  o  o  o  o  o  o  o  o
 o  o  o  o  o  o  o  o  o  o
 o  o  o  o  o  o  o  o  o  o
```

5. Now, make another right move:

```
>>> print(env.step(1))
>>> env.render()
(24, -1.0, False, {'prob': 1.0})
 o  o  o  o  o  o  o  o  o  o
 o  o  o  o  o  o  o  o  o  o
 o  o  o  o  x  o  o  o  o  o
 o  o  o  o  o  o  o  T  o  o
 o  o  o  o  o  o  o  o  o  o
 o  o  o  o  o  o  o  o  o  o
 o  o  o  o  o  o  o  o  o  o
```

With a 1-unit wind upward, the agent lands in state 24.

Feel free to play around with the environment until the goal is reached.

How it works...

We just developed a grid environment similar to Cliff Walking. The difference between Windy Gridworld and Cliff Walking is the extra upward push. Each action in a Windy Gridworld episode will result in a reward of -1. Hence, it is better to reach the goal earlier. In the next recipe, we will solve the Windy Gridworld problem with another TD control method.

Developing the SARSA algorithm

You will recall that Q-learning is an off-policy TD learning algorithm. In this recipe, we will solve an MDP with an on-policy TD learning algorithm, called **State-Action-Reward-State-Action (SARSA)**.

Similar to Q-learning, SARSA focuses on state-action values. It updates the Q-function based on the following equation:

$$Q(s,a) = Q(s,a) + \alpha(r + \gamma Q(s',a') - Q(s,a))$$

Here, s' is the resulting state after taking the action, a, in state s; r is the associated reward; α is the learning rate; and γ is the discount factor. You will recall that in Q-learning, a behavior-greedy policy, $max_{a'} Q(s',a')$, is used to update the Q value. In SARSA, we simply pick up the next action, a', by also following an epsilon-greedy policy to update the Q value. And the action a' is taken in the next step. Hence, SARSA is an on-policy algorithm.

How to do it...

We perform SARSA to solve the Windy Gridworld environment as follows:

1. Import PyTorch and `WindyGridworldEnvmodule` (assuming that it is in a file called `windy_gridworld.py`), and create an instance of the Windy Gridworld environment:

```
>>> import torch
>>> from windy_gridworld import WindyGridworldEnv
>>> env = WindyGridworldEnv()
```

2. Let's start by defining the epsilon-greedy behavior policy:

```
>>> def gen_epsilon_greedy_policy(n_action, epsilon):
...     def policy_function(state, Q):
...         probs = torch.ones(n_action) * epsilon / n_action
...         best_action = torch.argmax(Q[state]).item()
...         probs[best_action] += 1.0 - epsilon
...         action = torch.multinomial(probs, 1).item()
...         return action
...     return policy_function
```

3. We specify the number of episodes and initialize two variables used to track the length and total reward for each episode:

```
>>> n_episode = 500
>>> length_episode = [0] * n_episode
>>> total_reward_episode = [0] * n_episode
```

4. Now, we define the function that performs SARSA:

```
>>> from collections import defaultdict
>>> def sarsa(env, gamma, n_episode, alpha):
...         """
...         Obtain the optimal policy with on-policy SARSA algorithm
...         @param env: OpenAI Gym environment
...         @param gamma: discount factor
...         @param n_episode: number of episodes
...         @return: the optimal Q-function, and the optimal policy
...         """
...         n_action = env.action_space.n
...         Q = defaultdict(lambda: torch.zeros(n_action))
...         for episode in range(n_episode):
...             state = env.reset()
...             is_done = False
...             action = epsilon_greedy_policy(state, Q)
...             while not is_done:
...                 next_state, reward, is_done, info
                                         = env.step(action)
...                 next_action = epsilon_greedy_policy(next_state, Q)
...                 td_delta = reward +
                             gamma * Q[next_state][next_action]
                             - Q[state][action]
...                 Q[state][action] += alpha * td_delta
...                 length_episode[episode] += 1
...                 total_reward_episode[episode] += reward
...                 if is_done:
...                     break
...                 state = next_state
...                 action = next_action
...         policy = {}
...         for state, actions in Q.items():
...             policy[state] = torch.argmax(actions).item()
...         return Q, policy
```

5. We specify the discount rate as 1, the learning rate as 0.4, and epsilon as 0.1:

```
>>> gamma = 1
>>> alpha = 0.4
>>> epsilon = 0.1
```

6. Next, we create an instance of the epsilon-greedy policy:

```
>>> epsilon_greedy_policy =
gen_epsilon_greedy_policy(env.action_space.n, epsilon)
```

7. Finally, we perform SARSA with input parameters defined in the previous steps and print out the optimal policy:

```
>>> optimal_Q, optimal_policy = sarsa(env, gamma, n_episode, alpha)
>>> print('The optimal policy:\n', optimal_policy)
 The optimal policy:
 {30: 2, 31: 1, 32: 1, 40: 1, 50: 2, 60: 1, 61: 1, 51: 1, 41: 1,
42: 1, 20: 1, 21: 1, 62: 1, 63: 2, 52: 1, 53: 1, 43: 1, 22: 1, 11:
1, 10: 1, 0: 1, 33: 1, 23: 1, 12: 1, 13: 1, 2: 1, 1: 1, 3: 1, 24:
1, 4: 1, 5: 1, 6: 1, 14: 1, 7: 1, 8: 1, 9: 2, 19: 2, 18: 2, 29: 2,
28: 1, 17: 2, 39: 2, 38: 1, 27: 0, 49: 3, 48: 3, 37: 3, 34: 1, 59:
2, 58: 3, 47: 2, 26: 1, 44: 1, 15: 1, 69: 3, 68: 1, 57: 2, 36: 1,
25: 1, 54: 2, 16: 1, 35: 1, 45: 1}
```

How it works...

In *Step 4*, the SARSA function does the following tasks:

- It initializes the Q-table with all zeros.
- In each episode, it lets the agent follow the epsilon-greedy policy to choose what action to take. And for each step, it updates the Q function based on the equation $Q(s, a) = Q(s, a) + \alpha(r + \gamma Q(s', a') - Q(s, a))$, where a ' is selected on the basis of the epsilon-greedy policy. The new action, a', is then taken in the new state, s '.
- We run `n_episode` episodes.
- We obtain the optimal policy based on the optimal Q function.

As you can see in the SARSA method, it optimizes the Q function by taking the action chosen under the same policy, the epsilon-greedy policy. This is quite similar to the on-policy MC control method. The difference is that it updates the Q function by small derivatives in individual steps, rather than after the entire episode. It is considered advantageous for environments with long episodes where it is inefficient to delay learning until the end of an episode. In every single step in SARSA, we gain more information about the environment and use this information to update values right away. In our case, we obtained the optimal policy by running only 500 learning episodes.

There's more...

In fact, the optimal policy was obtained after around 200 episodes. We can plot the length and total reward for each episode over time to verify this:

1. Display a plot of episode lengths over time:

```
>>> import matplotlib.pyplot as plt
>>> plt.plot(length_episode)
>>> plt.title('Episode length over time')
>>> plt.xlabel('Episode')
>>> plt.ylabel('Length')
>>> plt.show()
```

This will result in the following plot:

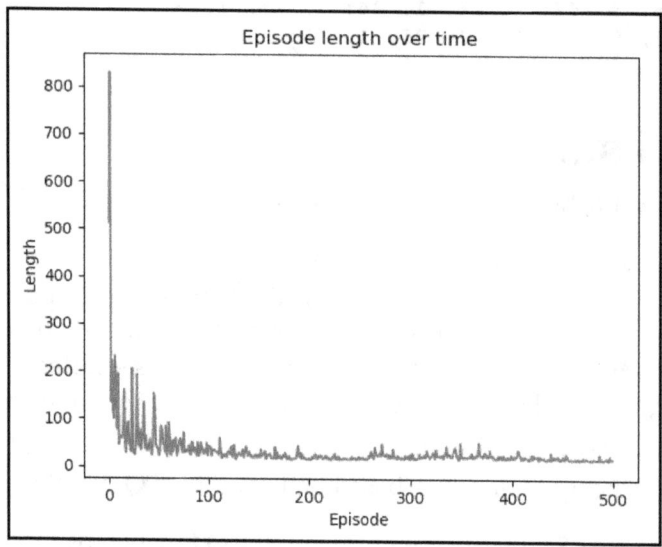

You can see that the episode length starts to saturate after 200 episodes. Note that those small fluctuations are due to random exploration in the epsilon-greedy policy.

2. Display a plot of episode rewards over time:

```
>>> plt.plot(total_reward_episode)
>>> plt.title('Episode reward over time')
>>> plt.xlabel('Episode')
>>> plt.ylabel('Total reward')
>>> plt.show()
```

This will result in the following plot:

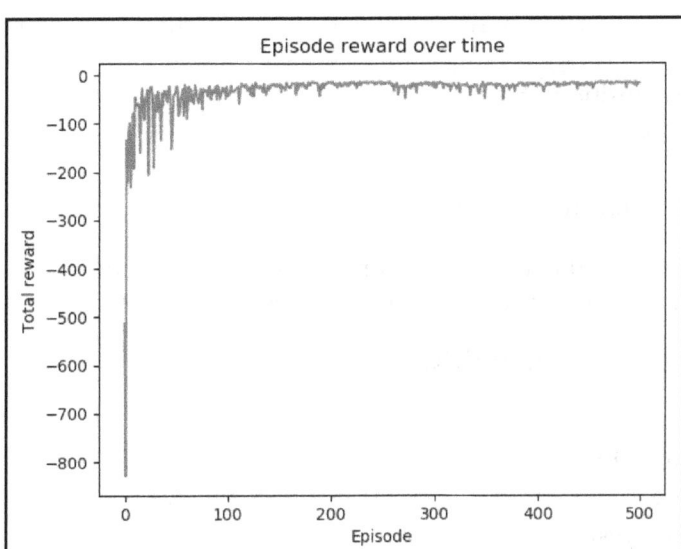

Again, if you reduce the value of epsilon, you will see smaller fluctuations, which are the effects of random exploration in the epsilon-greedy policy.

In the upcoming two recipes, we will use the two TD methods we just learned to solve a more complex environment with more possible states and actions. Let's start with Q-learning.

Solving the Taxi problem with Q-learning

The Taxi problem (https://gym.openai.com/envs/Taxi-v2/) is another popular grid world problem. In a 5 * 5 grid, the agent acts as a taxi driver to pick up a passenger at one location and then drop the passenger off at their destination. Take a look at the following example:

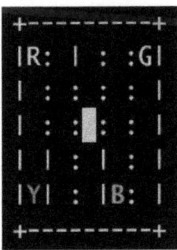

Colored tiles have the following meanings:

- **Yellow**: The starting position of the taxi. The starting location is random in each episode.
- **Blue**: The position of the passenger. It is also randomly selected in each episode.
- **Purple**: The destination of the passenger. Again, it is randomly selected in each episode.
- **Green**: The position of the taxi with the passenger.

The four letters R, Y, B, and G indicate the only tiles that allow picking up and dropping off the passenger. One of them is the destination, and one is where the passenger is located.

The taxi can take the following six deterministic actions:

- **0**: Moving south
- **1**: Moving north
- **2**: Moving east
- **3**: Moving west
- **4**: Picking up the passenger
- **5**: Dropping of the passenger

There is a pillar | between two tiles, which prevents the taxi from moving from one tile to another.

The reward for each step is generally -1, with the following exceptions:

- **+20**: The passenger is delivered to their destination. And an episode will end.
- **-10**: Attempted illegal pick-up or drop-off (not on any of R, Y, B, or G).

One more thing to note is that the observation space is a lot larger than 25 (5*5) since we should also consider the location of the passenger and the destination, and whether the taxi is empty or full. Hence, the observation space should be 25 * 5 (4 possible locations for the passenger or already in the taxi) * 4 (destinations) = 500 dimensions.

Getting ready

To run the Taxi environment, let's first search for its name in the table of environments, `https://github.com/openai/gym/wiki/Table-of-environments`. We get Taxi-v2 and also know that the observation space is represented by an integer ranging from 0 to 499, and that there are four possible actions (up = 0, right = 1, down = 2, and left = 3).

How to do it...

Let's start by simulating the Taxi environment in the following steps:

1. We import the Gym library and create an instance of the Taxi environment:

```
>>> import gym
>>> env = gym.make('Taxi-v2')
>>> n_state = env.observation_space.n
>>> print(n_state)
 500
>>> n_action = env.action_space.n
>>> print(n_action)
 6
```

2. Then, we reset the environment:

```
>>> env.reset()
 262
```

3. Then, we render the environment:

```
>>> env.render()
```

You will see a similar 5 * 5 matrix as follows:

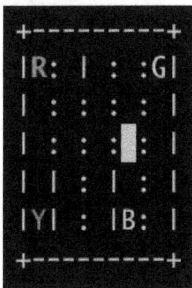

The passenger is in the R location, and the destination is in Y. You will see something different as the initial state is randomly generated.

4. Let's now go and pick up the passenger by heading west for three tiles and north for two tiles (you can adjust this according to your initial state) and then executing the pick-up. Then, we render the environment again:

```
>>> print(env.step(3))
(242, -1, False, {'prob': 1.0})
>>> print(env.step(3))
(222, -1, False, {'prob': 1.0})
>>> print(env.step(3))
(202, -1, False, {'prob': 1.0})
>>> print(env.step(1))
(102, -1, False, {'prob': 1.0})
>>> print(env.step(1))
(2, -1, False, {'prob': 1.0})
>>> print(env.step(4))
(18, -1, False, {'prob': 1.0})
Render the environment:
>>> env.render()
```

5. You will see the latest matrix updated (again, you may get different output depending on your initial state):

The taxi turns green.

6. Now, we go to the destination by heading south for four tiles (you can adjust this to your initial state) and then executing the drop-off:

```
>>> print(env.step(0))
(118, -1, False, {'prob': 1.0})
>>> print(env.step(0))
(218, -1, False, {'prob': 1.0})
>>> print(env.step(0))
(318, -1, False, {'prob': 1.0})
>>> print(env.step(0))
(418, -1, False, {'prob': 1.0})
>>> print(env.step(5))
(410, 20, True, {'prob': 1.0})
```

It finally receives a +20 reward and the episode ends.

Now, we render the environment:

```
>>> env.render()
```

You will see the following updated matrix:

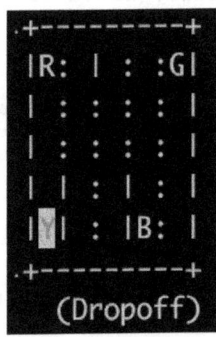

We will now perform Q-learning to solve the Taxi environment as follows:

1. Import the PyTorch library:

```
>>> import torch
```

2. Then, start defining the epsilon-greedy policy. We will reuse the `gen_epsilon_greedy_policy` function defined in the *Developing the Q-learning algorithm* recipe.

3. Now, we specify the number of episodes and initialize two variables used to track the length and total reward for each episode:

```
>>> n_episode = 1000
>>> length_episode = [0] * n_episode
>>> total_reward_episode = [0] * n_episode
```

4. Next, we define the function that performs Q-learning. We will reuse the `q_learning` function defined in the *Developing Q-learning algorithm* recipe.

5. Now, we specify the rest of the parameters, including the discount rate, learning rate, and epsilon, and create an instance of the epsilon-greedy-policy:

```
>>> gamma = 1
>>> alpha = 0.4
>>> epsilon = 0.1
>>> epsilon_greedy_policy =
gen_epsilon_greedy_policy(env.action_space.n, epsilon)
```

6. Finally, we perform Q-learning to obtain the optimal policy for the taxi problem:

```
>>> optimal_Q, optimal_policy = q_learning(env, gamma, n_episode,
alpha)
```

How it works...

In this recipe, we solve the Taxi problem via off-policy Q-learning.

After *Step 6*, you can plot the length and total reward for each episode over time to verify whether the model converges. The plot of episode lengths over time is displayed as follows:

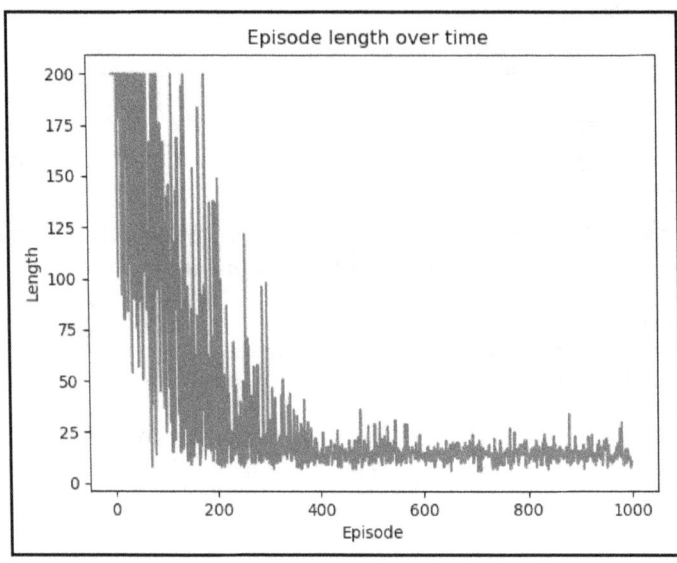

The plot of episode rewards over time is as follows:

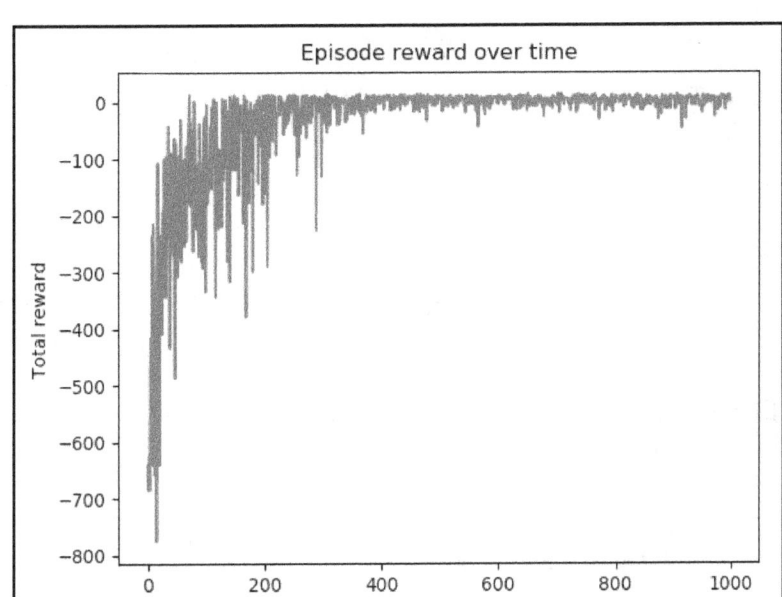

You can see that the optimization starts to saturate after 400 episodes.

The Taxi environment is a relatively complex grid problem with 500 discrete states and 6 possible actions. Q-learning optimizes the Q function in every single step in an episode by learning from the experience generated by a greedy policy. We gain information about the environment during the learning process and use this information to update the values right away by following the epsilon-greedy policy.

Solving the Taxi problem with SARSA

In this recipe, we will solve the Taxi environment with the SARSA algorithm and fine-tune the hyperparameters with the grid search algorithm.

We will start with our default set of hyperparameter values under the SARSA model. These are selected based on intuition and a number of trials. Moving on, we will come up with the best set of values.

How to do it...

We perform SARSA to solve the Taxi environment as follows:

1. Import PyTorch and the `gym` module, and create an instance of the Taxi environment:

   ```
   >>> import torch
   >>> import gym
   >>> env = gym.make('Taxi-v2')
   ```

2. Then, start defining the epsilon-greedy behavior policy. We will reuse the `gen_epsilon_greedy_policy` function defined in the *Developing the SARSA algorithm* recipe.

3. We then specify the number of episodes and initialize two variables used to track the length and total reward for each episode:

   ```
   >>> n_episode = 1000
   >>> length_episode = [0] * n_episode
   >>> total_reward_episode = [0] * n_episode
   ```

4. Now, we define the function that performs SARSA. We will reuse the `sarsa` function defined in the *Developing the SARSA algorithm* recipe.

5. We specify the discount rate as 1, the default learning rate as 0.4, and the default epsilon as 0.1:

   ```
   >>> gamma = 1
   >>> alpha = 0.4
   >>> epsilon = 0.01
   ```

6. Next, we create an instance of the epsilon-greedy-policy:

   ```
   >>> epsilon_greedy_policy =
   gen_epsilon_greedy_policy(env.action_space.n, epsilon)
   ```

7. Finally, we perform SARSA with input parameters defined in the previous steps:

   ```
   >>> optimal_Q, optimal_policy = sarsa(env, gamma, n_episode, alpha)
   ```

How it works...

After *Step 7*, you can plot the length and total reward for each episode over time to verify whether the model converges. A plot of episode lengths over time is displayed as follows:

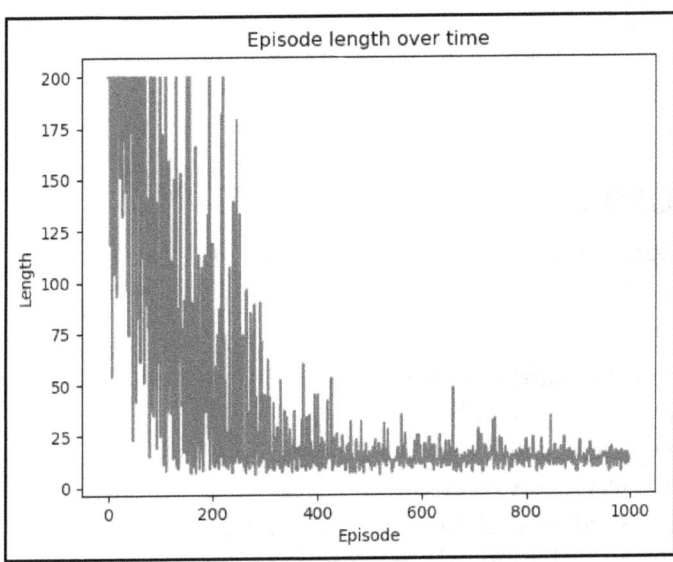

The plot of episode rewards over time is as follows:

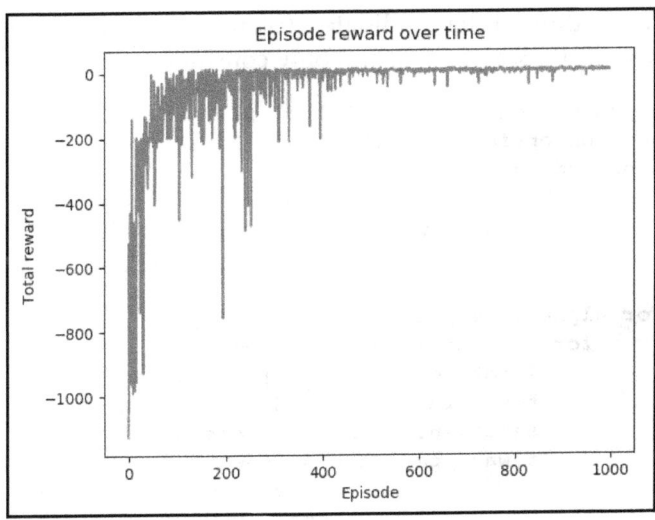

This SARSA model works fine, but is not necessarily the best. We will later use grid search to search for the best set of hyperparameters under the SARSA model.

The Taxi environment is a relatively complex grid problem with 500 discrete states and 6 possible actions. The SARSA algorithm optimizes the Q function in every single step in an episode by learning and optimizing the target policy. We gain information about the environment during the learning process and use this information to update values right away by following the epsilon-greedy policy.

There's more...

Grid search is a programmatic way to find the best set of values for hyperparameters in reinforcement learning. The performance of each set of hyperparameters is measured by the following three metrics:

- Average total reward over the first few episodes: We want to get the largest reward as early as possible.
- Average episode length over the first few episodes: We want the taxi to reach the destination as quickly as possible.
- Average reward for each time step over the first few episodes: We want to get the maximum reward as quickly as possible.

Let's go ahead and implement it:

1. We herein use three alpha candidates [0.4, 0.5, and 0.6] and three epsilon candidates [0.1, 0.03, and 0.01], and only consider the first 500 episodes:

```
>>> alpha_options = [0.4, 0.5, 0.6]
>>> epsilon_options = [0.1, 0.03, 0.01]
>>> n_episode = 500
```

2. We perform a grid search by training the SARSA model with each set of hyperparameters and evaluating the corresponding performance:

```
>>> for alpha in alpha_options:
...         for epsilon in epsilon_options:
...             length_episode = [0] * n_episode
...             total_reward_episode = [0] * n_episode
...             sarsa(env, gamma, n_episode, alpha)
...             reward_per_step = [reward/float(step) for
...                             reward, step in zip(
...                         total_reward_episode, length_episode)]
...             print('alpha: {}, epsilon: {}'.format(alpha, epsilon))
...             print('Average reward over {} episodes: {}'.format(
```

```
                    n_episode, sum(total_reward_episode) / n_episode))
...             print('Average length over {} episodes: {}'.format(
                    n_episode, sum(length_episode) / n_episode))
...             print('Average reward per step over {} episodes:
            {}\n'.format(n_episode, sum(reward_per_step) / n_episode))
```

Running the preceding code generates the following results:

```
alpha: 0.4, epsilon: 0.1
 Average reward over 500 episodes: -75.442
 Average length over 500 episodes: 57.682
 Average reward per step over 500 episodes: -0.32510755063660324
 alpha: 0.4, epsilon: 0.03
 Average reward over 500 episodes: -73.378
 Average length over 500 episodes: 56.53
 Average reward per step over 500 episodes: -0.2761201410280632
 alpha: 0.4, epsilon: 0.01
 Average reward over 500 episodes: -78.722
 Average length over 500 episodes: 59.366
 Average reward per step over 500 episodes: -0.3561815084186654
 alpha: 0.5, epsilon: 0.1
 Average reward over 500 episodes: -72.026
 Average length over 500 episodes: 55.592
 Average reward per step over 500 episodes: -0.25355404831497264
 alpha: 0.5, epsilon: 0.03
 Average reward over 500 episodes: -67.562
 Average length over 500 episodes: 52.706
 Average reward per step over 500 episodes: -0.20602525679639022
 alpha: 0.5, epsilon: 0.01
 Average reward over 500 episodes: -75.252
 Average length over 500 episodes: 56.73
 Average reward per step over 500 episodes: -0.2588407558703358
 alpha: 0.6, epsilon: 0.1
 Average reward over 500 episodes: -62.568
 Average length over 500 episodes: 49.488
 Average reward per step over 500 episodes: -0.1700284221229244
 alpha: 0.6, epsilon: 0.03
 Average reward over 500 episodes: -68.56
 Average length over 500 episodes: 52.804
 Average reward per step over 500 episodes: -0.24794191768600077
 alpha: 0.6, epsilon: 0.01
 Average reward over 500 episodes: -63.468
 Average length over 500 episodes: 49.752
 Average reward per step over 500 episodes: -0.14350124172091722
```

We can see that the best hyperparameter set in this case is alpha: 0.6, epsilon: 0.01, which achieves the largest reward per step and a large average reward and a short average episode length.

Developing the Double Q-learning algorithm

In this is a bonus recipe, in this chapter where we will develop the double Q-learning algorithm.

Q-learning is a powerful and popular TD control reinforcement learning algorithm. However, it may perform poorly in some cases, mainly because of the greedy component, $maxa'Q(s', a')$. It can overestimate action values and result in poor performance. Double Q-learning was invented to overcome this by utilizing two Q functions. We denote two Q functions as *Q1* and *Q2*. In each step, one Q function is randomly selected to be updated. If *Q1* is selected, *Q1* is updated as follows:

$$a^* = argmax_a Q1(s', a)$$
$$Q1(s, a) = Q1(s, a) + \alpha(r + \gamma Q2(s', a^*) - Q1(s, a))$$

If Q2 is selected, it is updated as follows:

$$a^* = argmax_a Q2(s', a)$$
$$Q2(s, a) = Q2(s, a) + \alpha(r + \gamma Q1(s', a^*) - Q2(s, a))$$

This means that each Q function is updated from another one following the greedy search, which reduces the overestimation of action values using a single Q function.

How to do it...

We now develop double Q-learning to solve the Taxi environment as follows:

1. Import the required libraries and create an instance of the Taxi environment:

```
>>> import torch
>>> import gym
>>> env = gym.make('Taxi-v2')
```

2. Then, start defining the epsilon-greedy policy. We will reuse the gen_epsilon_greedy_policy function defined in the *Developing Q-Learning algorithm* recipe.

3. We then specify the number of episodes and initialize two variables used to track the length and total reward for each episode:

```
>>> n_episode = 3000
>>> length_episode = [0] * n_episode
>>> total_reward_episode = [0] * n_episode
```

Here, we simulate 3,000 episodes as double Q-learning takes more episodes to converge.

4. Next, we define the function that performs double Q-learning:

```
>>> def double_q_learning(env, gamma, n_episode, alpha):
...         """
...         Obtain the optimal policy with off-policy double
...         Q-learning method
...         @param env: OpenAI Gym environment
...         @param gamma: discount factor
...         @param n_episode: number of episodes
...         @return: the optimal Q-function, and the optimal policy
...         """
...         n_action = env.action_space.n
...         n_state = env.observation_space.n
...         Q1 = torch.zeros(n_state, n_action)
...         Q2 = torch.zeros(n_state, n_action)
...         for episode in range(n_episode):
...             state = env.reset()
...             is_done = False
...             while not is_done:
...                 action = epsilon_greedy_policy(state, Q1 + Q2)
...                 next_state, reward, is_done, info
                                    = env.step(action)
...                 if (torch.rand(1).item() < 0.5):
...                     best_next_action =
torch.argmax(Q1[next_state])
...                     td_delta = reward +
                            gamma * Q2[next_state][best_next_action]
                            - Q1[state][action]
...                     Q1[state][action] += alpha * td_delta
...                 else:
...                     best_next_action =
torch.argmax(Q2[next_state])
...                     td_delta = reward +
                            gamma * Q1[next_state][best_next_action]
                            - Q2[state][action]
...                     Q2[state][action] += alpha * td_delta
...                 length_episode[episode] += 1
...                 total_reward_episode[episode] += reward
```

```
...                     if is_done:
...                         break
...                     state = next_state
...         policy = {}
...         Q = Q1 + Q2
...         for state in range(n_state):
...             policy[state] = torch.argmax(Q[state]).item()
...         return Q, policy
```

5. We then specify the rest of the parameters, including the discount rate, learning rate, and epsilon, and create an instance of the epsilon-greedy-policy:

```
>>> gamma = 1
>>> alpha = 0.4
>>> epsilon = 0.1
>>> epsilon_greedy_policy =
gen_epsilon_greedy_policy(env.action_space.n, epsilon)
```

6. Finally, we perform double Q-learning to obtain the optimal policy for the Taxi problem:

```
>>> optimal_Q, optimal_policy = double_q_learning(env, gamma,
n_episode, alpha)
```

How it works...

We have solved the Taxi problem using the double Q-learning algorithm in this recipe.

In *Step 4*, we conduct double Q-learning with the following tasks:

- Initialize the two Q-tables with all zeros.
- In each step of an episode, we randomly choose one Q function to update. Let the agent follow the epsilon-greedy policy to choose what action to take and update the selected Q function using another Q function.
- Run n_episode episodes.
- Obtain the optimal policy based on the optimal Q function by summing up (or averaging) two Q functions.

After *Step 6*, you can plot the length and total reward for each episode over time to verify whether the model converges. The plot of episode length over time is displayed as follows:

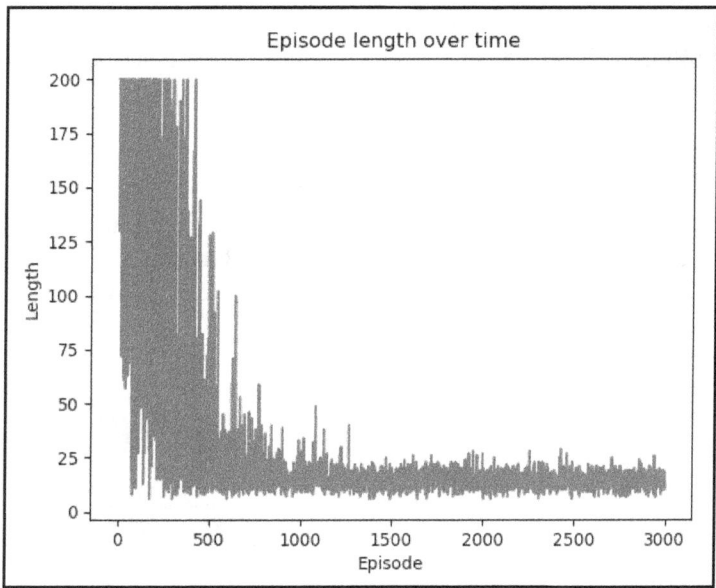

The plot of episode rewards over time is as follows:

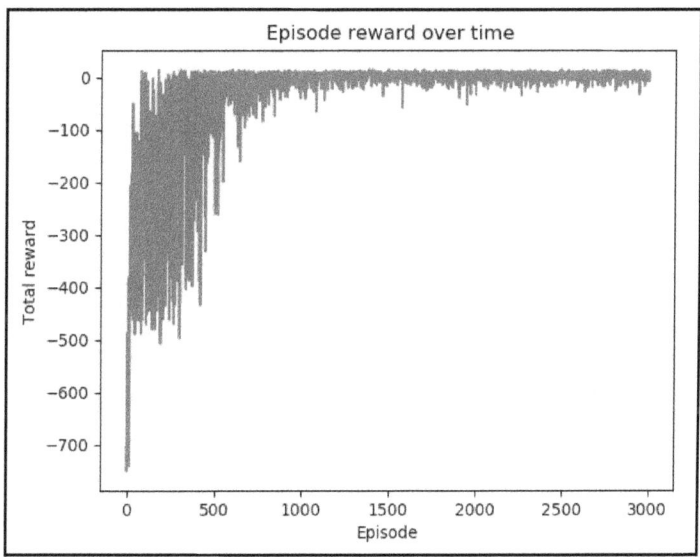

Double Q-learning overcomes the potential drawback of single Q-learning in complicated environments. It randomly rotates over two Q functions and updates them, which prevents action values from one Q function from being overestimated. At the same time, it might underestimate the Q function, since it doesn't update the same Q function over time steps. Hence, we can see that optimal action values take more episodes to converge.

See also

For the theory behind double Q-learning, check out the original paper, `https://papers.nips.cc/paper/3964-double-q-learning`, by Hado van Hasselt, published in *Advances in Neural Information Processing Systems 23* (NIPS 2010), 2613-2621, 2010.

5
Solving Multi-armed Bandit Problems

Multi-armed bandit algorithms are probably among the most popular algorithms in reinforcement learning. This chapter will start by creating a multi-armed bandit and experimenting with random policies. We will focus on how to solve the multi-armed bandit problem using four strategies, including epsilon-greedy, softmax exploration, upper confidence bound, and Thompson sampling. We will see how they deal with the exploration-exploitation dilemma in their own unique ways. We will also work on a billion-dollar problem, online advertising, and demonstrate how to solve it using a multi-armed bandit algorithm. Finally, we will solve the contextual advertising problem using contextual bandits to make more informed decisions in ad optimization.

The following recipes will be covered in this chapter:

- Creating a multi-armed bandit environment
- Solving multi-armed bandit problems with the epsilon-greedy policy
- Solving multi-armed bandit problems with softmax exploration
- Solving multi-armed bandit problems with an upper confidence bound algorithm
- Solving internet advertising problems with the multi-armed bandit
- Solving multi-armed bandit problems with the Thompson sampling algorithm
- Solving internet advertising problems with contextual bandits

Creating a multi-armed bandit environment

Let's get started with a simple project of estimating the value of π using the Monte Carlo method, which is the core of model-free reinforcement learning algorithms.

The multi-armed bandit problem is one of the simplest reinforcement learning problems. It is best described as a slot machine with multiple levers (arms), and each lever has a different payout and payout probability. Our goal is to discover the best lever with the maximum return so that we can keep choosing it afterward. Let's start with a simple multi-armed bandit problem in which the payout and payout probability is fixed for each arm. After creating the environment, we will solve it using the random policy algorithm.

How to do it...

Let's develop the multi-armed bandit environment as follows:

```
>>> import torch
>>> class BanditEnv():
...         """
...         Multi-armed bandit environment
...         payout_list:
...             A list of probabilities of the likelihood that a
...             particular bandit will pay out
...         reward_list:
...             A list of rewards of the payout that bandit has
...         """
...         def __init__(self, payout_list, reward_list):
...             self.payout_list = payout_list
...             self.reward_list = reward_list
...
...         def step(self, action):
...             if torch.rand(1).item() < self.payout_list[action]:
...                 return self.reward_list[action]
...             return 0
```

The step method executes an action and returns the reward if it pays out, otherwise it returns 0.

Now, we will use a multi-armed bandit as an example and solve it with random policy:

1. Define the payout probabilities and rewards for the three-armed bandit and create an instance of the bandit environment:

```
>>> bandit_payout = [0.1, 0.15, 0.3]
>>> bandit_reward = [4, 3, 1]
>>> bandit_env = BanditEnv(bandit_payout, bandit_reward)
```

For example, there is a 10% chance of getting a reward of 4 by choosing arm 0.

2. We specify the number of episodes to run and define the lists holding the total rewards accumulated by choosing individual arms, the number of times individual arms are chosen, and the average reward over time for each arm:

```
>>> n_episode = 100000
>>> n_action = len(bandit_payout)
>>> action_count = [0 for _ in range(n_action)]
>>> action_total_reward = [0 for _ in range(n_action)]
>>> action_avg_reward = [[] for action in range(n_action)]
```

3. Define the random policy, which randomly selects an arm:

```
>>> def random_policy():
...     action = torch.multinomial(torch.ones(n_action), 1).item()
...     return action
```

4. Now, we run 100,000 episodes. For each episode, we also update the statistics of each arm:

```
>>> for episode in range(n_episode):
...     action = random_policy()
...     reward = bandit_env.step(action)
...     action_count[action] += 1
...     action_total_reward[action] += reward
...     for a in range(n_action):
...         if action_count[a]:
...             action_avg_reward[a].append(
...                 action_total_reward[a] / action_count[a])
...         else:
...             action_avg_reward[a].append(0)
```

5. After running 100,000 episodes, we plot the results of average reward over time:

```
>>> import matplotlib.pyplot as plt
>>> for action in range(n_action):
...     plt.plot(action_avg_reward[action])
>>> plt.legend(['Arm {}'.format(action) for action in
```

```
range(n_action)])
>>> plt.title('Average reward over time')
>>> plt.xscale('log')
>>> plt.xlabel('Episode')
>>> plt.ylabel('Average reward')
>>> plt.show()
```

How it works...

In the example we just worked on, there are three slot machines. Each machine has a different payout (reward) and payout probability. In each episode, we randomly chose one arm of the machine to pull (one action to execute) and get a payout at a certain probability.

Run the lines of code in *Step 5*; you will see the following plot:

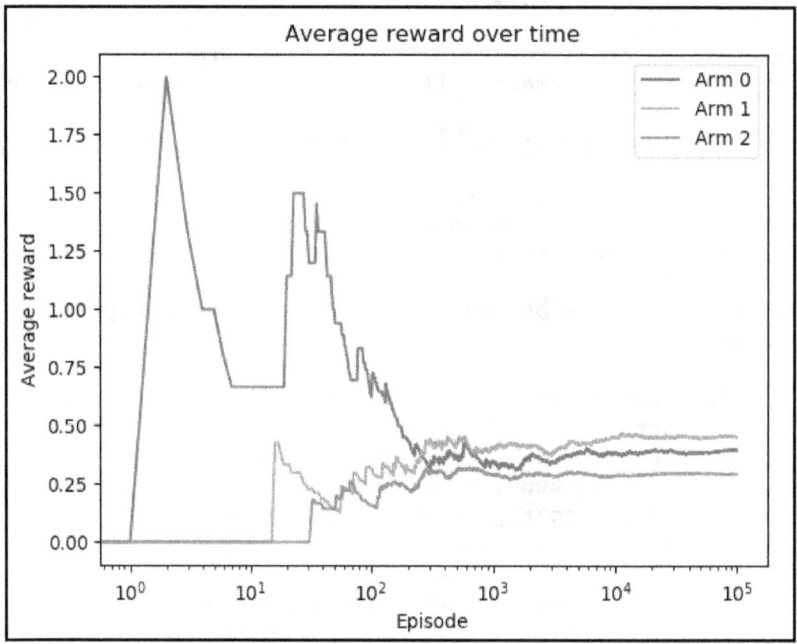

Arm 1 is the best arm with the largest average reward. Also, the average rewards start to saturate round 10,000 episodes.

This solution seems very naive as we only perform an exploration of all arms. We will come up with more intelligent strategies in the upcoming recipes.

Solving multi-armed bandit problems with the epsilon-greedy policy

Instead of exploring solely with random policy, we can do better with a combination of exploration and exploitation. Here comes the well-known epsilon-greedy policy.

Epsilon-greedy for multi-armed bandits exploits the best action the majority of the time and also keeps exploring different actions from time to time. Given a parameter, ε, with a value from 0 to 1, the probabilities of performing exploration and exploitation are ε and 1 - ε, respectively:

- **Epsilon**: Each action is taken with a probability calculated as follows:

$$\pi(s, a) = \epsilon/|A|$$

Here, |A| is the number of possible actions.

- **Greedy**: The action with the highest state-action value is favored, and its probability of being chosen is increased by 1 - ε:

$$\pi(s, a) = 1 - \epsilon + \epsilon/|A|$$

How to do it...

We solve the multi-armed bandit problem using the epsilon-greedy policy as follows:

1. Import the PyTorch and the bandit environment we developed in the previous recipe, *Creating a multi-armed bandit environment* (assuming the BanditEnv class is in a file called `multi_armed_bandit.py`):

```
>>> import torch
>>> from multi_armed_bandit import BanditEnv
```

2. Define the payout probabilities and rewards for the three-armed bandit and create an instance of the bandit environment:

```
>>> bandit_payout = [0.1, 0.15, 0.3]
>>> bandit_reward = [4, 3, 1]
>>> bandit_env = BanditEnv(bandit_payout, bandit_reward)
```

3. We specify the number of episodes to run and define the lists holding the total rewards accumulated by choosing individual arms, the number of times individual arms are chosen, and the average reward over time for each arm:

```
>>> n_episode = 100000
>>> n_action = len(bandit_payout)
>>> action_count = [0 for _ in range(n_action)]
>>> action_total_reward = [0 for _ in range(n_action)]
>>> action_avg_reward = [[] for action in range(n_action)]
```

4. Define the epsilon-greedy policy function, specify the value of epsilon, and create an epsilon-greedy policy instance:

```
>>> def gen_epsilon_greedy_policy(n_action, epsilon):
...         def policy_function(Q):
...             probs = torch.ones(n_action) * epsilon / n_action
...             best_action = torch.argmax(Q).item()
...             probs[best_action] += 1.0 - epsilon
...             action = torch.multinomial(probs, 1).item()
...             return action
...         return policy_function
>>> epsilon = 0.2
>>> epsilon_greedy_policy = gen_epsilon_greedy_policy(n_action,
epsilon)
```

5. Initialize the Q function, which is the average reward obtained by individual arms:

```
>>> Q = torch.zeros(n_action)
```

We will update the Q function over time.

6. Now, we run 100,000 episodes. For each episode, we also update the statistics of each arm:

```
>>> for episode in range(n_episode):
...        action = epsilon_greedy_policy(Q)
...        reward = bandit_env.step(action)
...        action_count[action] += 1
...        action_total_reward[action] += reward
...        Q[action] = action_total_reward[action] /
action_count[action]
...        for a in range(n_action):
...            if action_count[a]:
...                action_avg_reward[a].append(
                        action_total_reward[a] / action_count[a])
...            else:
...                action_avg_reward[a].append(0)
```

7. After running 100,000 episodes, we plot the results of the average reward over time:

```
>>> import matplotlib.pyplot as plt
 >>> for action in range(n_action):
...        plt.plot(action_avg_reward[action])
 >>> plt.legend(['Arm {}'.format(action) for action in
range(n_action)])
 >>> plt.title('Average reward over time')
 >>> plt.xscale('log')
 >>> plt.xlabel('Episode')
 >>> plt.ylabel('Average reward')
 >>> plt.show()
```

How it works...

Similar to other MDP problems, the epsilon-greedy policy selects the best arm with a probability of 1 - ε and performs random exploration with a probability of ε. Epsilon manages the trade-off between exploration and exploitation.

In *Step 7*, you will see the following plot:

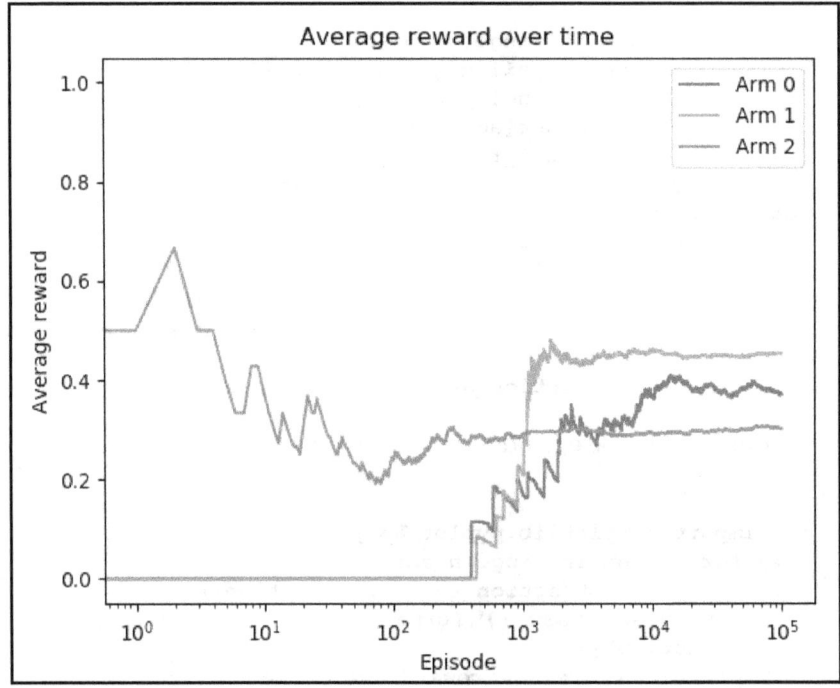

Arm 1 is the best arm, with the largest average reward at the end. Also, its average reward starts to saturate after around 1,000 episodes.

There's more...

You may wonder whether the epsilon-greedy policy actually outperforms the random policy. Besides the fact that the value for the optimal arm converges earlier with the epsilon-greedy policy, we can also prove that, on average, the reward we get during the course of training is higher with the epsilon-greedy policy than the random policy.

We can simply average the reward over all episodes:

```
>>> print(sum(action_total_reward) / n_episode)
0.43718
```

Over 100,000 episodes, the average payout is `0.43718` with the epsilon-greedy policy. Repeating the same computation for the random policy solution, we get 0.37902 as the average payout.

Solving multi-armed bandit problems with the softmax exploration

In this recipe, we will solve the multi-armed bandit problem using the softmax exploration, algorithm. We will see how it differs from the epsilon-greedy policy.

As we've seen with epsilon-greedy, when performing exploration we randomly select one of the non-best arms with a probability of ε/|A|. Each non-best arm is treated equivalently regardless of its value in the Q function. Also, the best arm is chosen with a fixed probability regardless of its value. In **softmax exploration**, an arm is chosen based on a probability from the **softmax distribution** of the Q function values. The probability is calculated as follows:

$$P(a) = \frac{exp(Q(a)/\tau)}{\sum_i^{|A|} exp(Q(i)/\tau)}$$

Here, the τ parameter is the temperature factor, which specifies the randomness of the exploration. The higher the value of τ, the closer to equal exploration it becomes; the lower the value of τ, the more likely the best arm is chosen.

How to do it...

We solve the multi-armed bandit problem using the softmax exploration algorithm as follows:

1. Import PyTorch and the bandit environment we developed in the first recipe, *Creating a multi-armed bandit environment* (assuming the BanditEnv class is in a file called multi_armed_bandit.py):

```
>>> import torch
>>> from multi_armed_bandit import BanditEnv
```

2. Define the payout probabilities and rewards for the three-armed bandit and create an instance of the bandit environment:

```
>>> bandit_payout = [0.1, 0.15, 0.3]
>>> bandit_reward = [4, 3, 1]
>>> bandit_env = BanditEnv(bandit_payout, bandit_reward)
```

3. We specify the number of episodes to run and define the lists holding the total rewards accumulated by choosing individual arms, the number of times individual arms are chosen, and the average reward over time for each arm:

```
>>> n_episode = 100000
>>> n_action = len(bandit_payout)
>>> action_count = [0 for _ in range(n_action)]
>>> action_total_reward = [0 for _ in range(n_action)]
>>> action_avg_reward = [[] for action in range(n_action)]
```

4. Define the softmax exploration policy function, specify the value of τ, and create a softmax exploration policy instance:

```
>>> def gen_softmax_exploration_policy(tau):
...     def policy_function(Q):
...         probs = torch.exp(Q / tau)
...         probs = probs / torch.sum(probs)
...         action = torch.multinomial(probs, 1).item()
...         return action
...     return policy_function
>>> tau = 0.1
>>> softmax_exploration_policy =
gen_softmax_exploration_policy(tau)
```

5. Initialize the Q function, which is the average reward obtained by the individual arms:

```
>>> Q = torch.zeros(n_action)
```

We will update the Q function over time.

6. Now, we run 100,000 episodes. For each episode, we also update the statistics of each arm:

```
>>> for episode in range(n_episode):
...     action = softmax_exploration_policy(Q)
...     reward = bandit_env.step(action)
...     action_count[action] += 1
...     action_total_reward[action] += reward
...     Q[action] = action_total_reward[action] /
action_count[action]
...     for a in range(n_action):
...         if action_count[a]:
...             action_avg_reward[a].append(
                     action_total_reward[a] / action_count[a])
...         else:
...             action_avg_reward[a].append(0)
```

7. After running 100,000 episodes, we plot the results of the average reward over time:

```
>>> import matplotlib.pyplot as plt
 >>> for action in range(n_action):
 ...        plt.plot(action_avg_reward[action])
 >>> plt.legend(['Arm {}'.format(action) for action in
range(n_action)])
 >>> plt.title('Average reward over time')
 >>> plt.xscale('log')
 >>> plt.xlabel('Episode')
 >>> plt.ylabel('Average reward')
 >>> plt.show()
```

How it works...

With the softmax exploration strategy, the dilemma of exploitation and exploration is solved with a softmax function based on the Q values. Instead of using a fixed pair of probabilities for the best arm and non-best arms, it adjusts the probabilities according to the softmax distribution with the τ parameter as a temperature factor. The higher the value of τ, the more focus will be shifted to exploration.

In *Step 7*, you will see the following plot:

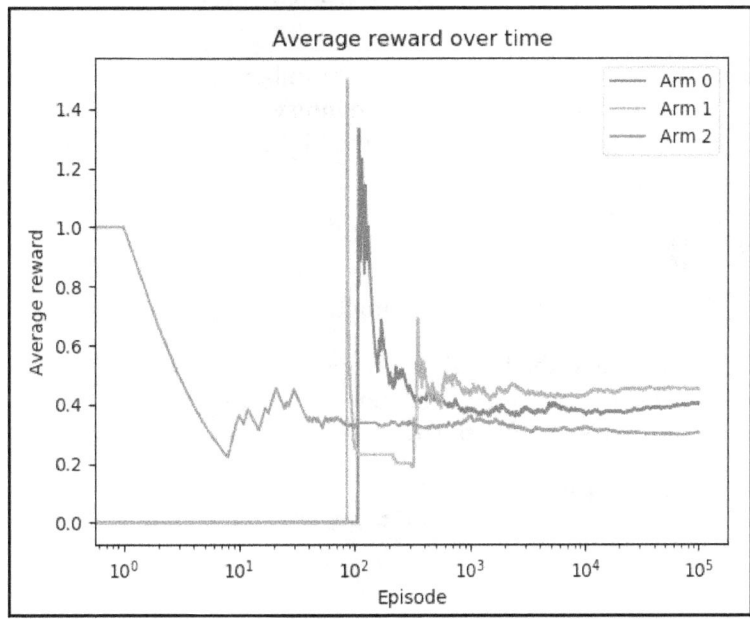

Arm 1 is the best arm, with the largest average reward at the end. Also, its average reward starts to saturate after around 800 episodes in this example.

Solving multi-armed bandit problems with the upper confidence bound algorithm

In the previous two recipes, we explored random actions in the multi-armed bandit problem with probabilities that are either assigned as fixed values in the epsilon-greedy policy or computed based on the Q-function values in the softmax exploration algorithm. In either algorithm, the probabilities of taking random actions are not adjusted over time. Ideally, we want less exploration as learning progresses. In this recipe, we will use a new algorithm called **upper confidence bound** to achieve this goal.

The **upper confidence bound (UCB)** algorithm stems from the idea of the confidence interval. In general, the confidence interval is a range of values where the true value lies. In the UCB algorithm, the confidence interval for an arm is a range where the mean reward obtained with this arm lies. The interval is in the form of [lower confidence bound, upper confidence bound] and we only use the upper bound, which is the UCB, to estimate the potential of the arm. The UCB is computed as follows:

$$UCB(a) = Q(a) + \sqrt{2log(t)/N(a)}$$

Here, t is the number of episodes, and N(a) is the number of times arm a is chosen among t episodes. As learning progresses, the confidence interval shrinks and becomes more and more accurate. The arm to pull is the one with the highest UCB.

How to do it...

We solve the multi-armed bandit problem using the UCB algorithm as follows:

1. Import PyTorch and the bandit environment we developed in the first recipe, *Creating a multi-armed bandit environment* (assuming the BanditEnv class is in a file called multi_armed_bandit.py):

```
>>> import torch
 >>> from multi_armed_bandit import BanditEnv
```

2. Define the payout probabilities and rewards for the three-armed bandit and create an instance of the bandit environment:

```
>>> bandit_payout = [0.1, 0.15, 0.3]
>>> bandit_reward = [4, 3, 1]
>>> bandit_env = BanditEnv(bandit_payout, bandit_reward)
```

3. We specify the number of episodes to run and define the lists holding the total rewards accumulated by choosing individual arms, the number of times individual arms are chosen, and the average reward over time for each arm:

```
>>> n_episode = 100000
>>> n_action = len(bandit_payout)
>>> action_count = torch.tensor([0. for _ in range(n_action)])
>>> action_total_reward = [0 for _ in range(n_action)]
>>> action_avg_reward = [[] for action in range(n_action)]
```

4. Define the UCB policy function, which computes the best arm based on the UCB formula:

```
>>> def upper_confidence_bound(Q, action_count, t):
...     ucb = torch.sqrt((2 * torch.log(torch.tensor(float(t))))
                                        / action_count) + Q
...     return torch.argmax(ucb)
```

5. Initialize the Q function, which is the average reward obtained with individual arms:

```
>>> Q = torch.empty(n_action)
```

We will update the Q function over time.

6. Now, we run 100,000 episodes with our UCB policy. For each episode, we also update the statistics of each arm:

```
>>> for episode in range(n_episode):
...         action = upper_confidence_bound(Q, action_count, episode)
...         reward = bandit_env.step(action)
...         action_count[action] += 1
...         action_total_reward[action] += reward
...         Q[action] = action_total_reward[action] /
action_count[action]
...         for a in range(n_action):
...             if action_count[a]:
...                 action_avg_reward[a].append(
                            action_total_reward[a] / action_count[a])
...             else:
...                 action_avg_reward[a].append(0)
```

7. After running 100,000 episodes, we plot the results of the average reward over time:

```
>>> import matplotlib.pyplot as plt
 >>> for action in range(n_action):
...         plt.plot(action_avg_reward[action])
 >>> plt.legend(['Arm {}'.format(action) for action in
range(n_action)])
 >>> plt.title('Average reward over time')
 >>> plt.xscale('log')
 >>> plt.xlabel('Episode')
 >>> plt.ylabel('Average reward')
 >>> plt.show()
```

How it works...

In this recipe, we solved the multi-armed bandit with the UCB algorithm. It adjusts the exploitation-exploration dilemma according to the number of episodes. For an action with a few data points, its confidence interval is relatively wide, hence, choosing this action is of relatively high uncertainty. With more episodes of the action being selected, the confidence interval becomes narrow and shrinks to its actual value. In this case, it is of high certainty to choose (or not) this action. Finally, the UCB algorithm pulls the arm with the highest UCB in each episode and gains more and more confidence over time.

After running the code in *Step 7*, you will see the following plot:

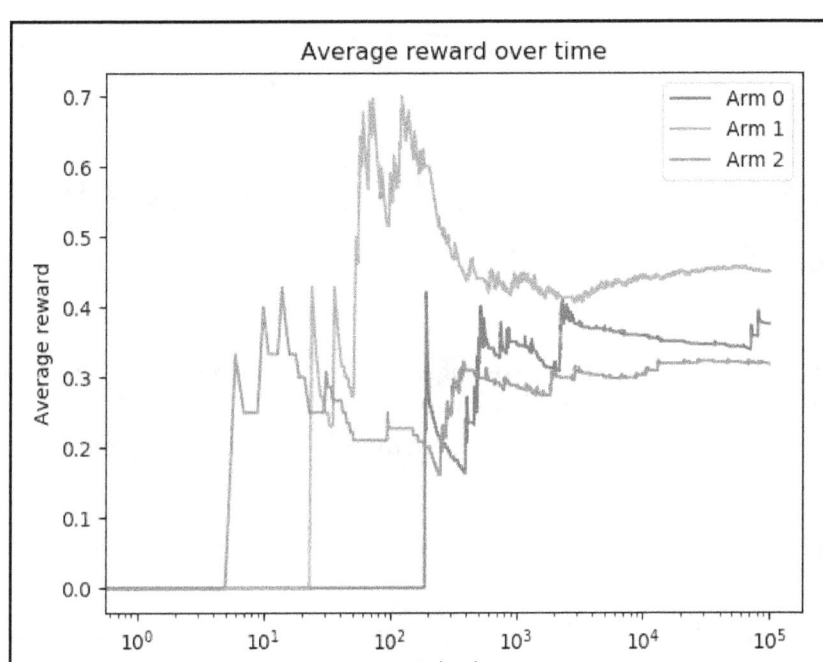

Arm 1 is the best arm, with the largest average reward in the end.

There's more...

You may wonder whether UCB actually outperforms the epsilon-greedy policy. We can compute the average reward over the entire training process, and the policy with the highest average reward learns faster.

We can simply average the reward over all episodes:

```
>>> print(sum(action_total_reward) / n_episode)
0.44605
```

Over 100,000 episodes, the average payout is 0.44605 with UCB, which is higher than 0.43718 with the epsilon-greedy policy.

See also

For those who want to brush up on confidence intervals, feel free to check out the following: `http://www.stat.yale.edu/Courses/1997-98/101/confint.htm`

Solving internet advertising problems with a multi-armed bandit

Imagine you are an advertiser working on ad optimization on a website:

- There are three different colors of ad background – red, green, and blue. Which one will achieve the best click-through rate (CTR)?
- There are three types of wordings of the ad – *learn ...*, *free ...*, and *try ....* Which one will achieve the best CTR?

For each visitor, we need to choose an ad in order to maximize the CTR over time. How can we solve this?

Perhaps you are thinking about A/B testing, where you randomly split the traffic into groups and assign each ad to a different group, and then choose the ad from the group with the highest CTR after a period of observation. However, this is basically a complete exploration, and we are usually unsure of how long the observation period should be and will end up losing a large portion of potential clicks. Besides, in A/B testing, the unknown CTR for an ad is assumed to not change over time. Otherwise, such A/B testing should be re-run periodically.

A multi-armed bandit can certainly do better than A/B testing. Each arm is an ad, and the reward for an arm is either 1 (click) or 0 (no click).

Let's try to solve it with the UCB algorithm.

How to do it...

We can solve the multi-armed bandit advertising problem using the UCB algorithm as follows:

1. Import PyTorch and the bandit environment we developed in the first recipe, *Creating a multi-armed bandit environment* (assuming the `BanditEnv` class is in a file called `multi_armed_bandit.py`):

```
>>> import torch
>>> from multi_armed_bandit import BanditEnv
```

2. Define the payout probabilities and rewards for the three-armed bandit (three ad candidates, for example) and create an instance of the bandit environment:

```
>>> bandit_payout = [0.01, 0.015, 0.03]
>>> bandit_reward = [1, 1, 1]
>>> bandit_env = BanditEnv(bandit_payout, bandit_reward)
```

Here, the true CTR for ad 0 is 1%, for ad 1 1.5%, and for ad 2 3%.

3. We specify the number of episodes to run and define the lists holding the total rewards accumulated by choosing individual arms, the number of times individual arms are chosen, and the average reward over time for each arm:

```
>>> n_episode = 100000
>>> n_action = len(bandit_payout)
>>> action_count = torch.tensor([0. for _ in range(n_action)])
>>> action_total_reward = [0 for _ in range(n_action)]
>>> action_avg_reward = [[] for action in range(n_action)]
```

4. Define the UCB policy function, which computes the best arm based on the UCB formula:

```
>>> def upper_confidence_bound(Q, action_count, t):
...     ucb = torch.sqrt((2 * torch.log(
                    torch.tensor(float(t)))) / action_count) + Q
...     return torch.argmax(ucb)
```

5. Initialize the Q function, which is the average reward obtained by individual arms:

```
>>> Q = torch.empty(n_action)
```

We will update the Q function over time.

6. Now, we run 100,000 episodes with the UCB policy. For each episode, we also update the statistics of each arm:

```
>>> for episode in range(n_episode):
...         action = upper_confidence_bound(Q, action_count, episode)
...         reward = bandit_env.step(action)
...         action_count[action] += 1
...         action_total_reward[action] += reward
...         Q[action] = action_total_reward[action] /
action_count[action]
...         for a in range(n_action):
...             if action_count[a]:
...                 action_avg_reward[a].append(
...                     action_total_reward[a] / action_count[a])
...             else:
...                 action_avg_reward[a].append(0)
```

7. After running 100,000 episodes, we plot the results of the average reward over time:

```
>>> import matplotlib.pyplot as plt
>>> for action in range(n_action):
...         plt.plot(action_avg_reward[action])
>>> plt.legend(['Arm {}'.format(action) for action in
range(n_action)])
>>> plt.title('Average reward over time')
>>> plt.xscale('log')
>>> plt.xlabel('Episode')
>>> plt.ylabel('Average reward')
>>> plt.show()
```

How it works...

In this recipe, we solved the ad optimization problem in a multi-armed bandit manner. It overcomes the challenges confronting the A/B testing approach. We used the UCB algorithm to solve the multi-armed (multi-ad) bandit problem; the reward for each arm is either 1 or 0. Instead of pure exploration and no interaction between action and reward, UCB (or other algorithms such as epsilon-greedy and softmax exploration) dynamically switches between exploitation and exploration where necessarly. For an ad with a few data points, the confidence interval is relatively wide, hence, choosing this action is of relatively high uncertainty. With more episodes of the ad being selected, the confidence interval becomes narrow and shrinks to its actual value.

You can see the resulting plot in *Step 7* as follows:

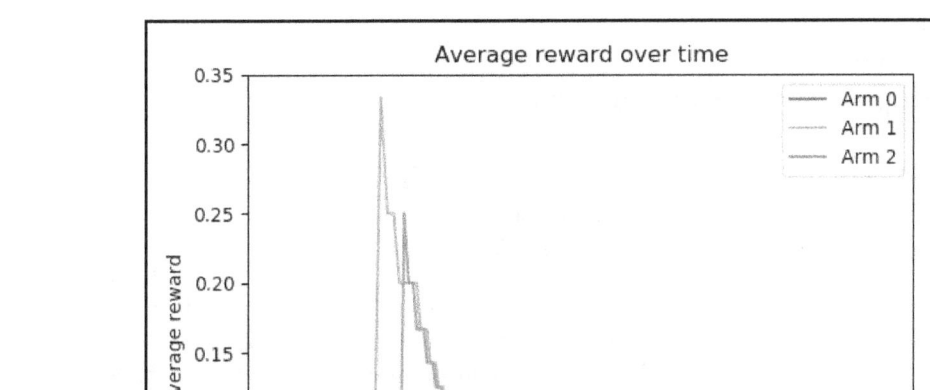

Ad 2 is the best ad with the highest predicted CTR (average reward) after the model converges.

Eventually, we found that ad 2 is the optimal one to choose, which is true. Also, the sooner we figure this out the better, because we will lose fewer potential clicks. In this example, ad 2 outperformed the others after around 100 episodes.

Solving multi-armed bandit problems with the Thompson sampling algorithm

In this recipe, we will tackle the exploitation and exploration dilemma in the advertising bandits problem using another algorithm, Thompson sampling. We will see how it differs greatly from the previous three algorithms.

Thompson sampling (TS) is also called Bayesian bandits as it applies the Bayesian way of thinking from the following perspectives:

- It is a probabilistic algorithm.
- It computes the prior distribution for each arm and samples a value from each distribution.
- It then selects the arm with the highest value and observes the reward.
- Finally, it updates the prior distribution based on the observed reward. This process is called **Bayesian updating**.

As we have seen that in our ad optimization case, the reward for each arm is either 1 or 0. We can use **beta distribution** for our prior distribution because the value of the beta distribution is from 0 to 1. The beta distribution is parameterized by two parameters, α and β. α represents the number of times we receive the reward of 1 and β, indicates the number of times we receive the reward of 0.

To help you understand the beta distribution better, we will start by looking at several beta distributions before we implement the TS algorithm.

How to do it...

Let's explore the beta distribution through the following steps:

1. Import PyTorch and matplotlib because we will visualize the shape of the distributions:

```
>>> import torch
>>> import matplotlib.pyplot as plt
```

2. We start by visualizing the shape of the beta distribution with the starting positions, $\alpha=1$ and $\beta=1$:

```
>>> beta1 = torch.distributions.beta.Beta(1, 1)
>>> samples1 = [beta1.sample() for _ in range(100000)]
>>> plt.hist(samples1, range=[0, 1], bins=10)
>>> plt.title('beta(1, 1)')
>>> plt.show()
```

You will see the following plot:

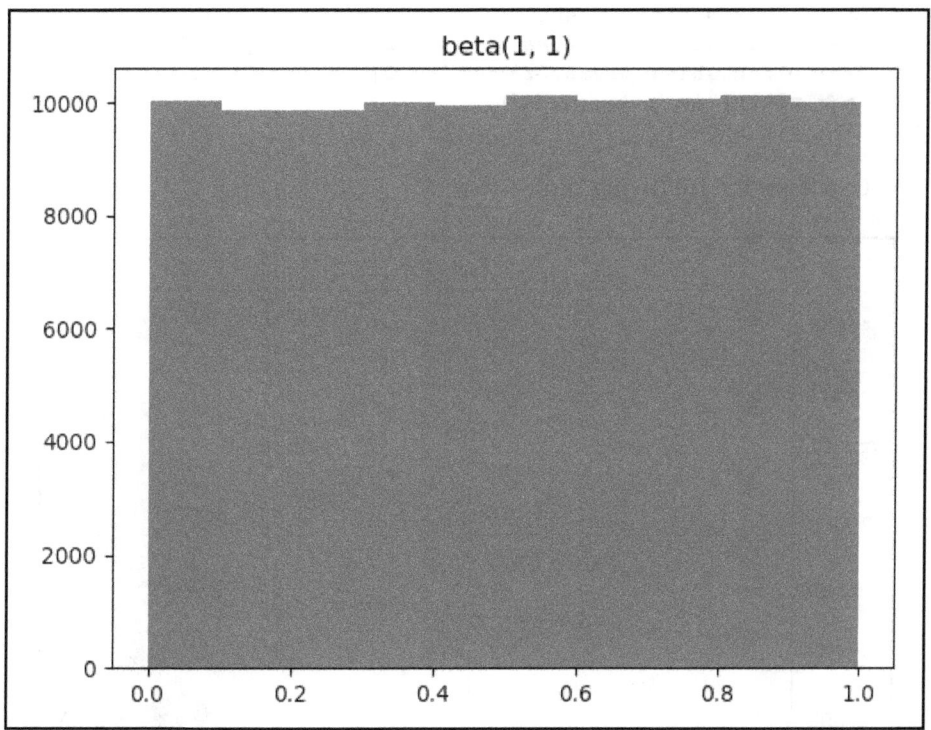

Obviously, when α=1 and β=1, it doesn't provide any information about where the true value lies in the range of 0 to 1. Hence, it becomes a uniform distribution.

3. We then visualize the shape of the beta distribution with α=5 and β=1:

```
>>> beta2 = torch.distributions.beta.Beta(5, 1)
>>> samples2 = [beta2.sample() for _ in range(100000)]
>>> plt.hist(samples2, range=[0, 1], bins=10)
>>> plt.title('beta(5, 1)')
>>> plt.show()
```

You will see the following plot:

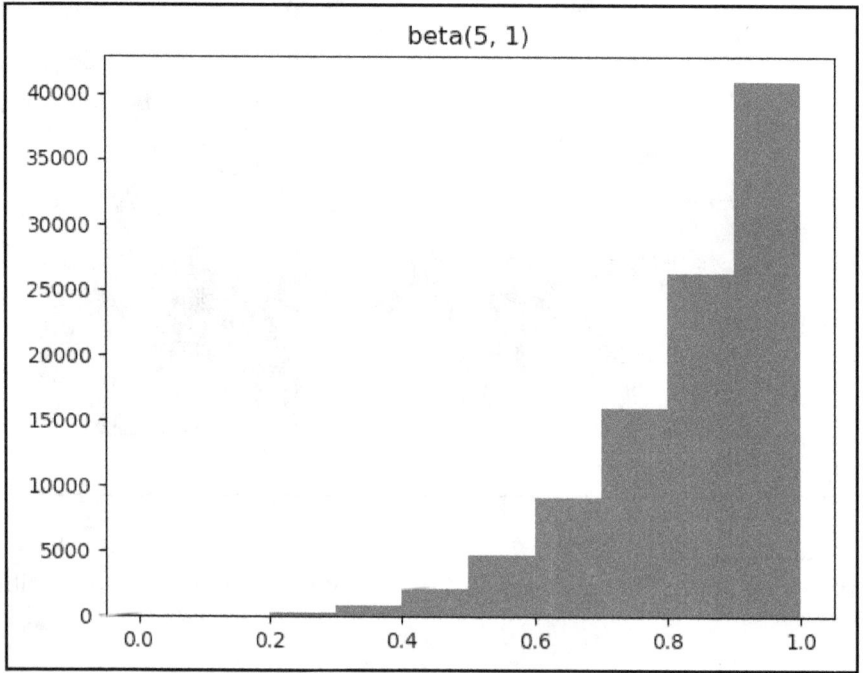

When α=5 and β=1, this means that there are 4 consecutive rewards of 1 in 4 experiments. The distribution shifts toward 1.

4. Now, let's experiment with α=1 and β=5:

```
>>> beta3 = torch.distributions.beta.Beta(1, 5)
>>> samples3= [beta3.sample() for _ in range(100000)]
>>> plt.hist(samples3, range=[0, 1], bins=10)
>>> plt.title('beta(1, 5)')
>>> plt.show()
```

You will see the following plot:

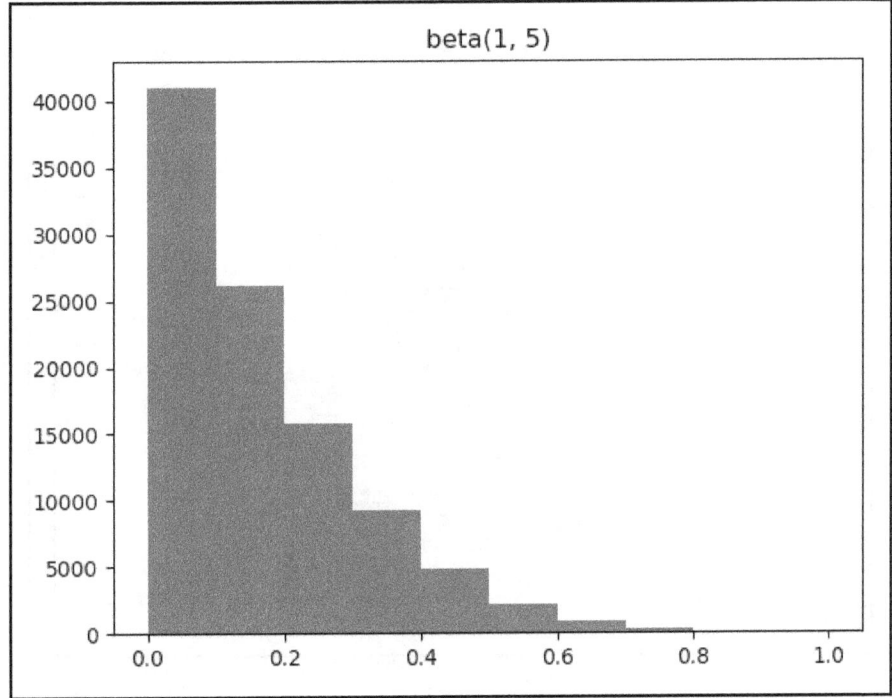

When α=1 and β=5, this means that there are 4 consecutive rewards of 0 in 4 experiments. The distribution shifts toward 0.

5. Finally, we take a look at the situation when α=5 and β=5:

```
>>> beta4 = torch.distributions.beta.Beta(5, 5)
>>> samples4= [beta4.sample() for _ in range(100000)]
>>> plt.hist(samples4, range=[0, 1], bins=10)
>>> plt.title('beta(5, 5)')
>>> plt.show()
```

You will see the following plot:

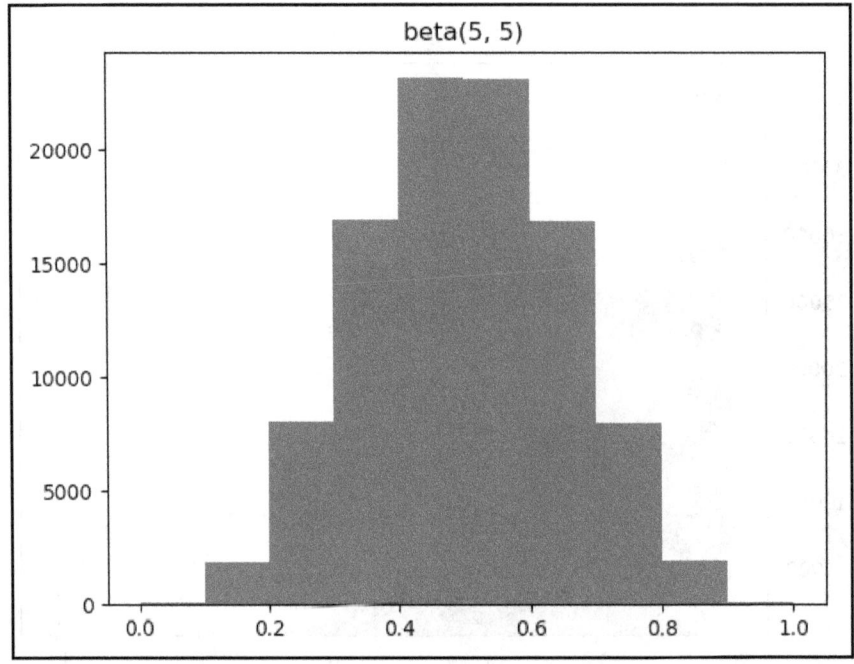

When α=5 and β=5, we observe the same numbers of clicks and no-clicks in 8 rounds. The distribution shifts toward the middle point, **0.5**.

Now it is time to solve the multi-armed bandit advertising problem using the Thompson sampling algorithm:

1. Import the bandit environment we developed in the first recipe, *Creating a multi-armed bandit environment* (assuming the `BanditEnv` class is in a file called `multi_armed_bandit.py`):

   ```
   >>> from multi_armed_bandit import BanditEnv
   ```

2. Define the payout probabilities and rewards for the three-armed bandit (three ad candidates) and create an instance of the bandit environment:

   ```
   >>> bandit_payout = [0.01, 0.015, 0.03]
   >>> bandit_reward = [1, 1, 1]
   >>> bandit_env = BanditEnv(bandit_payout, bandit_reward)
   ```

3. We specify the number of episodes to run and define the lists holding the total rewards accumulated by choosing individual arms, the number of times individual arms are chosen, and the average reward over time for each arm:

   ```
   >>> n_episode = 100000
   >>> n_action = len(bandit_payout)
   >>> action_count = torch.tensor([0. for _ in range(n_action)])
   >>> action_total_reward = [0 for _ in range(n_action)]
   >>> action_avg_reward = [[] for action in range(n_action)]
   ```

4. Define the TS function, which samples a value from the beta distribution of each arm and selects the arm with the highest value:

   ```
   >>> def thompson_sampling(alpha, beta):
   ...     prior_values = torch.distributions.beta.Beta(alpha,
   beta).sample()
   ...     return torch.argmax(prior_values)
   ```

5. Initialize α and β for each arm:

   ```
   >>> alpha = torch.ones(n_action)
   >>> beta = torch.ones(n_action)
   ```

   Note that each beta distribution should start with $\alpha=\beta=1$.

6. Now, we run 100,000 episodes with the TS algorithm. For each episode, we also update α and β of each arm based on the observed reward:

```
>>> for episode in range(n_episode):
...         action = thompson_sampling(alpha, beta)
...         reward = bandit_env.step(action)
...         action_count[action] += 1
...         action_total_reward[action] += reward
...         if reward > 0:
...             alpha[action] += 1
...         else:
...             beta[action] += 1
...         for a in range(n_action):
...             if action_count[a]:
...                 action_avg_reward[a].append(
...                     action_total_reward[a] / action_count[a])
...             else:
...                 action_avg_reward[a].append(0)
```

7. After running 100,000 episodes, we plot the results of the average reward over time:

```
>>> import matplotlib.pyplot as plt
>>> for action in range(n_action):
...         plt.plot(action_avg_reward[action])
>>> plt.legend(['Arm {}'.format(action) for action in
range(n_action)])
>>> plt.title('Average reward over time')
>>> plt.xscale('log')
>>> plt.xlabel('Episode')
>>> plt.ylabel('Average reward')
>>> plt.show()
```

How it works...

In this recipe, we solved the ad bandits problem with the TS algorithm. The biggest difference between TS and the three other approaches is the adoption of Bayesian optimization. It first computes the prior distribution for each possible arm, and then randomly draws a value from each distribution. It then picks the arm with the highest value and uses the observed outcome to update the prior distribution. The TS policy is both stochastic and greedy. If an ad is more likely to receive clicks, its beta distribution shifts toward 1 and, hence, the value of a random sample tends to be closer to 1.

After running the lines of code in *Step 7*, you will see the following plot:

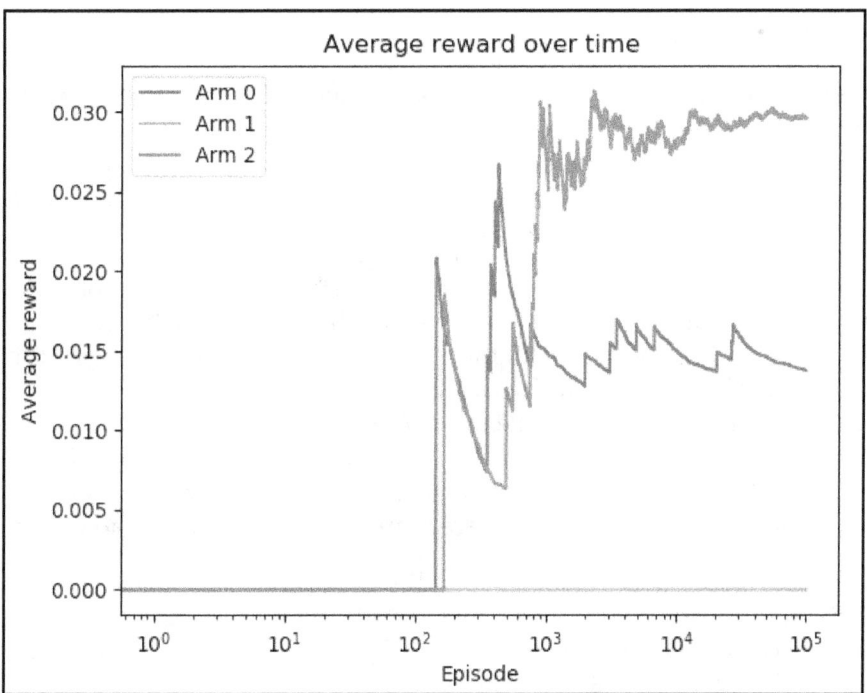

Ad 2 is the best ad, with the highest predicted CTR (average reward).

See also

For those who want to brush up on the beta distribution, feel free to check out the following:

- https://www.itl.nist.gov/div898/handbook/eda/section3/eda366h.htm
- http://varianceexplained.org/statistics/beta_distribution_and_baseball/

Solving internet advertising problems with contextual bandits

You may notice that in the ad optimization problem, we only care about the ad and ignore other information, such as user information and web page information, that might affect the ad being clicked on or not. In this recipe, we will talk about how we take more information into account beyond the ad itself and solve the problem with contextual bandits.

The multi-armed bandit problems we have worked with so far do not involve the concept of state, which is very different from MDPs. We only have several actions, and a reward will be generated that is associated with the action selected. **Contextual bandits** extend multi-armed bandits by introducing the concept of state. State provides a description of the environment, which helps the agent take more informed actions. In the advertising example, the state could be the user's gender (two states, male and female), the user's age group (four states, for example), or page category (such as sports, finance, or news). Intuitively, users of certain demographics are more likely to click on an ad on certain pages.

It is not difficult to understand contextual bandits. A multi-armed bandit is a single machine with multiple arms, while contextual bandits are a set of such machines (bandits). Each machine in contextual bandits is a state that has multiple arms. The learning goal is to find the best arm (action) for each machine (state).

We will work with an advertising example with two states for simplicity.

How to do it...

We solve the contextual bandits advertising problem using the UCB algorithm as follows:

1. Import PyTorch and the bandit environment we developed in the first recipe, *Creating a multi-armed bandit environment* (assuming the BanditEnv class is in a file called multi_armed_bandit.py):

```
>>> import torch
>>> from multi_armed_bandit import BanditEnv
```

2. Define the payout probabilities and rewards for the two three-armed bandits:

```
>>> bandit_payout_machines = [
...      [0.01, 0.015, 0.03],
...      [0.025, 0.01, 0.015]
... ]
```

```
>>> bandit_reward_machines = [
...     [1, 1, 1],
...     [1, 1, 1]
... ]
```

Here, the true CTR of ad 0 is 1%, of ad 1 is 1.5%, and of ad 2 is 3% for the first state, and [2.5%, 1%, and 1.5%] for the second state.

The number of slot machines in our case is two:

```
>>> n_machine = len(bandit_payout_machines)
```

Create a list of bandits given the corresponding payout information:

```
>>> bandit_env_machines = [BanditEnv(bandit_payout, bandit_reward)
...                         for bandit_payout, bandit_reward in
...                         zip(bandit_payout_machines, bandit_reward_machines)]
```

3. We specify the number of episodes to run and define the lists holding the total rewards accumulated by choosing individual arms in each state, the number of times individual arms are chosen in each state, and the average reward over time for each arm in each state:

```
>>> n_episode = 100000
>>> n_action = len(bandit_payout_machines[0])
>>> action_count = torch.zeros(n_machine, n_action)
>>> action_total_reward = torch.zeros(n_machine, n_action)
>>> action_avg_reward = [[[] for action in range(n_action)] for _
in range(n_machine)]
```

4. Define the UCB policy function, which computes the best arm based on the UCB formula:

```
>>> def upper_confidence_bound(Q, action_count, t):
...     ucb = torch.sqrt((2 * torch.log(
...              torch.tensor(float(t)))) / action_count) + Q
...     return torch.argmax(ucb)
```

5. Initialize the Q function, which is the average reward obtained with individual arms for individual states:

```
>>> Q_machines = torch.empty(n_machine, n_action)
```

We will update the Q-function over time.

6. Now, we run 100,000 episodes with the UCB policy. For each episode, we also update the statistics of each arm in each state:

```
>>> for episode in range(n_episode):
...         state = torch.randint(0, n_machine, (1,)).item()
...         action = upper_confidence_bound(
...                     Q_machines[state], action_count[state], episode)
...         reward = bandit_env_machines[state].step(action)
...         action_count[state][action] += 1
...         action_total_reward[state][action] += reward
...         Q_machines[state][action] =
...                             action_total_reward[state][action]
...                             / action_count[state][action]
...         for a in range(n_action):
...             if action_count[state][a]:
...                 action_avg_reward[state][a].append(
...                             action_total_reward[state][a]
...                             / action_count[state][a])
...             else:
...                 action_avg_reward[state][a].append(0)
```

7. After running 100,000 episodes, we plot the results of the average reward over time for each state:

```
>>> import matplotlib.pyplot as plt
>>> for state in range(n_machine):
...         for action in range(n_action):
...             plt.plot(action_avg_reward[state][action])
...         plt.legend(['Arm {}'.format(action)
...                         for action in range(n_action)])
...         plt.xscale('log')
...         plt.title(
...         'Average reward over time for state {}'.format(state))
...         plt.xlabel('Episode')
...         plt.ylabel('Average reward')
...         plt.show()
```

How it works...

In this recipe, we solved the contextual advertising problem with contextual bandits using the UCB algorithm.

Running the lines of code in *Step 7*, you will see the following plot.

We get this for the first state:

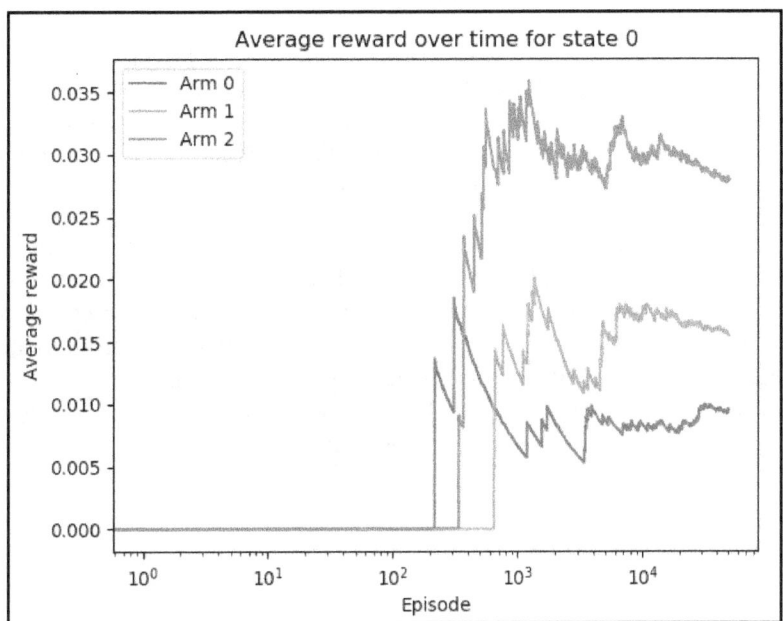

And we get this for the second state:

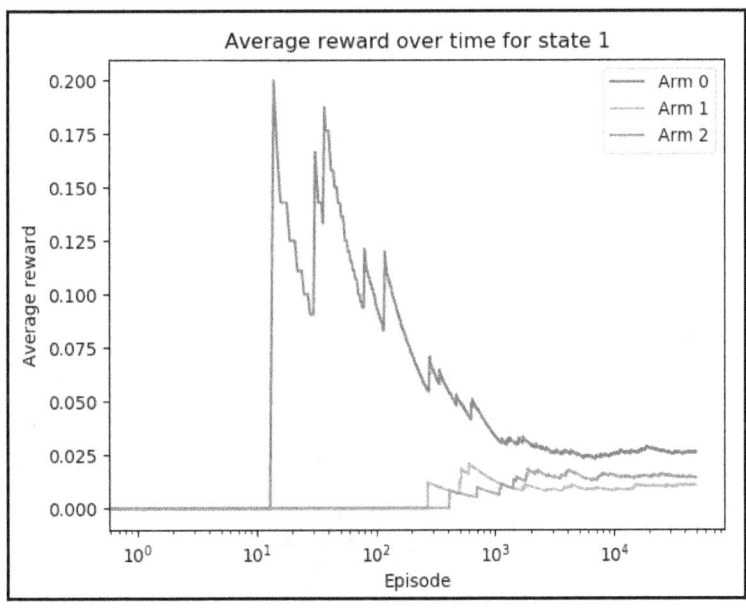

Given the first state, ad 2 is the best ad, with the highest predicted CTR. Given the second state, ad 0 is the optimal ad, with the highest average reward. And these are both true.

Contextual bandits are a set of multi-armed bandits. Each bandit represents a unique state of the environment. The state provides a description of the environment, which helps the agent take more informed actions. In our advertising example, male users might be more likely to click an ad than female users. We simply used two slot machines to incorporate two states and searched for the best arm to pull given each state.

One thing to note is that contextual bandits are still different from MDPs, although they involve the concept of state. First, the states in contextual bandits are not determined by the previous actions or states, but are simply observations of the environment. Second, there is no delayed or discounted reward in contextual bandits because a bandit episode is one step. However, compared to multi-armed bandits, contextual bandits are closer to MDP as the actions are conditional to the states in the environment. It is safe to say that contextual bandits are in between multi-armed bandits and full MDP reinforcement learning.

6
Scaling Up Learning with Function Approximation

So far, we have represented the value function in the form of a lookup table in the MC and TD methods. The TD method is able to update the Q-function on the fly during an episode, which is considered an advancement on the MC method. However, the TD method is still not sufficiently scalable for problems with many states and/or actions. It will be extremely slow at learning too many values for individual pairs of states and actions using the TD method.

This chapter will focus on function approximation, which can overcome the scaling issues in the TD method. We will begin by setting up the Mountain Car environment playground. After developing the linear function estimator, we will incorporate it into the Q-learning and SARSA algorithms. We will then improve the Q-learning algorithm using experience replay, and experiment with using neural works as a function estimator. Finally, we will cover how to solve the CartPole problem using what we have learned in the chapter as a whole.

The following recipes will be covered in this chapter:

- Setting up the Mountain Car environment playground
- Estimating Q-functions with gradient descent approximation
- Developing Q-learning with linear function approximation
- Developing SARSA with linear function approximation
- Incorporating batching using experience replay
- Developing Q-learning with neural net function approximation
- Solving the CartPole problem with function approximation

Setting up the Mountain Car environment playground

The TD method can learn the Q-function during an episode but is not scalable. For example, the number of states in a chess game is around 1,040, and 1,070 in a Go game. Moreover, it seems infeasible to learn the values for continuous state using the TD method. Hence, we need to solve such problems using **function approximation (FA)**, which approximates the state space using a set of features.

In this first recipe, we will begin by getting familiar with the Mountain Car environment, which we will solve with the help of FA methods in upcoming recipes.

Mountain Car (https://gym.openai.com/envs/MountainCar-v0/) is a typical Gym environment with continuous states. As shown in the following diagram, its goal is to get the car to the top of the hill:

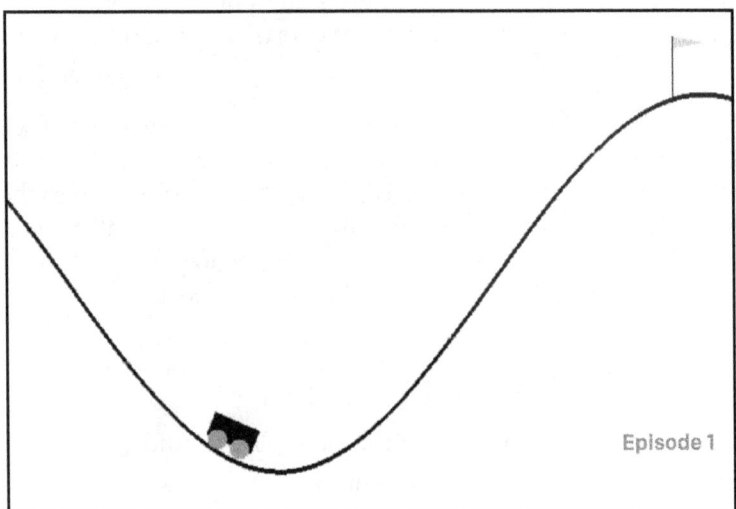

On a one-dimensional track, the car is positioned between -1.2 (leftmost) and 0.6 (rightmost), and the goal (yellow flag) is located at 0.5. The engine of the car is not strong enough to drive it to the top in a single pass, so it has to drive back and forth to build up momentum. Hence, there are three discrete actions for each step:

- Push left (0)
- No push (1)
- Push right (2)

And there are two states of the environment:

- Position of the car: this is a continuous variable from -1.2 to 0.6.
- Velocity of the car: this is a continuous variable from -0.07 to 0.07.

The reward associated with each step is -1, until the car reaches the goal (a position of 0.5).

An episode ends when the car reaches the goal position (obviously), or after 200 steps.

Getting ready

To run the Mountain Car environment, let's first search for its name in the table of environments – `https://github.com/openai/gym/wiki/Table-of-environments`. We get `MountainCar-v0` and also know that the observation space is represented by two floats and that there are three possible actions (left = 0, no push = 1, right = 2).

How to do it...

Let's simulate the Mountain Car environment in the following steps:

1. We import the Gym library and create an instance of the Mountain Car environment:

    ```
    >>> import gym
    >>> env = gym.envs.make("MountainCar-v0")
    >>> n_action = env.action_space.n
    >>> print(n_action)
    3
    ```

2. Reset the environment:

    ```
    >>> env.reset()
    array([-0.52354759,  0. ])
    ```

    The car starts with a state `[-0.52354759, 0.]`, which means that the initial position is around -0.5 and the velocity is 0. You may see a different initial position as it is randomly generated from -0.6 to -0.4.

3. Let's take a naive approach now: we just keep pushing the car to the right and hope it will reach the top:

    ```
    >>> is_done = False
    >>> while not is_done:
    ```

```
...          next_state, reward, is_done, info = env.step(2)
...          print(next_state, reward, is_done)
...          env.render()
>>> env.render()
[-0.49286453  0.00077561] -1.0 False
[-0.4913191   0.00154543] -1.0 False
[-0.48901538  0.00230371] -1.0 False
[-0.48597058  0.0030448 ] -1.0 False
......
......
[-0.29239555 -0.0046231 ] -1.0 False
[-0.29761694 -0.00522139] -1.0 False
[-0.30340632 -0.00578938] -1.0 True
```

4. Close the environment:

```
env.close()
```

How it works...

In *Step 3*, the state (position and velocity) keeps changing accordingly and the reward is -1 for each step.

You will also see in the video that the car is repeatedly moving to the right and back to the left, but doesn't reach the top in the end:

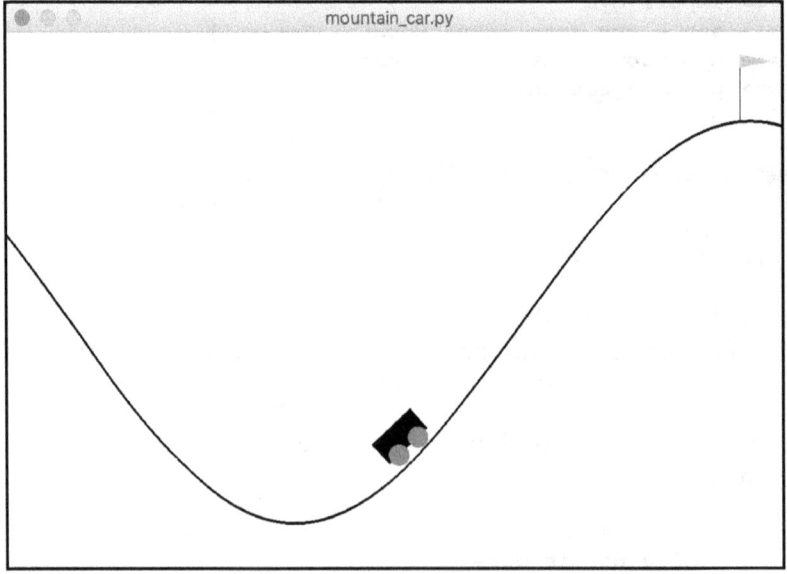

As you can imagine, the Mountain Car problem is not as easy as you thought. We need to drive the car back and forth to build up momentum. And the state variables are continuous, which means that a table `lookup/update` method (such as the TD method) will not work. In the next recipe, we will solve the Mountain Car problem with FA methods.

Estimating Q-functions with gradient descent approximation

Starting from this recipe, we will develop FA algorithms to solve environments with continuous state variables. We will begin by approximating Q-functions using linear functions and gradient descent.

The main idea of **FA** is to use a set of **features** to estimate Q values. This is extremely useful for processes with a large state space where the Q table becomes huge. There are several ways to map the features to the Q values; for example, linear approximations that are linear combinations of features and neural networks. With linear approximation, the state-value function for an action is expressed by a weighted sum of the features:

$$V(s) = \theta_1 F_1(s) + \theta_2 F_2(s) + \ldots\ldots + \theta_n F_n(s)$$

Here, F1(s), F2(s), ..., Fn(s) is a set of features given the input state, s; θ1, θ2,......, θn are the weights applied to corresponding features. Or we can put it as V(s)=θF(s).

As we have seen this in the TD method, we have the following formula to compute the future states:

$$V(s_t) := V(s_t) + \alpha[r + \gamma V(s_{t+1}) - V(s_t)]$$

Here, r is the associated reward obtained by transforming from state st to st+1, α is the learning rate, and γ is the discount factor. Let's denote δ as the TD error term, and now we have the following:

$$\delta = r + \gamma V(s_{t+1}) - V(s_t)$$
$$V(s_t) := V(s_t) + \alpha\delta$$

This is in the exact form of gradient descent. Hence, the goal of learning is to find the optimal weights, θ, to best approximate the state-value function V(s) for each possible action. The loss function we are trying to minimize in this case is similar to that in a regression problem, which is the mean squared error between the actual value and the estimated value. After each step in an episode, we have a new estimation of the true state value, and we move the weights, θ, a step toward their optimal value.

One more thing to note is the feature set, F(s), given the input state, s. A good feature set is one that can capture the dynamics of different inputs. Typically, we can generate a set of features with a set of Gaussian functions under various parameters, including mean and standard deviation.

How to do it...

We develop the Q-function approximator based on the linear function as follows:

1. Import all the necessary packages:

```
>>> import torch
>>> from torch.autograd import Variable
>>> import math
```

The variable wraps a tensor and supports backpropagation.

2. Then, start the __init__ method of the linear function's Estimator class:

```
>>> class Estimator():
...        def __init__(self, n_feat, n_state, n_action, lr=0.05):
...            self.w, self.b = self.get_gaussian_wb(n_feat, n_state)
...            self.n_feat = n_feat
...            self.models = []
...            self.optimizers = []
...            self.criterion = torch.nn.MSELoss()
...            for _ in range(n_action):
...                model = torch.nn.Linear(n_feat, 1)
...                self.models.append(model)
...                optimizer = torch.optim.SGD(model.parameters(),
lr)
...                self.optimizers.append(optimizer)
```

It takes in three parameters: the number of features, `n_feat`; the number of states; and the number of actions. It first generates a set of coefficients, `w` and `b`, for the feature function F(s) from Gaussian distributions, which we will define later. It then initializes `n_action` linear models, where each model corresponds to an action, and `n_action` optimizers, accordingly. For the linear model, we herein use the Linear module from PyTorch. It takes in `n_feat` units and generates one output, which is the predicted state-value for an action. The stochastic gradient descent optimizer is also initialized along with each linear model. The learning rate for each optimizer is 0.05. The loss function is the mean squared error.

3. We now continue defining the `get_gaussian_wb` method, which generates a set of coefficients, w and b, for the feature function, F(s):

```
>>>         def get_gaussian_wb(self, n_feat, n_state, sigma=.2):
...             """
...             Generate the coefficients of the feature set from
                Gaussian distribution
...             @param n_feat: number of features
...             @param n_state: number of states
...             @param sigma: kernel parameter
...             @return: coefficients of the features
...             """
...             torch.manual_seed(0)
...             w = torch.randn((n_state, n_feat)) * 1.0 / sigma
...             b = torch.rand(n_feat) * 2.0 * math.pi
...             return w, b
```

The coefficient, `w`, is an `n_feat` by `n_state` matrix, with values generated from a Gaussian distribution of variance defined by the parameter sigma; the bias, b, is a list of `n_feat` values generated from a uniform distribution of $[0, 2\pi]$.

Note that it is very important to set a specific random seed (`torch.manual_seed(0)`) so that a state can always be mapped to the same feature in different runs.

4. Next, we develop the function to map the state space to the feature space based on `w` and `b`:

```
>>>         def get_feature(self, s):
...             """
...             Generate features based on the input state
...             @param s: input state
...             @return: features
...             """
```

```
...            features = (2.0 / self.n_feat) ** .5 * torch.cos(
                   torch.matmul(torch.tensor(s).float(), self.w)
                   + self.b)
...            return features
```

The feature of a state, s, is generated as follows:

$$F(s) = \sqrt{2/n\_feat}\ cos(w * s + b)$$

Use cosine transformation to ensure that the feature is in the range of [-1, 1] despite the value of an input state.

5. Since we've defined model and feature generation, we now develop the training method, which updates the linear models with a data point:

```
>>>        def update(self, s, a, y):
...            """
...            Update the weights for the linear estimator with
               the given training sample
...            @param s: state
...            @param a: action
...            @param y: target value
...            """
...            features = Variable(self.get_feature(s))
...            y_pred = self.models[a](features)
...            loss = self.criterion(y_pred,
                       Variable(torch.Tensor([y])))
...            self.optimizers[a].zero_grad()
...            loss.backward()
...            self.optimizers[a].step()
```

Given a training data point, it first converts the state to feature space with the get_feature method. The resulting features are then fed into the current linear model of the given action, a. The predictive result, along with the target value, is used to compute the loss and gradients. The weights, θ, are then updated via backpropagation.

6. The next operation involves predicting the state-value for each action given a state using the current models:

```
>>>        def predict(self, s):
...            """
...            Compute the Q values of the state using
                   the learning model
...            @param s: input state
```

```
...              @return: Q values of the state
...              """
...              features = self.get_feature(s)
...              with torch.no_grad():
...                  return torch.tensor([model(features)
                                    for model in self.models])
```

That's all for the `Estimator` class.

7. Now, let's play around with some dummy data. First, create an `Estimator` object that maps a 2-dimensional state to a 10-dimensional feature and works with 1 possible action:

```
>>> estimator = Estimator(10, 2, 1)
```

8. Now, generate the feature out of a state [0.5, 0.1]:

```
>>> s1 = [0.5, 0.1]
>>> print(estimator.get_feature(s1))
tensor([ 0.3163, -0.4467, -0.0450, -0.1490,  0.2393, -0.4181,
-0.4426, 0.3074,
            -0.4451,  0.1808])
```

As you can see, the resulting feature is a 10-dimensional vector.

9. Train the estimator on a list of states and target state-values (and we only have one action in this example):

```
>>> s_list = [[1, 2], [2, 2], [3, 4], [2, 3], [2, 1]]
>>> target_list = [1, 1.5, 2, 2, 1.5]
>>> for s, target in zip(s_list, target_list):
...     feature = estimator.get_feature(s)
...     estimator.update(s, 0, target)
```

10. And finally, we use the trained linear model to predict the value for new states:

```
>>> print(estimator.predict([0.5, 0.1]))
tensor([0.6172])
>>> print(estimator.predict([2, 3]))
tensor([0.8733])
```

The predicted value for state [0.5, 0.1] with the action is 0.5847, while for [2, 3], it is 0.7969.

How it works...

The FA method approximates the state values with a more compact model than computing the exact values with a Q table in the TD method. FA first maps the state space to the feature space and then estimates the Q values using a regression model. In this way, the learning process becomes supervised. Type regression models include linear models and neural networks. In this recipe, we developed an estimator based on linear regression. It generates features according to coefficients sampled from a Gaussian distribution. It updates the weights for the linear model given training data via gradient descent and predicts Q values given a state.

FA dramatically reduces the number of states to learn, where learning millions of states is not feasible in the TD method. More importantly, it is able to generalize to unseen states, as the state-values are parameterized by the estimation functions given input states.

See also

If you are not familiar with linear regression or gradient descent, please check out the following material:

- https://towardsdatascience.com/step-by-step-tutorial-on-linear-regression-with-stochastic-gradient-descent-1d35b088a843
- https://machinelearningmastery.com/simple-linear-regression-tutorial-for-machine-learning/

Developing Q-learning with linear function approximation

In the previous recipe, we developed a value estimator based on linear regression. We will employ the estimator in Q-learning, as part of our FA journey.

As we have seen, Q-learning is an off-policy learning algorithm and it updates the Q-function based on the following equation:

$$Q(s,a) = Q(s,a) + \alpha(r + \gamma max_{a'} Q(s',a') - Q(s,a))$$

Here, s' is the resulting state after taking action, a, in state, s; r is the associated reward; α is the learning rate; and γ is the discount factor. Also, $max_{a'}Q(s',a')$ means that the behavior policy is greedy, where the highest Q-value among those in state s' is selected to generate learning data. In Q-learning, actions are taken on the basis of the epsilon-greedy policy. Similarly, Q-learning with FA has the following error term:

$$\delta = r + \gamma V(s_{t+1}) - V(s_t) = r + \gamma max_{a'} V(s') - V(s_t)$$

Our learning goal is to minimize the error term to zero, which means the estimated V(st) should satisfy the following equation:

$$V(s_t) = r + \gamma max_{a'} V(s')$$

Now, the goal becomes finding the optimal weights, θ, as in V(s)=θF(s), to best approximate the state-value function V(s) for each possible action. The loss function we are trying to minimize in this case is similar to that in a regression problem, which is the mean squared error between the actual value and the estimated value.

How to do it...

Let's develop Q-learning with FA using the linear estimator, `Estimator`, from `linear_estimator.py`, which we developed in the previous recipe, *Estimating Q-functions with gradient descent approximation*:

1. Import the necessary modules and create a Mountain Car environment:

```
>>> import gym
>>> import torch
>>> from linear_estimator import Estimator
>>> env = gym.envs.make("MountainCar-v0")
```

2. Then, start defining the epsilon-greedy policy:

```
>>> def gen_epsilon_greedy_policy(estimator, epsilon, n_action):
...         def policy_function(state):
...             probs = torch.ones(n_action) * epsilon / n_action
...             q_values = estimator.predict(state)
...             best_action = torch.argmax(q_values).item()
...             probs[best_action] += 1.0 - epsilon
...             action = torch.multinomial(probs, 1).item()
...             return action
...         return policy_function
```

This takes in a parameter, ε, with a value from 0 to 1, |A|, the number of possible actions, and the estimator used to predict state-action values. Each action is taken with a probability of ε/ |A|, and the action with the highest predicted state-action value is chosen with a probability of 1- ε + ε/ |A|.

3. Now, define the function that performs Q-learning with FA:

```
>>> def q_learning(env, estimator, n_episode, gamma=1.0,
                    epsilon=0.1, epsilon_decay=.99):
...         """
...         Q-Learning algorithm using Function Approximation
...         @param env: Gym environment
...         @param estimator: Estimator object
...         @param n_episode: number of episodes
...         @param gamma: the discount factor
...         @param epsilon: parameter for epsilon_greedy
...         @param epsilon_decay: epsilon decreasing factor
...         """
...         for episode in range(n_episode):
...             policy = gen_epsilon_greedy_policy(estimator,
...                 epsilon * epsilon_decay ** episode, n_action)
...             state = env.reset()
...             is_done = False
...             while not is_done:
...                 action = policy(state)
...                 next_state, reward, is_done, _ = env.step(action)
...                 q_values_next = estimator.predict(next_state)
...                 td_target = reward +
...                             gamma * torch.max(q_values_next)
...                 estimator.update(state, action, td_target)
...                 total_reward_episode[episode] += reward
...
...                 if is_done:
...                     break
...                 state = next_state
```

The `q_learning()` function does the following tasks:

- In each episode, creates an epsilon-greedy policy with an epsilon factor decayed to 99% (for example, if epsilon in the first episode is 0.1, it will be 0.099 in the second episode).
- Runs an episode: in each step, takes an action, *a*, in keeping with the epsilon-greedy policy; computes the Q values of the new state using the current estimator; then, computes the target value, $V(s_t) = r + \gamma max_{a'} V(s')$, and uses it to train the estimator.
- Runs `n_episode` episodes and records the total reward for each episode.

4. We specify the number of features as `200` and the learning rate as `0.03`, and create an estimator accordingly:

```
>>> n_state = env.observation_space.shape[0]
>>> n_action = env.action_space.n
>>> n_feature = 200
>>> lr = 0.03
>>> estimator = Estimator(n_feature, n_state, n_action, lr)
```

5. We perform Q-learning with FA for 300 episodes and also keep track of the total rewards for each episode:

```
>>> n_episode = 300
>>> total_reward_episode = [0] * n_episode
>>> q_learning(env, estimator, n_episode, epsilon=0.1)
```

6. Then, we display the plot of episode lengths over time:

```
>>> import matplotlib.pyplot as plt
>>> plt.plot(total_reward_episode)
>>> plt.title('Episode reward over time')
>>> plt.xlabel('Episode')
>>> plt.ylabel('Total reward')
>>> plt.show()
```

How it works...

As you can see, in Q-learning with FA, it tries to learn the optimal weights for the approximation models so that the Q values are best estimated. It is similar to TD Q-learning in the sense that they both generate learning data from another policy. It is more suitable for environments with large state space as the Q values are approximated by a set of regression models and latent features, while TD Q-learning requires exact table lookup to update the Q values. The fact that Q-learning with FA updates the regression models after every single step also makes it similar to the TD Q-learning method.

After the Q-learning model is trained, we just need to use the regression models to predict the state-action values for all possible actions and pick the action with the largest value given a state. In *Step 6*, we import `pyplot` to plot all the rewards, which will result in the following plot:

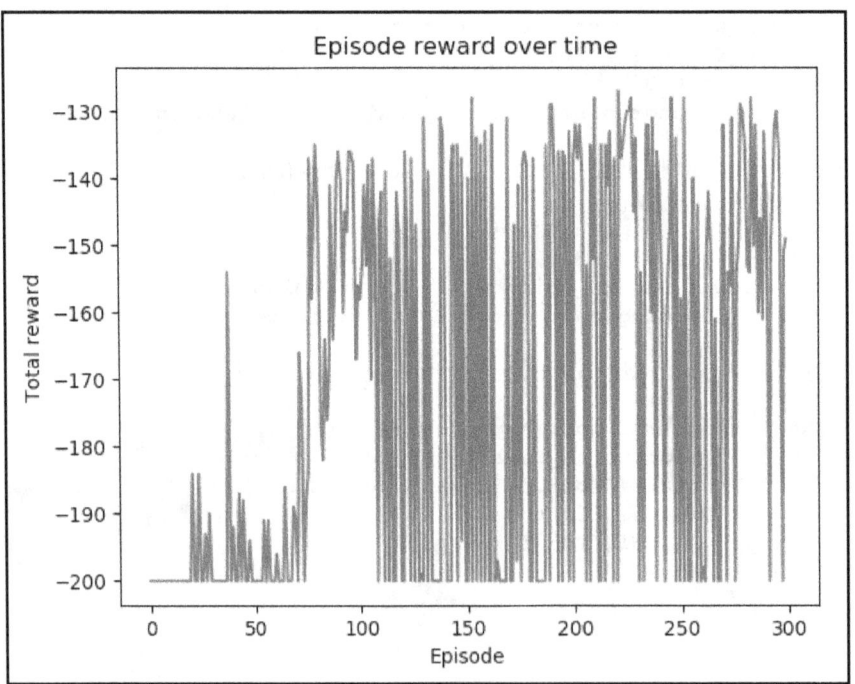

You can see that, in most episodes, after the first 25 iterations, the car reaches the mountain top in around 130 to 160 steps.

Developing SARSA with linear function approximation

We've just solved the Mountain Car problem using the off-policy Q-learning algorithm in the previous recipe. Now, we will do so with the on-policy **State-Action-Reward-State-Action (SARSA)** algorithm (the FA version of course).

In general, the SARSA algorithm updates the Q-function based on the following equation:

$$Q(s, a) = Q(s, a) + \alpha(r + \gamma Q(s', a') - Q(s, a))$$

Here, s' is the resulting state after taking action, a, in state s; r is the associated reward; α is the learning rate; and γ is the discount factor. We simply pick up the next action, a', by also following an epsilon-greedy policy to update the Q value. And the action, a', is taken in the next step. Accordingly, SARSA with FA has the following error term:

$$\delta = r + \gamma V(s_{t+1}) - V(s_t) = r + \gamma V(s', a') - V(s_t)$$

Our learning goal is to minimize the error term to zero, which means that the estimated V(st) should satisfy the following equation:

$$V(s_t) = r + \gamma V(s', a')$$

Now, the goal becomes finding the optimal weights, θ, as in V(s)=θF(s), to best approximate the state-value function V(s) for each possible action. The loss function we are trying to minimize in this case is similar to that in a regression problem, which is the mean squared error between the actual value and the estimated value.

How to do it...

Let's develop SARSA with FA using the linear estimator, `Estimator`, from `linear_estimator.py`, which we developed in the recipe, *Estimating Q-functions with gradient descent approximation*:

1. Import the necessary modules and create a Mountain Car environment:

```
>>> import gym
>>> import torch
>>> from linear_estimator import Estimator
>>> env = gym.envs.make("MountainCar-v0")
```

2. We will reuse the epsilon-greedy policy function developed in the previous recipe, *Developing Q-learning with linear function approximation*.

3. Now, define the function that performs the SARSA algorithm with FA:

```
>>> def sarsa(env, estimator, n_episode, gamma=1.0,
                 epsilon=0.1, epsilon_decay=.99):
...     """
...     SARSA algorithm using Function Approximation
...     @param env: Gym environment
...     @param estimator: Estimator object
...     @param n_episode: number of episodes
...     @param gamma: the discount factor
...     @param epsilon: parameter for epsilon_greedy
...     @param epsilon_decay: epsilon decreasing factor
...     """
...     for episode in range(n_episode):
...         policy = gen_epsilon_greedy_policy(estimator,
                         epsilon * epsilon_decay ** episode,
                         env.action_space.n)
...         state = env.reset()
...         action = policy(state)
...         is_done = False
...
...         while not is_done:
...             next_state, reward, done, _ = env.step(action)
...             q_values_next = estimator.predict(next_state)
...             next_action = policy(next_state)
...             td_target = reward +
                         gamma * q_values_next[next_action]
...             estimator.update(state, action, td_target)
...             total_reward_episode[episode] += reward
...
...             if done:
...                 break
...             state = next_state
...             action = next_action
```

The `sarsa()` function does the following tasks:

- In each episode, creates an epsilon-greedy policy with an epsilon factor decayed to 99%.
- Runs an episode: in each step, takes an action, *a*, in keeping with the epsilon-greedy policy; in the new state, chooses a new action according to the epsilon-greedy policy; then, compute the Q values of the new state using the current estimator; computes the target value, $V(s_t) = r + \gamma V(s', a')$, and uses it to update the estimator.
- Runs `n_episode` episodes and records the total reward for each episode.

4. We specify the number of features as 200, the learning rate as 0.03, and create an estimator accordingly:

```
>>> n_state = env.observation_space.shape[0]
>>> n_action = env.action_space.n
>>> n_feature = 200
>>> lr = 0.03
>>> estimator = Estimator(n_feature, n_state, n_action, lr)
```

5. We then perform SARSA with FA for 300 episodes and also keep track of the total rewards for each episode:

```
>>> n_episode = 300
>>> total_reward_episode = [0] * n_episode
>>> sarsa(env, estimator, n_episode, epsilon=0.1)
```

6. Then, we display the plot of episode lengths over time:

```
>>> import matplotlib.pyplot as plt
>>> plt.plot(total_reward_episode)
>>> plt.title('Episode reward over time')
>>> plt.xlabel('Episode')
>>> plt.ylabel('Total reward')
>>> plt.show()
```

How it works...

SARSA with FA tries to learn the optimal weights for the approximation models so that the Q values are best estimated. It optimizes the estimation by taking actions chosen under the same policy, as opposed to learning the experience from another policy in Q-learning.

Similarly, after the SARSA model is trained, we just need to use the regression models to predict the state-action values for all possible actions and pick the action with the largest value given a state.

In *Step 6*, we plot the rewards with `pyplot`, which will result in the following plot:

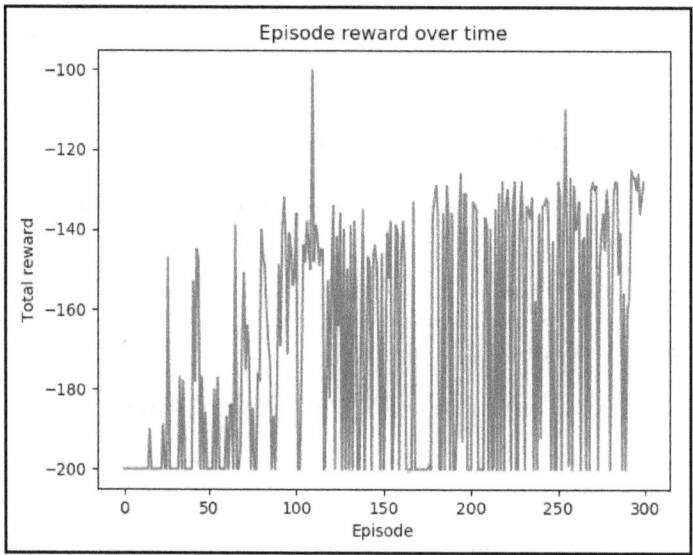

You can see that, in most episodes, after the first 100 episodes, the car reaches the mountain top in around 130 to 160 steps.

Incorporating batching using experience replay

In the previous two recipes, we developed two FA learning algorithms: off-policy and on-policy, respectively. In this recipe, we will improve the performance of off-policy Q-learning by incorporating experience replay.

Experience replay means we store the agent's experiences during an episode instead of running Q-learning. The learning phase with experience replay becomes two phases: gaining experience and updating models based on the experience obtained after an episode finishes.Specifically, the experience (also called the buffer, or memory) includes the past state, the action taken, the reward received, and the next state for individual steps in an episode.

In the learning phase, a certain number of data points are randomly sampled from the experience and are used to train the learning models. Experience replay can stabilize training by providing a set of samples with low correlation, which, as a result, increases learning efficiency.

How to do it...

Let's apply experience replay to FA Q-learning using the linear estimator, `Estimator`, from `linear_estimator.py`, which we developed in the previous recipe, *Estimating Q-functions with gradient descent approximation*:

1. Import the necessary modules and create a Mountain Car environment:

```
>>> import gym
 >>> import torch
 >>> from linear_estimator import Estimator
 >>> from collections import deque
 >>> import random
 >>> env = gym.envs.make("MountainCar-v0")
```

2. We will reuse the epsilon-greedy policy function developed in the previous, *Developing Q-learning with linear function approximation* recipe.

3. Then, specify the number of features as `200`, the learning rate as `0.03`, and create an estimator accordingly:

```
>>> n_state = env.observation_space.shape[0]
 >>> n_action = env.action_space.n
 >>> n_feature = 200
 >>> lr = 0.03
 >>> estimator = Estimator(n_feature, n_state, n_action, lr)
```

4. Next, define the buffer holding the experience:

```
>>> memory = deque(maxlen=400)
```

New samples will be appended to the queue, and the old ones will be removed as long as there are more than 400 samples in the queue.

5. Now, define the function that performs FA Q-learning with experience replay:

```
>>> def q_learning(env, estimator, n_episode, replay_size,
                    gamma=1.0, epsilon=0.1, epsilon_decay=.99):
 ...        """
 ...        Q-Learning algorithm using Function Approximation,
              with experience replay
```

```
...        @param env: Gym environment
...        @param estimator: Estimator object
...        @param replay_size: number of samples we use to
                               update the model each time
...        @param n_episode: number of episode
...        @param gamma: the discount factor
...        @param epsilon: parameter for epsilon_greedy
...        @param epsilon_decay: epsilon decreasing factor
...        """
...        for episode in range(n_episode):
...            policy = gen_epsilon_greedy_policy(estimator,
                             epsilon * epsilon_decay ** episode,
                             n_action)
...            state = env.reset()
...            is_done = False
...            while not is_done:
...                action = policy(state)
...                next_state, reward, is_done, _ = env.step(action)
...                total_reward_episode[episode] += reward
...                if is_done:
...                    break

...                q_values_next = estimator.predict(next_state)
...                td_target = reward +
                             gamma * torch.max(q_values_next)
...                memory.append((state, action, td_target))
...                state = next_state

...            replay_data = random.sample(memory,
                             min(replay_size, len(memory)))
...            for state, action, td_target in replay_data:
...                estimator.update(state, action, td_target)
```

The function does the following tasks:

- In each episode, creates an epsilon-greedy policy with an epsilon factor decayed to 99% (for example, if epsilon in the first episode is 0.1, it will be 0.099 in the second episode).
- Runs an episode: in each step, takes an action, *a*, in keeping with the epsilon-greedy policy; compute the *Q* values of the new state using the current estimator; then, computes the target value, $V(s_t) = r + \gamma max_{a'} V(s')$, and stores the state, action, and target value tuple in the buffer memory.

- After each episode, randomly selects `replay_size` samples from the buffer memory and uses them to train the estimator.
- Runs `n_episode` episodes and records the total reward for each episode.

6. We perform Q-learning with experience replay for 1,000 episodes:

```
>>> n_episode = 1000
```

We need more episodes simply because the models are not sufficiently trained, so the agent takes random steps in early episodes.

We set 190 as the replay sample size:

```
>>> replay_size = 190
```

We also keep track of the total rewards for each episode:

```
>>> total_reward_episode = [0] * n_episode
>>> q_learning(env, estimator, n_episode, replay_size, epsilon=0.1)
```

7. Now, we display the plot of episode lengths over time:

```
>>> import matplotlib.pyplot as plt
>>> plt.plot(total_reward_episode)
>>> plt.title('Episode reward over time')
>>> plt.xlabel('Episode')
>>> plt.ylabel('Total reward')
>>> plt.show()
```

This will result in the following plot:

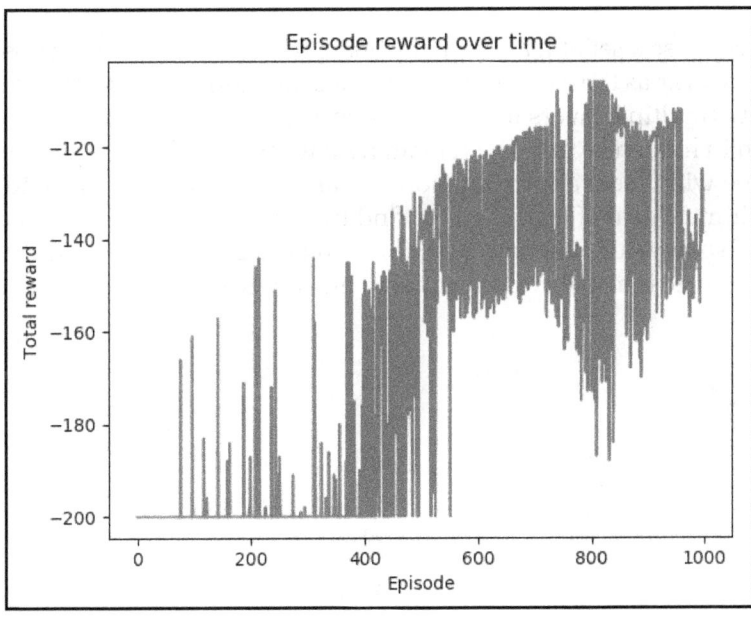

You can see that the performance of Q-learning with experience replay becomes much more stable. The rewards in most episodes after the first 500 episodes stay in the range of -160 to -120.

How it works...

In this recipe, we solved the Mountain Car problem with the help of FA Q-learning, along with experience replay. It outperforms pure FA Q-learning because we collect less corrected training data with experience replay. Instead of rushing in and training the estimator, we first store the data points we observe during episodes in a buffer, and then we randomly select a batch of samples from the buffer and train the estimator. This forms an input dataset where samples are more independent of one another, thereby making training more stable and efficient.

Developing Q-learning with neural network function approximation

As we mentioned before, we can also use neural networks as the approximating function. In this recipe, we will solve theMountain Car environment using Q-learning with neural networks for approximation.

The goal of FA is to use a set of features to estimate the Q values via a regression model. Using neural networks as the estimation model, we increase the regression power by adding flexibility (multiple layers in neural networks) and non-linearity introduced by non-linear activation in hidden layers. The remaining part of the Q-learning model is very similar to the one with linear approximation. We also use gradient descent to train the network. The ultimate goal of learning is to find the optimal weights of the network to best approximate the state-value function, $V(s)$, for each possible action. The loss function we are trying to minimize is also the mean squared error between the actual value and the estimated value.

How to do it...

Let's start by implementing the neural network-based estimator. We will reuse most parts of the linear estimator we developed in the *Estimating Q-functions with gradient descent approximation* recipe. The difference is that we connect the input layer and output layer with a hidden layer, followed by an activation function, which is a ReLU (rectified linear unit) function in this case. So, we only need to modify the __init__ method as follows:

```
>>> class Estimator():
...       def __init__(self, n_feat, n_state, n_action, lr=0.05):
...           self.w, self.b = self.get_gaussian_wb(n_feat, n_state)
...           self.n_feat = n_feat
...           self.models = []
...           self.optimizers = []
...           self.criterion = torch.nn.MSELoss()
...           for _ in range(n_action):
...               model = torch.nn.Sequential(
...                               torch.nn.Linear(n_feat, n_hidden),
...                               torch.nn.ReLU(),
...                               torch.nn.Linear(n_hidden, 1)
...               )
...               self.models.append(model)
...               optimizer = torch.optim.Adam(model.parameters(), lr)
...               self.optimizers.append(optimizer)
```

As you can see, the hidden layer has n_hidden nodes, and a ReLU activation, torch.nn.ReLU(), comes after the hidden layer, followed by the output layer producing the estimated value.

The other parts of the neural network Estimator are the same as the linear Estimator. You can copy them into the nn_estimator.py file.

Now, we continue with Q-learning using neural networks with experience replay as follows:

1. Import the necessary modules, including the neural network estimator, Estimator, from nn_estimator.py, which we just developed, and create a Mountain Car environment:

```
>>> import gym
>>> import torch
>>> from nn_estimator import Estimator
>>> from collections import deque
>>> import random
>>> env = gym.envs.make("MountainCar-v0")
```

2. We will reuse the epsilon-greedy policy function developed in the *Developing Q-learning with linear function approximation* recipe.

3. We then specify the number of features as 200, the learning rate as 0.001, the size of the hidden layer as 50, and create an estimator accordingly:

```
>>> n_state = env.observation_space.shape[0]
>>> n_action = env.action_space.n
>>> n_feature = 200
>>> n_hidden = 50
>>> lr = 0.001
>>> estimator = Estimator(n_feature, n_state, n_action, n_hidden,
lr)
```

4. Next, define the buffer holding the experience:

```
>>> memory = deque(maxlen=300)
```

New samples will be appended to the queue, and the old ones will be removed as long as there are more than 300 samples in the queue.

5. We will reuse the `q_learning` function we developed in the previous recipe, *Incorporating batching using experience replay*. It performs FA Q-learning with experience replay.

6. We perform Q-learning with experience replay for 1,000 episodes, and set 200 as the replay sample size.

```
>>> n_episode = 1000
>>> replay_size = 200
```

We also keep track of the total rewards for each episode:

```
>>> total_reward_episode = [0] * n_episode
>>> q_learning(env, estimator, n_episode, replay_size, epsilon=0.1)
```

7. Then, we display the plot of episode lengths over time:

```
>>> import matplotlib.pyplot as plt
>>> plt.plot(total_reward_episode)
>>> plt.title('Episode reward over time')
>>> plt.xlabel('Episode')
>>> plt.ylabel('Total reward')
>>> plt.show()
```

How it works...

FA using neural networks is very similar to linear function approximation. Instead of using a simple linear function, it uses neural networks to map the features to target values. The remaining parts of the algorithm are essentially the same, but it has higher flexibility because of the more complex architecture of neural networks and non-linear activation, and, hence, more predictive power.

In *Step 7*, we plot the episode lengths over time, which will result in the following plot:

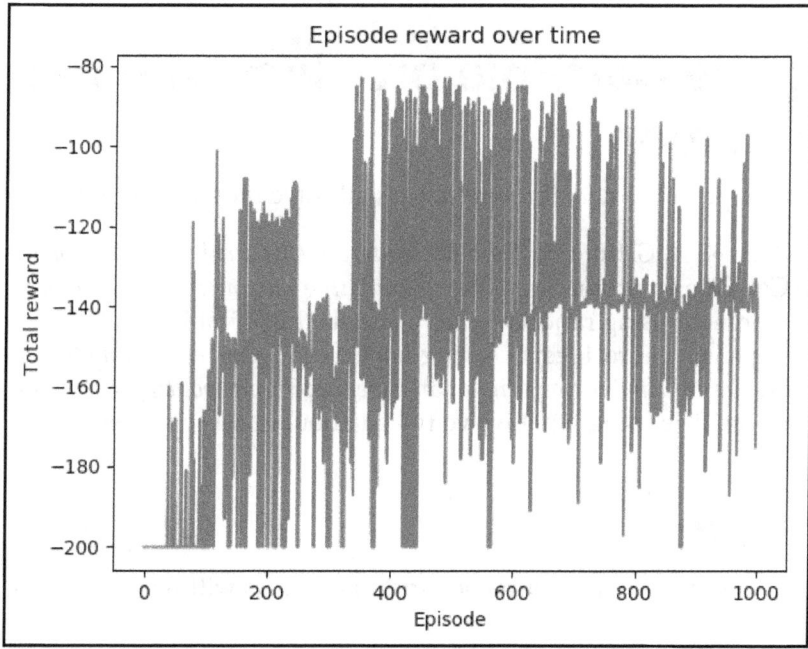

You can see that the performance of Q-learning with neural networks is better than using linear functions. The rewards in most episodes after the first 500 episodes stay in the range of -140 to -85.

See also

If you want to brush up on your knowledge of neural networks, please check out the following material:

- https://pytorch.org/tutorials/beginner/blitz/neural_networks_tutorial.html
- https://www.cs.toronto.edu/~jlucas/teaching/csc411/lectures/tut5_handout.pdf

Solving the CartPole problem with function approximation

This is a bonus recipe in this chapter, where we will solve the CartPole problem using FA.

As we saw in Chapter 1, *Getting started with reinforcement learning and PyTorch*, we simulated the CartPole environment in the , *Simulating the CartPole environment* recipe, and solved the environment using random search, and the hill climbing and policy gradient algorithms, respectively, in recipes including *Implementing and evaluating the random search policy, Developing the hill climbing algorithm*, and *Developing the policy gradient algorithm*. Now, let's try to solve CartPole using what we've talked about in this chapter.

How to do it...

We demonstrate the solution for neural network-based FAs without experience replay as follows:

1. Import the necessary modules, including the neural network, Estimator, from nn_estimator.py which we developed in the previous recipe, *Developing Q-learning with neural net function approximation*, and create a CartPole environment:

```
>>> import gym
>>> import torch
>>> from nn_estimator import Estimator
>>> env = gym.envs.make("CartPole-v0")
```

2. We will reuse the epsilon-greedy policy function developed in the previous recipe, *Developing Q-learning with linear function approximation*.

3. We then specify the number of features as 400 (note that the state space of the
   CartPole environment is 4-dimensional), the learning rate as 0.01, the size of the
   hidden layer as 100, and create a neural network estimator accordingly:

```
>>> n_state = env.observation_space.shape[0]
>>> n_action = env.action_space.n
>>> n_feature = 400
>>> n_hidden = 100
>>> lr = 0.01
>>> estimator = Estimator(n_feature, n_state, n_action, n_hidden,
lr)
```

4. We will reuse the `q_learning` function we developed in the previous
   recipe, *Developing Q-learning with linear function approximation*. This performs FA
   Q-learning.

5. We perform Q-learning with FA for 1,000 episodes and also keep track of the
   total rewards for each episode:

```
>>> n_episode = 1000
>>> total_reward_episode = [0] * n_episode
>>> q_learning(env, estimator, n_episode, epsilon=0.1)
```

6. Finally, we display the plot of episode lengths over time:

```
>>> import matplotlib.pyplot as plt
>>> plt.plot(total_reward_episode)
>>> plt.title('Episode reward over time')
>>> plt.xlabel('Episode')
>>> plt.ylabel('Total reward')
>>> plt.show()
```

How it works...

We have solved the CartPole problem using the FA algorithm with neural networks in this
recipe. Note that the environment has a four dimensional observation space, which is
double that of the Mountain Car, so we intuitively double up the number of features we
use, and the size of the hidden layer accordingly. Feel free to experiment with SARSA with
neural networks, or Q-learning with experience replay, and see whether either of them
perform better.

In *Step 6*, we plot the episode lengths over time, which will result in the following plot:

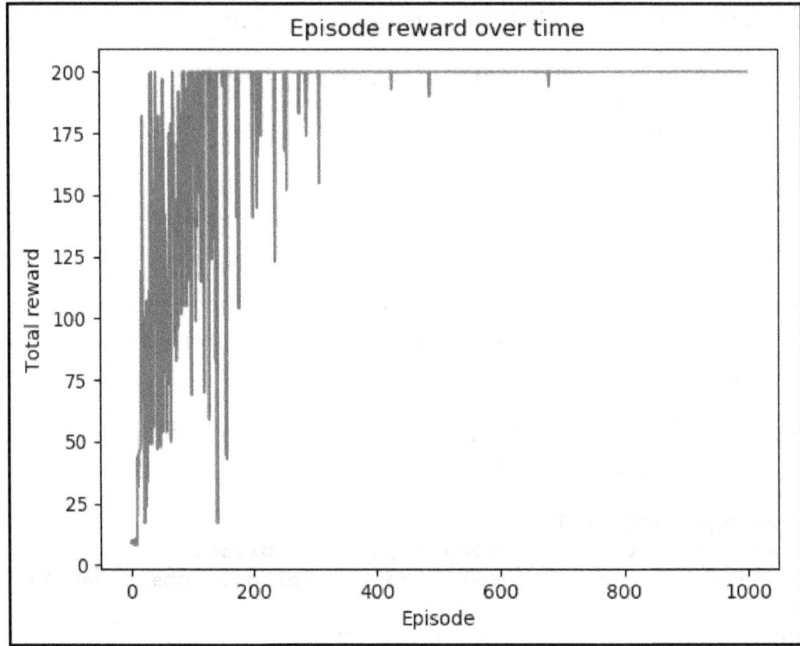

You can see that the total rewards in most episodes after the first 300 episodes are the maximum value of +200.

Deep Q-Networks in Action

7

Deep Q-learning, or using deep Q-networks, is considered the most modern reinforcement learning technique. In this chapter, we will develop various deep Q-network models step by step and apply them to solve several reinforcement learning problems. We will start with vanilla Q-networks and enhance them with experience replay. We will improve robustness by using an additional target network and demonstrate how to fine-tune a Deep Q-Network. We will also experiment with dueling deep Q-networks and see how their value functions differs from other types of Deep Q-Networks. In the last two recipes, we will solve complex Atari game problems by incorporating convolutional neural networks into Deep Q-Networks.

The following recipes will be covered in this chapter:

- Developing deep Q-networks
- Improving DQNs with experience replay
- Developing double deep Q-Networks
- Tuning double DQN hyperparameters for CartPole
- Developing Dueling deep Q-Networks
- Applying deep Q-Networks to Atari games
- Using convolutional neural networks for Atari games

Developing deep Q-networks

You will recall that **Function Approximation (FA)** approximates the state space using a set of features generated from the original states. **Deep Q-Networks (DQNs)** are very similar to FA with neural networks, but they use neural networks to map the states to action values directly instead of using a set of generated features as media.

In Deep Q-learning, a neural network is trained to output the appropriate $Q(s,a)$ values for each action given the input state, s. The action, a, of the agent is chosen based on the output $Q(s,a)$ values following the epsilon-greedy policy. The structure of a DQN with two hidden layers is depicted in the following diagram:

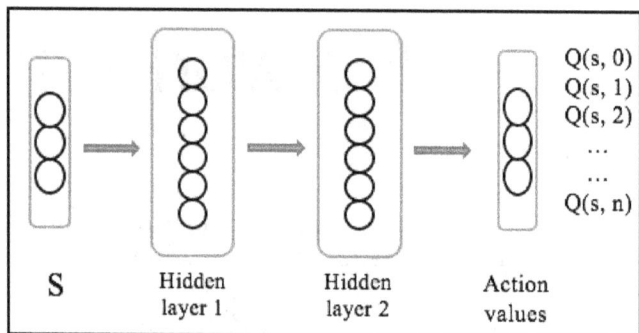

You will recall that Q-learning is an off-policy learning algorithm and that it updates the Q-function based on the following equation:

$$Q(s,a) = Q(s,a) + \alpha(r + \gamma max_{a'} Q(s', a') - Q(s,a))$$

Here, s' is the resulting state after taking action, a, in state, s; r is the associated reward; α is the learning rate; and γ is the discount factor. Also, $max_{a'} Q(s', a')$ means that the behavior policy is greedy where the highest Q-value among those in state s' is selected to generate learning data. Similarly, DQNs learn to minimize the following error term:

$$\delta = r + \gamma max_{a'} Q(s') - Q(s)$$

Now, the goal becomes one of finding the optimal network model to best approximate the state-value function, $Q(s, a)$, for each possible action. The loss function we are trying to minimize in this case is similar to that in a regression problem, which is the mean squared error between the actual value and the estimated value.

Now, we will develop a DQN model to solve the Mountain Car (https://gym.openai.com/envs/MountainCar-v0/) problem.

How to do it...

We develop deep Q-learning using DQN as follows:

1. Import all the necessary packages:

```
>>> import gym
>>> import torch
>>> from torch.autograd import Variable
>>> import random
```

The variable wraps a tensor and supports backpropagation.

2. Let's start with the __init__ method of the DQN class:

```
>>> class DQN():
...         def __init__(self, n_state, n_action, n_hidden=50,
                    lr=0.05):
...             self.criterion = torch.nn.MSELoss()
...             self.model = torch.nn.Sequential(
                            torch.nn.Linear(n_state, n_hidden),
                            torch.nn.ReLU(),
                            torch.nn.Linear(n_hidden, n_action)
                        )
...             self.optimizer = torch.optim.Adam(
                            self.model.parameters(), lr)
```

3. We now develop the training method, which updates the neural network with a data point:

```
>>>         def update(self, s, y):
...             """
...             Update the weights of the DQN given a training sample
...             @param s: state
...             @param y: target value
...             """
...             y_pred = self.model(torch.Tensor(s))
...             loss = self.criterion(y_pred,
                        Variable(torch.Tensor(y)))
...             self.optimizer.zero_grad()
...             loss.backward()
...             self.optimizer.step()
```

4. Next is the prediction of the state value for each action given a state:

```
>>>     def predict(self, s):
...         """
...         Compute the Q values of the state for all
                    actions using the learning model
...         @param s: input state
...         @return: Q values of the state for all actions
...         """
...         with torch.no_grad():
...             return self.model(torch.Tensor(s))
```

That's all for the DQN class! And now we can move on to develop the learning algorithm.

5. We begin by creating a Mountain Car environment:

```
>>> env = gym.envs.make("MountainCar-v0")
```

6. Then, we define the epsilon-greedy policy:

```
>>> def gen_epsilon_greedy_policy(estimator, epsilon, n_action):
...     def policy_function(state):
...         if random.random() < epsilon:
...             return random.randint(0, n_action - 1)
...         else:
...             q_values = estimator.predict(state)
...             return torch.argmax(q_values).item()
...     return policy_function
```

7. Now, define the deep Q-learning algorithm with DQN:

```
>>> def q_learning(env, estimator, n_episode, gamma=1.0,
                        epsilon=0.1, epsilon_decay=.99):
...     """
...     Deep Q-Learning using DQN
...     @param env: Gym environment
...     @param estimator: Estimator object
...     @param n_episode: number of episodes
...     @param gamma: the discount factor
...     @param epsilon: parameter for epsilon_greedy
...     @param epsilon_decay: epsilon decreasing factor
...     """
...     for episode in range(n_episode):
...         policy = gen_epsilon_greedy_policy(
                        estimator, epsilon, n_action)
...         state = env.reset()
...         is_done = False
```

```
...                 while not is_done:
...                     action = policy(state)
...                     next_state, reward, is_done, _ = env.step(action)
...                     total_reward_episode[episode] += reward
...                     modified_reward = next_state[0] + 0.5
...                     if next_state[0] >= 0.5:
...                         modified_reward += 100
...                     elif next_state[0] >= 0.25:
...                         modified_reward += 20
...                     elif next_state[0] >= 0.1:
...                         modified_reward += 10
...                     elif next_state[0] >= 0:
...                         modified_reward += 5
...
...                     q_values = estimator.predict(state).tolist()
...
...                     if is_done:
...                         q_values[action] = modified_reward
...                         estimator.update(state, q_values)
...                         break
...                     q_values_next = estimator.predict(next_state)
...                     q_values[action] = modified_reward + gamma * \
                                torch.max(q_values_next).item()
...                     estimator.update(state, q_values)
...                     state = next_state
...                 print('Episode: {}, total reward: {}, epsilon:
                        {}'.format(episode,
                        total_reward_episode[episode], epsilon))
...             epsilon = max(epsilon * epsilon_decay, 0.01)
```

8. We then specify the size of the hidden layer and the learning rate, and create a DQN instance accordingly:

```
>>> n_state = env.observation_space.shape[0]
>>> n_action = env.action_space.n
>>> n_hidden = 50
>>> lr = 0.001
>>> dqn = DQN(n_state, n_action, n_hidden, lr)
```

9. We then perform Deep Q-learning with the DQN we just developed for 1,000 episodes and also keep track of the total (original) rewards for each episode:

```
>>> n_episode = 1000
>>> total_reward_episode = [0] * n_episode
>>> q_learning(env, dqn, n_episode, gamma=.99, epsilon=.3)
 Episode: 0, total reward: -200.0, epsilon: 0.3
 Episode: 1, total reward: -200.0, epsilon: 0.297
 Episode: 2, total reward: -200.0, epsilon: 0.29402999999999996
```

```
......
......
Episode: 993, total reward: -177.0, epsilon: 0.01
Episode: 994, total reward: -200.0, epsilon: 0.01
Episode: 995, total reward: -172.0, epsilon: 0.01
Episode: 996, total reward: -200.0, epsilon: 0.01
Episode: 997, total reward: -200.0, epsilon: 0.01
Episode: 998, total reward: -173.0, epsilon: 0.01
Episode: 999, total reward: -200.0, epsilon: 0.01
```

10. Now, let's display the plot of episode reward over time:

```
>>> import matplotlib.pyplot as plt
>>> plt.plot(total_reward_episode)
>>> plt.title('Episode reward over time')
>>> plt.xlabel('Episode')
>>> plt.ylabel('Total reward')
>>> plt.show()
```

How it works...

In *Step 2*, the DQN class takes in four parameters: the number of input states and output actions, the number of hidden nodes (we herein just use one hidden layer as an example), and the learning rate. It initializes a neural network with one hidden layer, followed by a ReLU activation function. It takes in n_state units and generates one n_action output, which are the predicted state values for individual actions. An optimizer, Adam, is initialized along with each linear model. The loss function is the mean squared error.

Step 3 is for updating the network: given a training data point, the predictive result, along with the target value, is used to compute the loss and gradients. The neural network model is then updated via backpropagation.

In *Step 7*, the deep Q-learning function does the following tasks:

- In each episode, creates an epsilon-greedy policy with an epsilon factor decayed to 99% (for example, if epsilon in the first episode is 0.1, it will be 0.099 in the second episode). We also set 0.01 as the lower epsilon limit.
- Runs an episode: In each step in state s, takes an action, a, by following the epsilon-greedy policy; then, compute the Q values q_value, of the previous state using the predict method from DQN.

- Computes the Q values, `q_values_next`, for the new state, s'; then, computes the target value by updating the old Q values, `q_values`, for the action, $Q(s, a) = r + \gamma max_{a'} Q(s', a')$.
- Use the data point *(s, Q(s))*, to train the neural network. Note that *Q(s)* is composed of the values for all actions.
- Runs `n_episode` episodes and records the total reward for each episode.

You may notice that we use a modified version of reward in training the model. It is based on the position of the car since we want it to reach the position of +0.5. And we also give tiered incentives for positions greater than or equal to +0.5, +0.25, +0.1, and 0, respectively. This modified reward setting differentiates different car positions and favors positions that are closer to the goal; hence, it largely speeds up learning compared to the original monotonous -1 reward for each step.

Finally, in *Step 10*, you will see the resulting plot as follows:

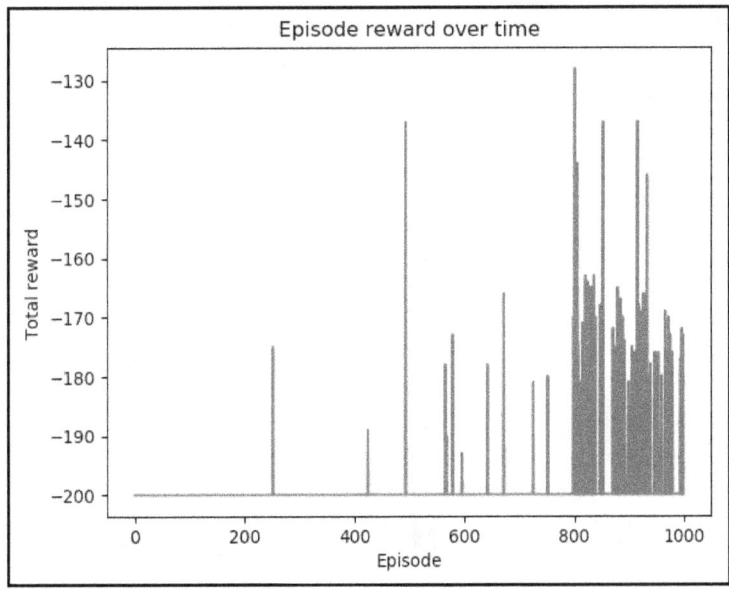

You can see that in the last 200 episodes, the car reaches the mountain top after around 170 to 180 steps.

Deep Q-learning approximates the state values with a more direct model, a neural network, than using a set of intermediate artificial features. Given one step, where an old state transfers to a new state by taking an action and receives a reward, training the DQN involves the following phases:

- Use the neural network model to estimate the Q values of the old state.
- Use the neural network model to estimate the Q values of the new state.
- Update the target Q value for the action using the reward and the new Q values, as in $r + \gamma max_{a'} Q(s', a')$
- Note that if it is a terminal state, the target Q value is updated as r.
- Train the neural network model with the old state as the input, and the target Q values as the output.

It updates the weights for the network via gradient descent and can predict the Q values given a state.

DQN dramatically reduces the number of states to learn, where learning millions of states is not feasible in the TD method. Moreover, it directly maps the input state to the Q values, and does not require any additional functions to generate artificial features.

See also

If you are not familiar with the Adam optimizer as an advanced gradient descent method, please check out the following material:

- https://towardsdatascience.com/adam-latest-trends-in-deep-learning-optimization-6be9a291375c
- https://arxiv.org/abs/1412.6980

Improving DQNs with experience replay

The approximation of Q-values using neural networks with one sample at a time is not very stable. You will recall that, in FA, we incorporated experience replay to improve stability. Similarly, in this recipe, we will apply experience replay to DQNs.

With experience replay, we store the agent's experiences (an experience is composed of an old state, a new state, an action, and a reward) during episodes in a training session in a memory queue. Every time we gain sufficient experience, batches of experiences are randomly sampled from the memory and are used to train the neural network. Learning with experience replay becomes two phases: gaining experience, and updating models based on the past experiences randomly selected. Otherwise, the model will keep learning from the most recent experience and the neural network model could get stuck in a local minimum.

We will develop DQN with experience replay to solve the Mountain Car problem.

How to do it...

We'll develop a DQN with experience replay as follows:

1. Import the necessary modules and create a Mountain Car environment:

```
>>> import gym
>>> import torch
>>> from collections import deque
>>> import random
>>> from torch.autograd import Variable
>>> env = gym.envs.make("MountainCar-v0")
```

2. To incorporate experience replay, we add a `replay` method to the `DQN` class:

```
>>> def replay(self, memory, replay_size, gamma):
...         """
...         Experience replay
...         @param memory: a list of experience
...         @param replay_size: the number of samples we use to
...             update the model each time
...         @param gamma: the discount factor
...         """
...         if len(memory) >= replay_size:
...             replay_data = random.sample(memory, replay_size)
...             states = []
...             td_targets = []
...             for state, action, next_state, reward,
...                                 is_done in replay_data:
...                 states.append(state)
...                 q_values = self.predict(state).tolist()
...                 if is_done:
...                     q_values[action] = reward
...                 else:
```

```
...                       q_values_next = self.predict(next_state)
...                       q_values[action] = reward + gamma *
                               torch.max(q_values_next).item()
...              td_targets.append(q_values)
...
...          self.update(states, td_targets)
```

The rest of the DQN class remains unchanged.

3. We will reuse the `gen_epsilon_greedy_policy` function we developed in the, *Developing Deep Q-Networks* recipe and will not repeat it here.

4. We then specify the shape of the neural network, including the size of the input, the output, and the hidden layer, set 0.001 as the learning rate, and create a DQN accordingly:

```
>>> n_state = env.observation_space.shape[0]
>>> n_action = env.action_space.n
>>> n_hidden = 50
>>> lr = 0.001
>>> dqn = DQN(n_state, n_action, n_hidden, lr)
```

5. Next, we define the buffer holding the experience:

```
>>> memory = deque(maxlen=10000)
```

New samples will be appended to the queue, and the old ones will be removed as long as there are more than `10000` samples in the queue.

6. Now, we define the deep Q-learning function that performs experience replay:

```
>>> def q_learning(env, estimator, n_episode, replay_size,
               gamma=1.0, epsilon=0.1, epsilon_decay=.99):
...      """
...      Deep Q-Learning using DQN, with experience replay
...      @param env: Gym environment
...      @param estimator: Estimator object
...      @param replay_size: the number of samples we use to
...              update the model each time
...      @param n_episode: number of episodes
...      @param gamma: the discount factor
...      @param epsilon: parameter for epsilon_greedy
...      @param epsilon_decay: epsilon decreasing factor
...      """
...      for episode in range(n_episode):
...          policy = gen_epsilon_greedy_policy(
                      estimator, epsilon, n_action)
...          state = env.reset()
```

```
...            is_done = False
...            while not is_done:
...                action = policy(state)
...                next_state, reward, is_done, _ = env.step(action)
...                total_reward_episode[episode] += reward
...                modified_reward = next_state[0] + 0.5
...                if next_state[0] >= 0.5:
...                    modified_reward += 100
...                elif next_state[0] >= 0.25:
...                    modified_reward += 20
...                elif next_state[0] >= 0.1:
...                    modified_reward += 10
...                elif next_state[0] >= 0:
...                    modified_reward += 5
...                memory.append((state, action, next_state,
                                 modified_reward, is_done))
...                if is_done:
...                    break
...                estimator.replay(memory, replay_size, gamma)
...                state = next_state
...            print('Episode: {}, total reward: {}, epsilon:
               {}'.format(episode, total_reward_episode[episode],
               epsilon))
...            epsilon = max(epsilon * epsilon_decay, 0.01)
```

7. We then perform deep Q-learning with experience replay for 600 episodes:

```
>>> n_episode = 600
```

We set 20 as the replay sample size for each step:

```
>>> replay_size = 20
```

We also keep track of the total rewards for each episode:

```
>>> total_reward_episode = [0] * n_episode
>>> q_learning(env, dqn, n_episode, replay_size, gamma=.9,
epsilon=.3)
```

8. Now, it is time to display the plot of episode rewards over time:

```
>>> import matplotlib.pyplot as plt
>>> plt.plot(total_reward_episode)
>>> plt.title('Episode reward over time')
>>> plt.xlabel('Episode')
>>> plt.ylabel('Total reward')
>>> plt.show()
```

How it works...

In *Step 2*, the experience replay function first randomly selects `replay_size` samples of experience. It then converts each experience into a training sample composed of the input state and output target values. And finally, it updates the neural network using the selected batch.

In *Step 6*, deep Q-learning with experience replay is performed with the following tasks:

- In each episode, create an epsilon-greedy policy with an epsilon factor decayed to 99%.
- Run an episode: in each step, take an action, *a*, following the epsilon-greedy policy; store this experience (old state, action, new state, reward) in memory.
- In each step, conduct experience replay to train the neural network, provided we have sufficient training samples to randomly pick from.
- Run `n_episode` episodes and record the total reward for each episode.

Executing the lines of code in *Step 8* will result in the following plot:

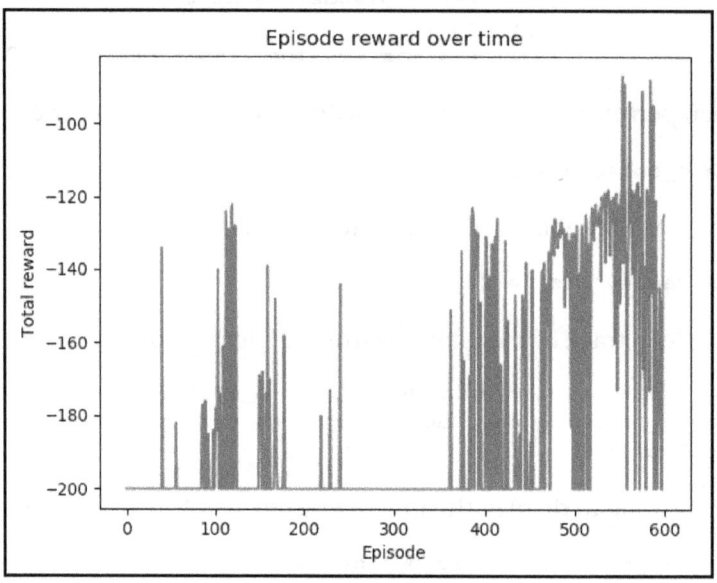

You can see that, in most episodes in the last 200 episodes, the car reaches the mountain top in around 120 to 160 steps.

In deep Q-learning, experience replay means we store the agent's experience for each step and randomly draw some samples of past experience to train the DQN. The learning in this case is split into two phases: accumulating experience, and updating models based on batches of past experience. Specifically, the experience (also called the **buffer**, or **memory**) includes the past state, the action taken, the reward received, and the next state. Experience replay can stabilize training by providing a set of samples with low correlation, which, as a result, increases learning efficiency.

Developing double deep Q-Networks

In the deep Q-learning algorithms we have developed so far, the same neural network is used to calculate the predicted values and the target values. This may cause a lot of divergence as the target values keep on changing and the prediction has to chase it. In this recipe, we will develop a new algorithm using two neural networks instead of one.

In **double DQNs**, we use a separate network to estimate the target rather than the prediction network. The separate network has the same structure as the prediction network. And its weights are fixed for every T episode (T is a hyperparameter we can tune), which means they are only updated after every T episode. The update is simply done by copying the weights of the prediction network. In this way, the target function is fixed for a while, which results in a more stable training process.

Mathematically, double DQNs are trained to minimize the following error term:

$$\delta = r + \gamma max_{a'} Q_T(s') - Q(s)$$

Here, s' is the resulting state after taking action, a, in state s; r is the associated reward; α is the learning rate; and γ is the discount factor. Also, Q_T is the function for the target network, and Q is the function for the prediction network.

Let's now solve the Mountain Car problem using double DQNs.

How to do it...

We develop deep Q-learning using double DQNs as follows:

1. Import the necessary modules and create a Mountain Car environment:

```
>>> import gym
>>> import torch
>>> from collections import deque
```

```
>>> import random
>>> import copy
>>> from torch.autograd import Variable
>>> env = gym.envs.make("MountainCar-v0")
```

2. To incorporate the target network in the experience replay phase, we first initialize it in the ___init___ method of the DQN class:

```
>>> class DQN():
...         def __init__(self, n_state, n_action,
                         n_hidden=50, lr=0.05):
...             self.criterion = torch.nn.MSELoss()
...             self.model = torch.nn.Sequential(
...                             torch.nn.Linear(n_state, n_hidden),
...                             torch.nn.ReLU(),
...                             torch.nn.Linear(n_hidden, n_action)
...                     )
...             self.optimizer = torch.optim.Adam(
...                             self.model.parameters(), lr)
...             self.model_target = copy.deepcopy(self.model)
```

The target network has the same structure as the prediction network.

3. Accordingly, we add the calculation of values using the target network:

```
>>>     def target_predict(self, s):
...         """
...         Compute the Q values of the state for all actions
            using the target network
...         @param s: input state
...         @return: targeted Q values of the state for all
actions
...         """
...         with torch.no_grad():
...             return self.model_target(torch.Tensor(s))
```

4. We also add the method to synchronize the weights of the target network:

```
>>>     def copy_target(self):
...
self.model_target.load_state_dict(self.model.state_dict())
```

5. In experience replay, we use the target network to calculate the target value instead of the prediction network:

```
>>>     def replay(self, memory, replay_size, gamma):
...         """
...         Experience replay with target network
```

```
    ...             @param memory: a list of experience
    ...             @param replay_size: the number of samples
                    we use to update the model each time
    ...             @param gamma: the discount factor
    ...             """
    ...             if len(memory) >= replay_size:
    ...                 replay_data = random.sample(memory, replay_size)
    ...                 states = []
    ...                 td_targets = []
    ...                 for state, action, next_state, reward, is_done
                                                    in replay_data:
    ...                     states.append(state)
    ...                     q_values = self.predict(state).tolist()
    ...                     if is_done:
    ...                         q_values[action] = reward
    ...                     else:
    ...                         q_values_next = self.target_predict(
                                            next_state).detach()
    ...                         q_values[action] = reward + gamma *
                                    torch.max(q_values_next).item()
    ...
    ...                     td_targets.append(q_values)
    ...
    ...                 self.update(states, td_targets)
```

The rest of the DQN class remains unchanged.

6. We will reuse the gen_epsilon_greedy_policy function we developed in the, *Developing Deep Q-Networks* recipe, and will not repeat it here.

7. We then specify the shape of the neural network, including the size of the input, the output, and the hidden layer, set 0.01 as the learning rate, and create a DQN accordingly:

```
>>> n_state = env.observation_space.shape[0]
>>> n_action = env.action_space.n
>>> n_hidden = 50
>>> lr = 0.01
>>> dqn = DQN(n_state, n_action, n_hidden, lr)
```

8. Next, we define the buffer holding the experience:

```
>>> memory = deque(maxlen=10000)
```

New samples will be appended to the queue, and the old ones will be removed as long as there are more than 10000 samples in the queue.

9. Now, we'll develop deep Q-learning with double DQN:

```
>>> def q_learning(env, estimator, n_episode, replay_size,
        target_update=10, gamma=1.0, epsilon=0.1,
        epsilon_decay=.99):
...     """
...         Deep Q-Learning using double DQN, with experience replay
...         @param env: Gym environment
...         @param estimator: DQN object
...         @param replay_size: number of samples we use
...             to update the model each time
...         @param target_update: number of episodes before
...             updating the target network
...         @param n_episode: number of episodes
...         @param gamma: the discount factor
...         @param epsilon: parameter for epsilon_greedy
...         @param epsilon_decay: epsilon decreasing factor
...     """
...     for episode in range(n_episode):
...         if episode % target_update == 0:
...             estimator.copy_target()
...         policy = gen_epsilon_greedy_policy(
...                     estimator, epsilon, n_action)
...         state = env.reset()
...         is_done = False
...         while not is_done:
...             action = policy(state)
...             next_state, reward, is_done, _ = env.step(action)
...             total_reward_episode[episode] += reward
...             modified_reward = next_state[0] + 0.5
...             if next_state[0] >= 0.5:
...                 modified_reward += 100
...             elif next_state[0] >= 0.25:
...                 modified_reward += 20
...             elif next_state[0] >= 0.1:
...                 modified_reward += 10
...             elif next_state[0] >= 0:
...                 modified_reward += 5
...             memory.append((state, action, next_state,
...                     modified_reward, is_done))
...             if is_done:
...                 break
...             estimator.replay(memory, replay_size, gamma)
...             state = next_state
...         print('Episode: {}, total reward: {}, epsilon:
{}'.format(episode, total_reward_episode[episode],
epsilon))
...         epsilon = max(epsilon * epsilon_decay, 0.01)
```

10. We perform deep Q-learning with double DQN for 1000 episodes:

```
>>> n_episode = 1000
```

We set 20 as the replay sample size for each step:

```
>>> replay_size = 20
```

We update the target network for every 10 episodes:

```
>>> target_update = 10
```

We also keep track of the total rewards for each episode:

```
>>> total_reward_episode = [0] * n_episode
>>> q_learning(env, dqn, n_episode, replay_size, target_update,
gamma=.9, epsilon=1)
Episode: 0, total reward: -200.0, epsilon: 1
Episode: 1, total reward: -200.0, epsilon: 0.99
Episode: 2, total reward: -200.0, epsilon: 0.9801
......
......
Episode: 991, total reward: -151.0, epsilon: 0.01
Episode: 992, total reward: -200.0, epsilon: 0.01
Episode: 993, total reward: -158.0, epsilon: 0.01
Episode: 994, total reward: -160.0, epsilon: 0.01
Episode: 995, total reward: -200.0, epsilon: 0.01
Episode: 996, total reward: -200.0, epsilon: 0.01
Episode: 997, total reward: -200.0, epsilon: 0.01
Episode: 998, total reward: -151.0, epsilon: 0.01
Episode: 999, total reward: -200.0, epsilon: 0.01
```

11. We then display the plot of episode rewards over time:

```
>>> import matplotlib.pyplot as plt
>>> plt.plot(total_reward_episode)
>>> plt.title('Episode reward over time')
>>> plt.xlabel('Episode')
>>> plt.ylabel('Total reward')
>>> plt.show()
```

How it works...

In *Step 5*, the experience replay function first randomly selects `replay_size` samples of experience. It then converts each experience into a training sample composed of the input state and output target values. And finally, it updates the prediction network using the selected batch.

Step 9 is the most important step in a double DQN: it uses a different network to calculate the target values and then this network is updated periodically. The rest of the function is similar to deep Q-learning with experience replay.

The visualization function in *Step 11* will result in the following plot:

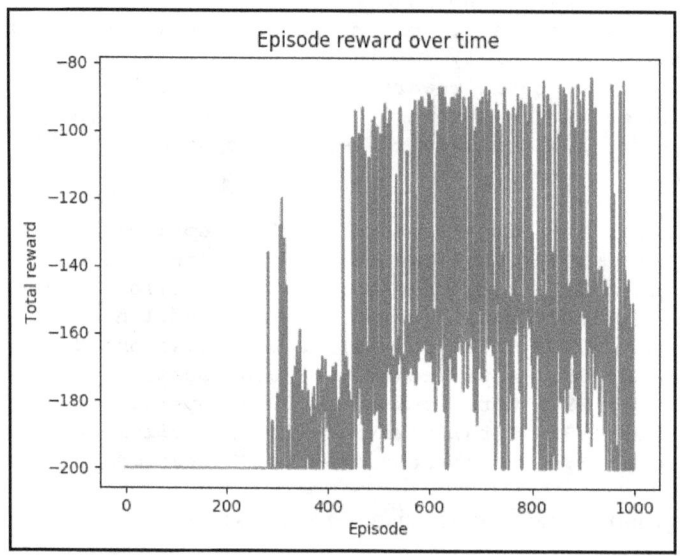

You can see that, in most episodes, after the first **400** episodes, the car reaches the mountain top in around **80** to **160** steps.

In deep Q-learning with a double DQN, we create two separate networks for prediction and target calculation, respectively. The first one is used to predict and retrieve Q values, while the second one is used to provide a stable target Q value. And, after a while (let's say every 10 episodes, or 1,500 training steps), we synchronize the prediction network with the target network. In this double network setting, the target values are temporarily fixed instead of being modified constantly, so the prediction network has more stable targets to learn against. The results we obtained show that double DQNs outperform single DQNs.

Tuning double DQN hyperparameters for CartPole

In this recipe, let's solve the CartPole environment using double DQNs. We will demonstrate how to fine-tune the hyperparameters in a double DQN to achieve the best performance.

In order to fine-tune the hyperparameters, we can apply the **grid search** technique to explore a set of different combinations of values and pick the one achieving the best average performance. We can start with a coarse range of values and continue to narrow it down gradually. And don't forget to fix the random number generators for all of the following in order to ensure reproducibility:

- The Gym environment random number generator
- The epsilon-greedy random number generator
- The initial weights for the neural network in PyTorch

How to do it...

We solve the CartPole environment using double DQNs as follows:

1. Import the necessary modules and create a CartPole environment:

```
>>> import gym
>>> import torch
>>> from collections import deque
>>> import random
>>> import copy
>>> from torch.autograd import Variable
>>> env = gym.envs.make("CartPole-v0")
```

2. We will reuse the DQN class developed in the last, *Developing double deep Q-networks* recipe.
3. We will reuse the gen_epsilon_greedy_policy function we developed in the, *Developing Deep Q-Networks* recipe, and will not repeat it here.
4. Now, we'll develop deep Q-learning with a double DQN:

```
>>> def q_learning(env, estimator, n_episode, replay_size,
                   target_update=10, gamma=1.0, epsilon=0.1,
                   epsilon_decay=.99):
...        """
...        Deep Q-Learning using double DQN, with experience replay
```

```
...        @param env: Gym environment
...        @param estimator: DQN object
...        @param replay_size: number of samples we use to
                   update the model each time
...        @param target_update: number of episodes before
                   updating the target network
...        @param n_episode: number of episodes
...        @param gamma: the discount factor
...        @param epsilon: parameter for epsilon_greedy
...        @param epsilon_decay: epsilon decreasing factor
...        """
...        for episode in range(n_episode):
...            if episode % target_update == 0:
...                estimator.copy_target()
...            policy = gen_epsilon_greedy_policy(
                       estimator, epsilon, n_action)
...            state = env.reset()
...            is_done = False
...            while not is_done:
...                action = policy(state)
...                next_state, reward, is_done, _ = env.step(action)
...                total_reward_episode[episode] += reward
...                memory.append((state, action,
                           next_state, reward, is_done))
...                if is_done:
...                    break
...                estimator.replay(memory, replay_size, gamma)
...                state = next_state
...            epsilon = max(epsilon * epsilon_decay, 0.01)
```

5. We then specify the shape of the neural network, including the size of the input, the output, the hidden layer, and the number of episodes, as well as the number of episodes used to evaluate the performance:

```
>>> n_state = env.observation_space.shape[0]
>>> n_action = env.action_space.n
>>> n_episode = 600
>>> last_episode = 200
```

6. We then define a few values for the following hyperparameters to explore in a grid search:

```
>>> n_hidden_options = [30, 40]
>>> lr_options = [0.001, 0.003]
>>> replay_size_options = [20, 25]
>>> target_update_options = [30, 35]
```

7. Finally, we perform a grid search where, in each iteration, we create a DQN according to the set of hyperparameters and allow it to learn for 600 episodes. We then evaluate its performance by averaging the total rewards for the last 200 episodes:

```
>>> for n_hidden in n_hidden_options:
...        for lr in lr_options:
...            for replay_size in replay_size_options:
...                for target_update in target_update_options:
...                    env.seed(1)
...                    random.seed(1)
...                    torch.manual_seed(1)
...                    dqn = DQN(n_state, n_action, n_hidden, lr)
...                    memory = deque(maxlen=10000)
...                    total_reward_episode = [0] * n_episode
...                    q_learning(env, dqn, n_episode, replay_size,
...                        target_update, gamma=.9, epsilon=1)
...                    print(n_hidden, lr, replay_size,
target_update,
                sum(total_reward_episode[-
last_episode:])/last_episode)
```

How it works...

Having executed *Step 7*, we get the following grid search results:

```
30 0.001 20 30 143.15
30 0.001 20 35 156.165
30 0.001 25 30 180.575
30 0.001 25 35 192.765
30 0.003 20 30 187.435
30 0.003 20 35 122.42
30 0.003 25 30 169.32
30 0.003 25 35 172.65
40 0.001 20 30 136.64
40 0.001 20 35 160.08
40 0.001 25 30 141.955
40 0.001 25 35 122.915
40 0.003 20 30 143.855
40 0.003 20 35 178.52
40 0.003 25 30 125.52
40 0.003 25 35 178.85
```

We can see that the best average reward, `192.77`, is achieved with the combination of `n_hidden=30, lr=0.001, replay_size=25,` and `target_update=35`.

Feel free to fine-tune the hyperparameters further in order to get a better DQN model.

In this recipe, we solved the CartPole problem with double DQNs. We fine-tuned the values of hyperparameters using a grid search. In our example, we optimized the size of the hidden layer, the learning rate, the replay batch size, and the target network update frequency. There are other hyperparameters we could also explore, such as the number of episodes, the initial epsilon, and the value of epsilon decay. For each experiment, we kept the random seeds fixed so that the randomness of the Gym environment, and the epsilon-greedy action, as well as the weight initialization of the neural network, remain the same. This is to ensure the reproducibility and comparability of performance. The performance of each DQN model is measured by the average total reward for the last few episodes.

Developing Dueling deep Q-Networks

In this recipe, we are going to develop another advanced type of DQNs, **Dueling DQNs (DDQNs)**. In particularly, we will see how the computation of the Q value is split into two parts in DDQNs.

In DDQNs, the Q value is computed with the following two functions:

$$Q(s,a) = V(s) + A(s,a) - \frac{1}{|A|} \sum_{a=1}^{|A|} A(s,a)$$

Here, *V(s)* is the state-value function, calculating the value of being at state *s*; *A(s, a)* is the state-dependent action advantage function, estimating how much better it is to take an action, *a*, rather than taking other actions at a state, *s*. By decoupling the `value` and `advantage` functions, we are able to accommodate the fact that our agent may not necessarily look at both the value and advantage at the same time during the learning process. In other words, the agent using DDQNs can efficiently optimize either or both functions as it prefers.

How to do it...

We solve the Mountain Car problem using DDQNs as follows:

1. Import the necessary modules and create a Mountain Car environment:

```
>>> import gym
>>> import torch
>>> from collections import deque
>>> import random
>>> from torch.autograd import Variable
>>> import torch.nn as nn
>>> env = gym.envs.make("MountainCar-v0")
```

2. Next, we define the DDQN model as follows:

```
>>> class DuelingModel(nn.Module):
...        def __init__(self, n_input, n_output, n_hidden):
...            super(DuelingModel, self).__init__()
...            self.adv1 = nn.Linear(n_input, n_hidden)
...            self.adv2 = nn.Linear(n_hidden, n_output)
...            self.val1 = nn.Linear(n_input, n_hidden)
...            self.val2 = nn.Linear(n_hidden, 1)
...
...        def forward(self, x):
...            adv = nn.functional.relu(self.adv1(x))
...            adv = self.adv2(adv)
...            val = nn.functional.relu(self.val1(x))
...            val = self.val2(val)
...            return val + adv - adv.mean()
```

3. Accordingly, we use the DDQN model in the DQN class:

```
>>> class DQN():
...        def __init__(self, n_state, n_action, n_hidden=50,
lr=0.05):
...            self.criterion = torch.nn.MSELoss()
...            self.model = DuelingModel(n_state, n_action, n_hidden)
...            self.optimizer =
torch.optim.Adam(self.model.parameters(), lr)
```

The rest of the DQN class remains unchanged.

4. We will reuse the `gen_epsilon_greedy_policy` function we developed in the, *Developing deep Q-Networks* recipe, and will not repeat it here.

5. We will reuse the `q_learning` function we developed in the, *Improving DQNs with experience replay* recipe, and will not repeat it here.

6. We then specify the shape of the neural network, including the size of the input, the output, and the hidden layer, set `0.001` as the learning rate, and create a DQN accordingly:

```
>>> n_state = env.observation_space.shape[0]
>>> n_action = env.action_space.n
>>> n_hidden = 50
>>> lr = 0.001
>>> dqn = DQN(n_state, n_action, n_hidden, lr)
```

7. Next, we define the buffer holding the experience:

```
>>> memory = deque(maxlen=10000)
```

New samples will be appended to the queue, and the old ones will be removed as long as there are more than `10000` samples in the queue.

8. We then perform Deep Q-learning with DDQN for `600` episodes:

```
>>> n_episode = 600
```

We set `20` as the replay sample size for each step:

```
>>> replay_size = 20
```

We also keep track of the total rewards for each episode:

```
>>> total_reward_episode = [0] * n_episode
>>> q_learning(env, dqn, n_episode, replay_size, gamma=.9,
epsilon=.3)
```

9. Now, we can display the plot of episode rewards over time:

```
>>> import matplotlib.pyplot as plt
>>> plt.plot(total_reward_episode)
>>> plt.title('Episode reward over time')
>>> plt.xlabel('Episode')
>>> plt.ylabel('Total reward')
>>> plt.show()
```

How it works...

Step 2 is the core part of the Dueling DQN. It is composed of two parts, the action **advantage** (**adv**), and the **state-value** (**val**). Again, we use one hidden layer as an example.

Executing *Step 9* will result in the following plot:

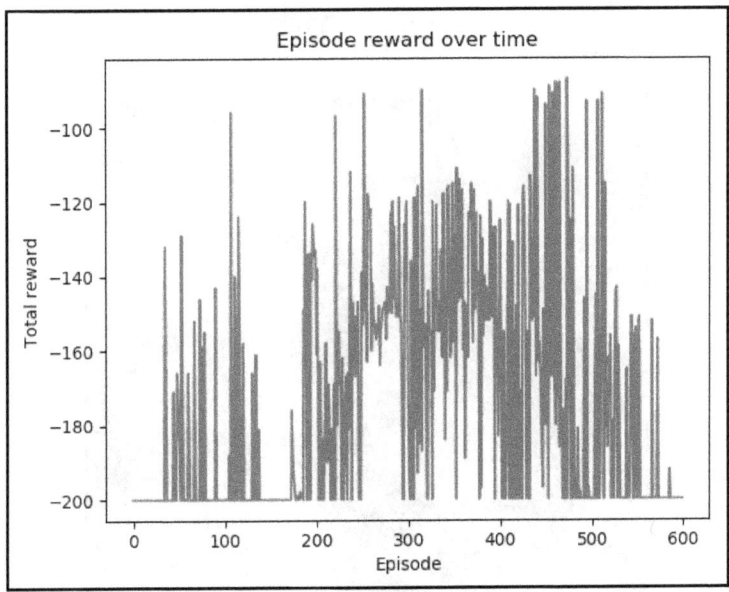

In DDQNs, the predicted Q value is the result of two elements: state-value and action advantage. The first one estimates how good it is to be at a certain state. The second one indicates how much better it is to take a particular action as opposed to the alternatives. These two elements are computed separately and combined into the last layer of the DQN. You will recall that traditional DQNs update the Q value for a given action at a state only. DDQNs update the state-value that all actions (not just the given one) can take advantage of, as well as the advantage for the action. Hence, DDQNs are thought to be more robust.

Applying Deep Q-Networks to Atari games

The problems we have worked with so far are fairly simple, and applying DQNs is sometimes overkill. In this and the next recipe, we'll use DQNs to solve Atari games, which are far more complicated problems.

We will use Pong (`https://gym.openai.com/envs/Pong-v0/`) as an example in this recipe. It simulates the Atari 2600 game Pong, where the agent plays table tennis with another player. The observation in this environment is an RGB image of the screen (refer to the following screenshot):

This is a matrix of shape (210, 160, 3), which means that the image is of size *210 * 160* and in three RGB channels.

The agent (on the right-hand side) moves up and down during the game to hit the ball. If it misses it, the other player (on the left-hand side) will get 1 point; similarly, if the other player misses it, the agent will get 1 point. The winner of the game is whoever scores 21 points first. The agent can take the following 6 possible actions in the Pong environment:

- **0: NOOP**: The agent stays still
- **1: FIRE**: Not a meaningful action
- **2: RIGHT**: The agent moves up

- **3: LEFT**: The agent moves down
- **4: RIGHTFIRE**: The same as 2
- **5: LEFTFIRE**: The same as 5

Each action is repeatedly performed for a duration of *k* frames (*k* can be 2, 3, 4, or 16, depending on the specific variant of the Pong environment). The reward is any of the following:

- *-1*: The agent misses the ball.
- *1*: The opponent misses the ball.
- *0*: Otherwise.

The observation space *210 * 160 * 3* in Pong is a lot larger than what we are used to dealing with. Therefore, we will downsize the image to *84 * 84* and convert it to grayscale, before using DQNs to solve it.

How to do it...

We'll begin by exploring the Pong environment as follows:

1. Import the necessary modules and create a Pong environment:

```
>>> import gym
>>> import torch
>>> import random
>>> env = gym.envs.make("PongDeterministic-v4")
```

In this Pong environment variant, an action is deterministic and is repeatedly performed for a duration of 16 frames.

2. Take a look at the observation space and action space:

```
>>> state_shape = env.observation_space.shape
>>> n_action = env.action_space.n
>>> print(state_shape)
(210, 160, 3)
>>> print(n_action)
6
>>> print(env.unwrapped.get_action_meanings())
['NOOP', 'FIRE', 'RIGHT', 'LEFT', 'RIGHTFIRE', 'LEFTFIRE']
```

3. Specify three actions:

```
>>> ACTIONS = [0, 2, 3]
>>> n_action = 3
```

These actions are not moving, moving up, and moving down.

4. Let's take random actions and render the screen:

```
>>> env.reset()
>>> is_done = False
>>> while not is_done:
...         action = ACTIONS[random.randint(0, n_action - 1)]
...         obs, reward, is_done, _ = env.step(action)
...         print(reward, is_done)
...         env.render()
0.0 False
0.0 False
0.0 False
......
......
0.0 False
0.0 False
0.0 False
-1.0 True
```

You will see in the screen that two players are playing table tennis, even though the agent is losing.

5. Now, we develop a screen processing function to downsize the image and convert it to grayscale:

```
>>> import torchvision.transforms as T
>>> from PIL import Image
>>> image_size = 84
>>> transform = T.Compose([T.ToPILImage(),
...                        T.Grayscale(num_output_channels=1),
...                        T.Resize((image_size, image_size),
...                            interpolation=Image.CUBIC),
...                        T.ToTensor(),
...                        ])
```

Now, we just define a resizer that downsizes the image to *84 * 84*:

```
>>> def get_state(obs):
...         state = obs.transpose((2, 0, 1))
...         state = torch.from_numpy(state)
...         state = transform(state)
...         return state
```

This function reshapes the resized image to size (1, 84, 84):

```
>>> state = get_state(obs)
>>> print(state.shape)
torch.Size([1, 84, 84])
```

Now, we can start solving the environment using double DQNs as follows:

1. We will use a larger neural network with two hidden layers at this time, as the input size is around 21,000:

```
>>> from collections import deque
>>> import copy
>>> from torch.autograd import Variable
>>> class DQN():
...         def __init__(self, n_state, n_action, n_hidden, lr=0.05):
...             self.criterion = torch.nn.MSELoss()
...             self.model = torch.nn.Sequential(
...                     torch.nn.Linear(n_state, n_hidden[0]),
...                     torch.nn.ReLU(),
...                     torch.nn.Linear(n_hidden[0], n_hidden[1]),
...                     torch.nn.ReLU(),
...                     torch.nn.Linear(n_hidden[1], n_action)
...                     )
...             self.model_target = copy.deepcopy(self.model)
...             self.optimizer = torch.optim.Adam(
...                     self.model.parameters(), lr)
```

2. The rest of the DQN class is the same as the one in the, *Developing double deep Q-networks* recipe, with a small change to the replay method:

```
>>> def replay(self, memory, replay_size, gamma):
...         """
...         Experience replay with target network
...         @param memory: a list of experience
...         @param replay_size: the number of samples we use
...                             to update the model each time
...         @param gamma: the discount factor
...         """
...         if len(memory) >= replay_size:
```

```
...         replay_data = random.sample(memory, replay_size)
...         states = []
...         td_targets = []
...         for state, action, next_state, reward,
                                is_done in replay_data:
...             states.append(state.tolist())
...             q_values = self.predict(state).tolist()
...             if is_done:
...                 q_values[action] = reward
...             else:
...                 q_values_next = self.target_predict(
                                next_state).detach()
...                 q_values[action] = reward + gamma *
                        torch.max(q_values_next).item()
...             td_targets.append(q_values)
...         self.update(states, td_targets)
```

3. We will reuse the `gen_epsilon_greedy_policy` function we developed in the, *Developing Deep Q-Networks* recipe, and will not repeat it here.

4. Now, we'll develop deep Q-learning with a double DQN:

```
>>> def q_learning(env, estimator, n_episode, replay_size,
            target_update=10, gamma=1.0, epsilon=0.1,
            epsilon_decay=.99):
...     """
...     Deep Q-Learning using double DQN, with experience replay
...     @param env: Gym environment
...     @param estimator: DQN object
...     @param replay_size: number of samples we use to
                            update the model each time
...     @param target_update: number of episodes before
                            updating the target network
...     @param n_episode: number of episodes
...     @param gamma: the discount factor
...     @param epsilon: parameter for epsilon_greedy
...     @param epsilon_decay: epsilon decreasing factor
...     """
...     for episode in range(n_episode):
...         if episode % target_update == 0:
...             estimator.copy_target()
...         policy = gen_epsilon_greedy_policy(
                        estimator, epsilon, n_action)
...         obs = env.reset()
...         state = get_state(obs).view(image_size *
image_size)[0]
...         is_done = False
...         while not is_done:
...             action = policy(state)
```

```
...                next_obs, reward, is_done, _ =
                              env.step(ACTIONS[action])
...                total_reward_episode[episode] += reward
...                next_state = get_state(obs).view(
                              image_size * image_size)
...                memory.append((state, action, next_state,
                              reward, is_done))
...                if is_done:
...                    break
...                estimator.replay(memory, replay_size, gamma)
...                state = next_state
...           print('Episode: {}, total reward: {}, epsilon:
              {}'.format(episode, total_reward_episode[episode],
              epsilon))
...           epsilon = max(epsilon * epsilon_decay, 0.01)
```

Given an observation of size *[210, 160, 3]*, this transforms it to a grayscale matrix of a smaller size *[84, 84]* and flattens it so that we can feed it into our network.

5. Now, we specify the shape of the neural network, including the size of the input and hidden layers:

```
>>> n_state = image_size * image_size
>>> n_hidden = [200, 50]
```

The remaining hyperparameters are as follows:

```
>>> n_episode = 1000
>>> lr = 0.003
>>> replay_size = 32
>>> target_update = 10
```

Now, we create a DQN accordingly:

```
>>> dqn = DQN(n_state, n_action, n_hidden, lr)
```

6. Next, we define the buffer holding the experience:

```
>>> memory = deque(maxlen=10000)
```

7. Finally, we perform deep Q-learning and also keep track of the total rewards for each episode:

```
>>> total_reward_episode = [0] * n_episode
>>> q_learning(env, dqn, n_episode, replay_size, target_update,
gamma=.9, epsilon=1)
```

How it works...

The observation in Pong is much more complicated than the environments we have worked with so far in this chapter. It is a three-channel image of *210 * 160* screen size. So, we first transform it into a grayscale image, downsize it to *84 * 84*, and then flatten it so that it can be fed into the fully connected neural network. As we have inputs of around 6,000 dimensions, we use two hidden layers to accommodate the complexity.

Using convolutional neural networks for Atari games

In the previous recipe, we treated each observed image in the Pong environment as a grayscale array and fed it to a fully connected neural network. Flattening an image may actually result in information loss. Why don't we use the image as input instead? In this recipe, we will incorporate **convolutional neural networks** (**CNNs**) into the DQN model.

A CNN is one of the best neural network architectures to deal with image inputs. In a CNN, the convolutional layers are able to effectively extract features from images, which will be passed on to downstream, fully connected layers. An example of a CNN with two convolutional layers is depicted here:

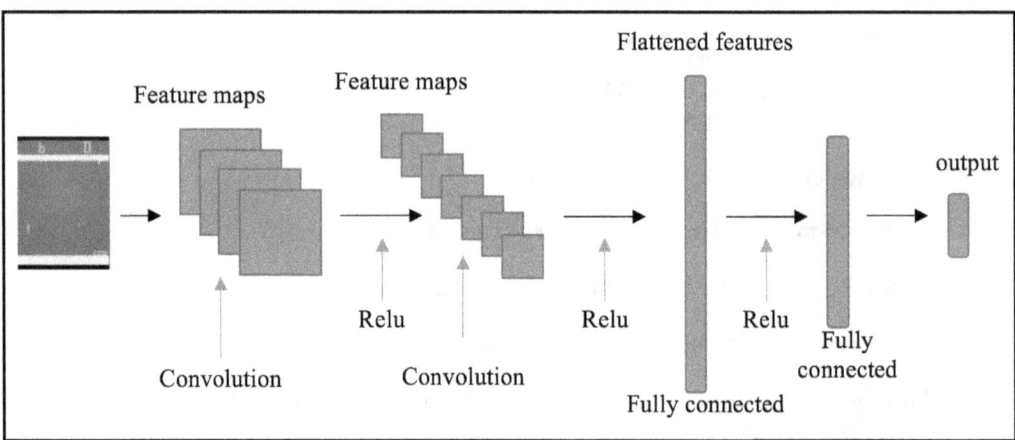

As you can imagine, if we simply flatten an image into a vector, we will lose some information on where the ball is located, and where the two players are. Such information is significant to the model learning. With convolutional operations in a CNN, such information about represented by a set of feature maps generated from multiple filters.

Again, we downsize the image from *210 * 160* to *84 * 84*, but retain three RGB channels without flattening them into an array this time.

How to do it...

Let's solve the Pong environment using a CNN-based DQN as follows:

1. Import the necessary modules and create a Pong environment:

```
>>> import gym
>>> import torch
>>> import random
>>> from collections import deque
>>> import copy
>>> from torch.autograd import Variable
>>> import torch.nn as nn
>>> import torch.nn.functional as F
>>> env = gym.envs.make("PongDeterministic-v4")
```

2. Then, we specify three actions:

```
>>> ACTIONS = [0, 2, 3]
>>> n_action = 3
```

These actions are not moving, moving up, and moving down.

3. Now, we develop an image processing function to downsize the image:

```
>>> import torchvision.transforms as T
>>> from PIL import Image
>>> image_size = 84
>>> transform = T.Compose([T.ToPILImage(),
...                        T.Resize((image_size, image_size),
...                            interpolation=Image.CUBIC),
...                        T.ToTensor()])
```

We now define a resizer that downsizes the image to *84 * 84*, and then we reshape the image to (*3, 84, 84*):

```
>>> def get_state(obs):
...         state = obs.transpose((2, 0, 1))
...         state = torch.from_numpy(state)
...         state = transform(state).unsqueeze(0)
...         return state
```

4. Now, we start to solve the Pong environment by developing the CNN model:

```
>>> class CNNModel(nn.Module):
...       def __init__(self, n_channel, n_action):
...           super(CNNModel, self).__init__()
...           self.conv1 = nn.Conv2d(in_channels=n_channel,
...                   out_channels=32, kernel_size=8, stride=4)
...           self.conv2 = nn.Conv2d(32, 64, 4, stride=2)
...           self.conv3 = nn.Conv2d(64, 64, 3, stride=1)
...           self.fc = torch.nn.Linear(7 * 7 * 64, 512)
...           self.out = torch.nn.Linear(512, n_action)
...
...       def forward(self, x):
...           x = F.relu(self.conv1(x))
...           x = F.relu(self.conv2(x))
...           x = F.relu(self.conv3(x))
...           x = x.view(x.size(0), -1)
...           x = F.relu(self.fc(x))
...           output = self.out(x)
...           return output
```

5. We will now use the CNN model we just defined in our DQN model:

```
>>> class DQN():
...       def __init__(self, n_channel, n_action, lr=0.05):
...           self.criterion = torch.nn.MSELoss()
...           self.model = CNNModel(n_channel, n_action)
...           self.model_target = copy.deepcopy(self.model)
...           self.optimizer = torch.optim.Adam(
...                       self.model.parameters(), lr)
```

6. The rest of the DQN class is the same as the one in the, *Developing double deep Q-networks* recipe, with a small change to the replay method:

```
>>> def replay(self, memory, replay_size, gamma):
...       """
...       Experience replay with target network
...       @param memory: a list of experience
...       @param replay_size: the number of samples we use
...                       to update the model each time
...       @param gamma: the discount factor
...       """
...       if len(memory) >= replay_size:
...           replay_data = random.sample(memory, replay_size)
...           states = []
...           td_targets = []
...           for state, action, next_state, reward,
...                       is_done in replay_data:
```

```
...            states.append(state.tolist()[0])
...            q_values = self.predict(state).tolist()[0]
...            if is_done:
...                q_values[action] = reward
...            else:
...                q_values_next = self.target_predict(
...                                next_state).detach()
...                q_values[action] = reward + gamma *
...                        torch.max(q_values_next).item()
...            td_targets.append(q_values)
...        self.update(states, td_targets)
```

7. We will reuse the `gen_epsilon_greedy_policy` function we developed in the, *Developing Deep Q-Networks* recipe, and will not repeat it here.

8. Now, we develop deep Q-learning with a double DQN:

```
>>> def q_learning(env, estimator, n_episode, replay_size,
...        target_update=10, gamma=1.0, epsilon=0.1,
...        epsilon_decay=.99):
...     """
...     Deep Q-Learning using double DQN, with experience replay
...     @param env: Gym environment
...     @param estimator: DQN object
...     @param replay_size: number of samples we use to
...                         update the model each time
...     @param target_update: number of episodes before
...                         updating the target network
...     @param n_episode: number of episodes
...     @param gamma: the discount factor
...     @param epsilon: parameter for epsilon_greedy
...     @param epsilon_decay: epsilon decreasing factor
...     """
...     for episode in range(n_episode):
...         if episode % target_update == 0:
...             estimator.copy_target()
...         policy = gen_epsilon_greedy_policy(
...                 estimator, epsilon, n_action)
...         obs = env.reset()
...         state = get_state(obs)
...         is_done = False
...         while not is_done:
...             action = policy(state)
...             next_obs, reward, is_done, _ =
...                         env.step(ACTIONS[action])
...             total_reward_episode[episode] += reward
...             next_state = get_state(obs)
...             memory.append((state, action, next_state,
...                         reward, is_done))
```

```
...                          if is_done:
...                              break
...                          estimator.replay(memory, replay_size, gamma)
...                          state = next_state
...                      print('Episode: {}, total reward: {}, epsilon: {}'
                     .format(episode, total_reward_episode[episode], epsilon))
...                      epsilon = max(epsilon * epsilon_decay, 0.01)
```

9. We then specify the remaining hyperparameters as follows:

```
>>> n_episode = 1000
>>> lr = 0.00025
>>> replay_size = 32
>>> target_update = 10
```

Create a DQN accordingly:

```
>>> dqn = DQN(3, n_action, lr)
```

10. Next, we define the buffer holding the experience:

```
>>> memory = deque(maxlen=100000)
```

11. Finally, we perform deep Q-learning and also keep track of the total rewards for each episode:

```
>>> total_reward_episode = [0] * n_episode
>>> q_learning(env, dqn, n_episode, replay_size, target_update,
gamma=.9, epsilon=1)
```

How it works...

The image preprocessing function in *Step 3* first downsizes the image for each channel to *84 * 84*, and then it changes its dimensions to *(3, 84, 84)*. This is to make sure that the image with the right dimensions is fed to the network.

In *Step 4*, the CNN model has three convolutional layers and a ReLU activation function that follows each convolutional layer. The resulting feature maps from the last convolutional layer are then flattened and fed to a fully connected hidden layer with 512 nodes, followed by the output layer.

Incorporating CNNs in DQNs was first introduced by DeepMind, as published in *Playing Atari with Deep Reinforcement Learning* (`https://www.cs.toronto.edu/~vmnih/docs/dqn.pdf`). The model takes in image pixels as inputs and outputs estimated future reward values. It also works well for other Atari game environments where the observation is an image of the game screen. The convolutional components are a set of effective hierarchical feature extractors. They can learn the feature representations from raw image data in complex environments and feed them the fully connected layers to learn successful control policies.

Keep in mind that the training in the preceding example usually takes a couple of days, even on a GPU, and around 90 hours on a 2.9 GHz Intel i7 Quad-Core CPU.

See also

If you are not familiar with CNNs, please check out the following material:

- Chapter 4, *CNN Architecture* from *Hands-On Deep Learning Architectures with Python* (Packt Publishing, by Yuxi (Hayden) Liu and Saransh Mehta)
- Chapter 1, *Handwritten Digit Recognition Using Convolutional Neural Networks,* and Chapter 2, *Traffic Sign Recognition for Intelligent Vehicles* from *R Deep Learning Projects* (Packt Publishing, by Yuxi (Hayden) Liu and Pablo Maldonado)

8
Implementing Policy Gradients and Policy Optimization

In this chapter, we will focus on policy gradient methods as one of the most popular reinforcement learning techniques over recent years. We will start with implementing the fundamental REINFORCE algorithm and will proceed with an improvement algorithm baseline. We will also implement a more powerful algorithm, actor-critic, and its variations, and apply it to solve the CartPole and Cliff Walking problems. We will also experience an environment with continuous action space and resort to Gaussian distribution to solve it. By way of a fun section at the end, we will train an agent based on the cross-entropy method to play the CartPole game.

The following recipes will be covered in this chapter:

- Implementing the REINFORCE algorithm
- Developing the REINFORCE algorithm with baseline
- Implementing the actor-critic algorithm
- Solving Cliff Walking with the actor-critic algorithm
- Setting up the continuous Mountain Car environment
- Solving the continuous Mountain Car environment with the advantage actor-critic network
- Playing CartPole through the cross-entropy method

Implementing the REINFORCE algorithm

A recent publication stipulated that policy gradient methods are becoming more and more popular. Their learning goal is to optimize the probability distribution of actions so that given a state, a more rewarding action will have a higher probability value. In the first recipe of the chapter, we will talk about the REINFORCE algorithm, which is foundational to advanced policy gradient methods.

The REINFORCE algorithm is also known as the **Monte Carlo policy gradient**, as it optimizes the policy based on Monte Carlo methods. Specifically, it collects trajectory samples from one episode using its current policy and uses them to the policy parameters, θ . The learning objective function for policy gradients is as follows:

$$J(\theta) = E[\sum_{t=0}^{T-1} r_{t+1}] = \sum_{t=0}^{T-1} P(s_t, a_t) * r_{t+1}$$

Its gradient can be derived as follows:

$$\nabla J(\theta) = \sum_{t=0}^{T-1} \nabla log\pi(a_t|s_t) * Gt$$

Here, G_t is the return, which is the cumulative discounted reward until time, $\pi(a_t|s_t)$ t, and is the stochastic policy, which determines the probabilities of taking certain actions at a given state. Since a policy update is conducted after the entire episode finishes and all samples are collected, REINFORCE is an off-policy algorithm.

After we compute the policy gradients, we use backpropagation to update the policy parameters. With the updated policy, we roll out an episode, collect a set of samples, and use them to repeatedly update the policy parameters.

We will now develop the REINFORCE algorithm to solve the CartPole (`https://gym.openai.com/envs/CartPole-v0/`) environment.

How to do it...

We develop the REINFORCE algorithm to solve the CartPole environment as follows:

1. Import all the necessary packages and create a CartPole instance:

```
>>> import gym
>>> import torch
>>> import torch.nn as nn
>>> env = gym.make('CartPole-v0')
```

2. Let's start with the __init__method of the PolicyNetwork class, which approximates the policy using a neural network:

```
>>> class PolicyNetwork():
...         def __init__(self, n_state, n_action, n_hidden=50,
lr=0.001):
...             self.model = nn.Sequential(
...                         nn.Linear(n_state, n_hidden),
...                         nn.ReLU(),
...                         nn.Linear(n_hidden, n_action),
...                         nn.Softmax(),
...                 )
...             self.optimizer = torch.optim.Adam(
...                         self.model.parameters(), lr)
```

3. Next, add the predict method, which computes the estimated policy:

```
>>>         def predict(self, s):
...             """
...             Compute the action probabilities of state s using
...                 the learning model
...             @param s: input state
...             @return: predicted policy
...             """
...             return self.model(torch.Tensor(s))
```

4. We now develop the training method, which updates the neural network with samples collected in an episode:

```
>>>         def update(self, returns, log_probs):
...             """
...             Update the weights of the policy network given
...                 the training samples
...             @param returns: return (cumulative rewards) for
...                 each step in an episode
...             @param log_probs: log probability for each step
...             """
```

```
...         policy_gradient = []
...         for log_prob, Gt in zip(log_probs, returns):
...             policy_gradient.append(-log_prob * Gt)
...
...         loss = torch.stack(policy_gradient).sum()
...         self.optimizer.zero_grad()
...         loss.backward()
...         self.optimizer.step()
```

5. The final method for the `PolicyNetwork` class is `get_action`, which samples an action given a state based on the predicted policy:

```
>>>     def get_action(self, s):
...         """
...         Estimate the policy and sample an action,
...             compute its log probability
...         @param s: input state
...         @return: the selected action and log probability
...         """
...         probs = self.predict(s)
...         action = torch.multinomial(probs, 1).item()
...         log_prob = torch.log(probs[action])
...         return action, log_prob
```

It also returns the log probability of the selected action, which will be used as part of the training sample.

That's all for the `PolicyNetwork` class!

6. Now, we can move on to developing the **REINFORCE** algorithm with a policy network model:

```
>>> def reinforce(env, estimator, n_episode, gamma=1.0):
...         """
...         REINFORCE algorithm
...         @param env: Gym environment
...         @param estimator: policy network
...         @param n_episode: number of episodes
...         @param gamma: the discount factor
...         """
...         for episode in range(n_episode):
...             log_probs = []
...             rewards = []
...             state = env.reset()
...             while True:
...                 action, log_prob = estimator.get_action(state)
...                 next_state, reward, is_done, _ = env.step(action)
...                 total_reward_episode[episode] += reward
```

```
...              log_probs.append(log_prob)
...              rewards.append(reward)
...
...              if is_done:
...                  returns = []
...                  Gt = 0
...                  pw = 0
...                  for reward in rewards[::-1]:
...                      Gt += gamma ** pw * reward
...                      pw += 1
...                      returns.append(Gt)
...                  returns = returns[::-1]
...                  returns = torch.tensor(returns)
...                  returns = (returns - returns.mean()) / (
...                      returns.std() + 1e-9)
...                  estimator.update(returns, log_probs)
...                  print('Episode: {}, total reward: {}'.format(
...                      episode, total_reward_episode[episode]))
...                  break
...
...              state = next_state
```

7. We specify the size of the policy network (input, hidden, and output layers), the learning rate, and then create a `PolicyNetwork` instance accordingly:

```
>>> n_state = env.observation_space.shape[0]
>>> n_action = env.action_space.n
>>> n_hidden = 128
>>> lr = 0.003
>>> policy_net = PolicyNetwork(n_state, n_action, n_hidden, lr)
```

We set the discount factor as `0.9`:

```
>>> gamma = 0.9
```

8. We perform learning with the REINFORCE algorithm using the policy network we just developed for 500 episodes, and we also keep track of the total rewards for each episode:

```
>>> n_episode = 500
>>> total_reward_episode = [0] * n_episode
>>> reinforce(env, policy_net, n_episode, gamma)
```

9. Let's now display the plot of episode reward over time:

```
>>> import matplotlib.pyplot as plt
>>> plt.plot(total_reward_episode)
>>> plt.title('Episode reward over time')
```

```
>>> plt.xlabel('Episode')
>>> plt.ylabel('Total reward')
>>> plt.show()
```

How it works...

In *Step 2*, we use a neural network with one hidden layer for simplicity. The input of the policy network is a state, followed by a hidden layer, while the output is the probability of taking possible individual actions. Therefore, we use the softmax function as the activation for the output layer.

Step 4 is for updating the network parameters: given all the data gathered in an episode, including the returns and the log probabilities of all steps, we compute the policy gradients, and then update the policy parameters accordingly via backpropagation.

In *Step 6*, the REINFORCE algorithm does the following tasks:

- It runs an episode: for each step in the episode, it samples an action based on the current estimated policy; it stores the reward and the log policy at each step.
- Once an episode finishes, it calculates the discounted cumulative rewards at each step; it normalizes the resulting returns by subtracting their mean and then dividing them by their standard deviation.
- It computes policy gradients using the returns and log probabilities, and then updates the policy parameters. We also display the total reward for each episode.
- It runs n_episode episodes by repeating the aforementioned steps.

Step 8 will generate the following training logs:

```
Episode: 0, total reward: 12.0
 Episode: 1, total reward: 18.0
 Episode: 2, total reward: 23.0
 Episode: 3, total reward: 23.0
 Episode: 4, total reward: 11.0
......
......
 Episode: 495, total reward: 200.0
 Episode: 496, total reward: 200.0
 Episode: 497, total reward: 200.0
 Episode: 498, total reward: 200.0
 Episode: 499, total reward: 200.0
```

You will observe the following plot in *Step 9*:

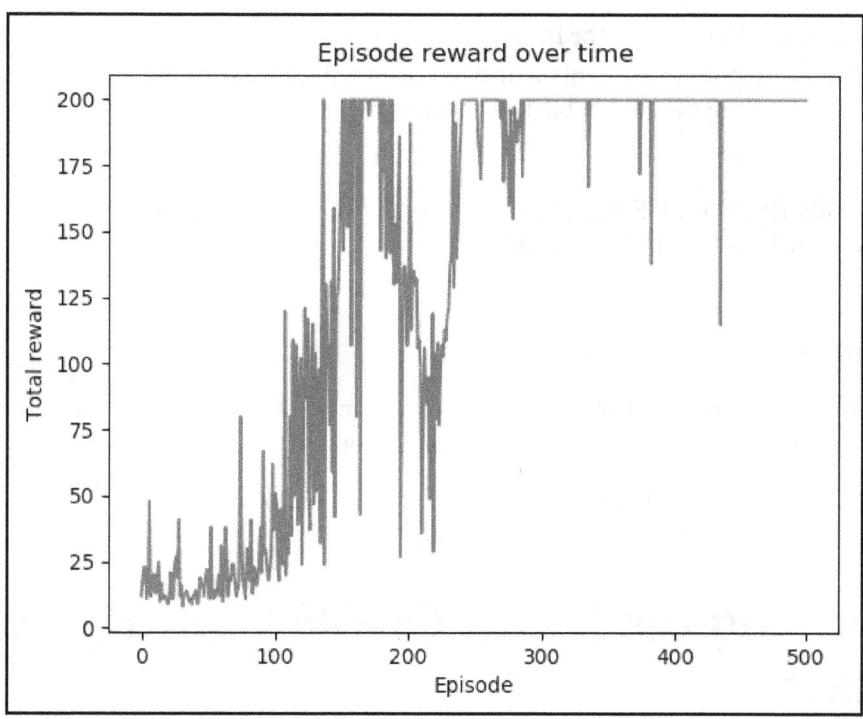

You can see that most of the last 200 episodes have rewards with a maximum value of +200.

The REINFORCE algorithm is a family of policy gradient methods that updates the policy parameters directly through the following rule:

$$\Delta\theta = \alpha \sum_{t=0}^{T-1} \nabla log\pi(a_t|s_t) * Gt$$

Here, α is the learning rate, $\pi(a_t|s_t)$, as the probability mappings of actions, and G_t, as the cumulative discounted rewards, are experiences collected in an episode. Since the set of training samples is constructed only after the full episode is completed, learning in REINFORCE is in an off-policy manner. The learning process can be summarized as follows:

1. Randomly initialize the policy parameter, θ.
2. Perform an episode by selecting actions based on the current policy.

3. At each step, store the log probability of the chosen action as well as the resulting reward.

4. Calculate the returns for individual steps.

5. Compute policy gradients using log probabilities and returns, and update the policy parameter, θ, via backpropagation.

6. Repeat *Steps 2 to 5*.

Again, since the REINFORCE algorithm relies on a full trajectory generated by a stochastic policy, it constitutes a Monte Carlo method.

See also

It is quite tricky to derive the policy gradient equation. It utilizes the log-derivative trick. In case you are wondering, here is a detailed explanation:

- http://www.1-4-5.net/~dmm/ml/log_derivative_trick.pdf

Developing the REINFORCE algorithm with baseline

In the REINFORCE algorithm, Monte Carlo plays out the whole trajectory in an episode that is used to update the policy afterward. However, the stochastic policy may take different actions at the same state in different episodes. This can confuse the training, since one sampled experience wants to increase the probability of choosing one action while another sampled experience may want to decrease it. To reduce this high variance problem in vanilla REINFORCE, we will develop a variation algorithm, REINFORCE with baseline, in this recipe.

In REINFORCE with baseline, we subtract the baseline state-value from the return, G. As a result, we use an advantage function A in the gradient update, which is described as follows:

$$A_t = G_t - V(s_t)$$
$$\nabla J(\theta) = \sum_{t=0}^{T-1} \nabla log\pi(a_t|s_t) * At$$

Here, V(s) is the value function that estimates the state-value given a state. Typically, we can use a linear function, or a neural network, to approximate the state-value. By introducing the baseline value, we can calibrate the rewards with respect to the average action given a state.

We develop the REINFORCE with baseline algorithm using two neural networks, one for policy, and another one for value estimation, in order to solve the CartPole environment.

How to do it...

We solve the CartPole environment using the REINFORCE with baseline algorithm as follows:

1. Import all the necessary packages and create a CartPole instance:

```
>>> import gym
>>> import torch
>>> import torch.nn as nn
>>> from torch.autograd import Variable
>>> env = gym.make('CartPole-v0')
```

2. For the policy network part, it is basically the same as the `PolicyNetwork` class we used in the *Implementing the REINFORCE algorithm* recipe. Keep in mind that the advantage values are used in the `update` method:

```
>>> def update(self, advantages, log_probs):
...         """
...         Update the weights of the policy network given
...             the training samples
...         @param advantages: advantage for each step in an episode
...         @param log_probs: log probability for each step
...         """
...         policy_gradient = []
...         for log_prob, Gt in zip(log_probs, advantages):
...             policy_gradient.append(-log_prob * Gt)
...
...         loss = torch.stack(policy_gradient).sum()
...         self.optimizer.zero_grad()
...         loss.backward()
...         self.optimizer.step()
```

3. For the value network part, we use a regression neural network with one hidden layer:

```
>>> class ValueNetwork():
...        def __init__(self, n_state, n_hidden=50, lr=0.05):
...            self.criterion = torch.nn.MSELoss()
...            self.model = torch.nn.Sequential(
...                            torch.nn.Linear(n_state, n_hidden),
...                            torch.nn.ReLU(),
...                            torch.nn.Linear(n_hidden, 1)
...                         )
...            self.optimizer = torch.optim.Adam(
...                            self.model.parameters(), lr)
```

Its learning goal is to approximate state-values; hence, we use the mean squared error as the loss function.

The `update` method trains the value regression model with a set of input states and target outputs, via backpropagation of course:

```
...        def update(self, s, y):
...            """
...            Update the weights of the DQN given a training sample
...            @param s: states
...            @param y: target values
...            """
...            y_pred = self.model(torch.Tensor(s))
...            loss = self.criterion(y_pred,
Variable(torch.Tensor(y)))
...            self.optimizer.zero_grad()
...            loss.backward()
...            self.optimizer.step()
```

And the `predict` method estimates the state-value:

```
...        def predict(self, s):
...            """
...            Compute the Q values of the state for all actions
...                using the learning model
...            @param s: input state
...            @return: Q values of the state for all actions
...            """
...            with torch.no_grad():
...                return self.model(torch.Tensor(s))
```

4. Now, we can move on to developing the REINFORCE with baseline algorithm with a policy and value network model:

```
>>> def reinforce(env, estimator_policy, estimator_value,
                   n_episode, gamma=1.0):
...     """
...     REINFORCE algorithm with baseline
...     @param env: Gym environment
...     @param estimator_policy: policy network
...     @param estimator_value: value network
...     @param n_episode: number of episodes
...     @param gamma: the discount factor
...     """
...     for episode in range(n_episode):
...         log_probs = []
...         states = []
...         rewards = []
...         state = env.reset()
...         while True:
...             states.append(state)
...             action, log_prob =
                    estimator_policy.get_action(state)
...             next_state, reward, is_done, _ = env.step(action)
...             total_reward_episode[episode] += reward
...             log_probs.append(log_prob)
...             rewards.append(reward)
...
...             if is_done:
...                 Gt = 0
...                 pw = 0
...                 returns = []
...                 for t in range(len(states)-1, -1, -1):
...                     Gt += gamma ** pw * rewards[t]
...                     pw += 1
...                     returns.append(Gt)
...                 returns = returns[::-1]
...                 returns = torch.tensor(returns)
...                 baseline_values =
                        estimator_value.predict(states)
...                 advantages = returns - baseline_values
...                 estimator_value.update(states, returns)
...                 estimator_policy.update(advantages, log_probs)
...                 print('Episode: {}, total reward: {}'.format(
                        episode, total_reward_episode[episode]))
...                 break
...             state = next_state
```

5. We specify the size of the policy network (input, hidden, and output layers), the learning rate, and then create a `PolicyNetwork` instance accordingly:

```
>>> n_state = env.observation_space.shape[0]
>>> n_action = env.action_space.n
>>> n_hidden_p = 64
>>> lr_p = 0.003
>>> policy_net = PolicyNetwork(n_state, n_action, n_hidden_p, lr_p)
```

As for the value network, we also set its size and create an instance:

```
>>> n_hidden_v = 64
>>> lr_v = 0.003
>>> value_net = ValueNetwork(n_state, n_hidden_v, lr_v)
```

We set the discount factor as 0.9:

```
>>> gamma = 0.9
```

6. We perform learning using the REINFORCE with baseline algorithm for 2,000 episodes, and we also keep track of the total rewards for each episode:

```
>>> n_episode = 2000
>>> total_reward_episode = [0] * n_episode
>>> reinforce(env, policy_net, value_net, n_episode, gamma)
```

7. Now, we display the plot of episode reward over time:

```
>>> import matplotlib.pyplot as plt
>>> plt.plot(total_reward_episode)
>>> plt.title('Episode reward over time')
>>> plt.xlabel('Episode')
>>> plt.ylabel('Total reward')
>>> plt.show()
```

How it works...

REINFORCE relies heavily on Monte Carlo methods to generate a whole trajectory used to train the policy network. However, different actions may be taken in different episodes under the same stochastic policy. To reduce the variance for the sampled experience, we subtract the state-value from the return . The resulting advantage measures the reward relative to the average action, which will be used in the gradient update.

In *Step 4*, REINFORCE with a baseline algorithm does the following tasks:

- It runs an episode—es the state, reward, and the log policy at each step.
- Once an episode finishes, it calculates the discounted cumulative reward at each step; it estimates the baseline values using the value network; it computes the advantage values by subtracting the baseline values from the returns.
- It computes policy gradients using the advantage values and log probabilities, and updates the policy and value networks. We also display the total reward for each episode.
- It runs `n_episode` episodes by repeating the aforementioned steps.

Executing the code in *Step 7* will result in the following plot:

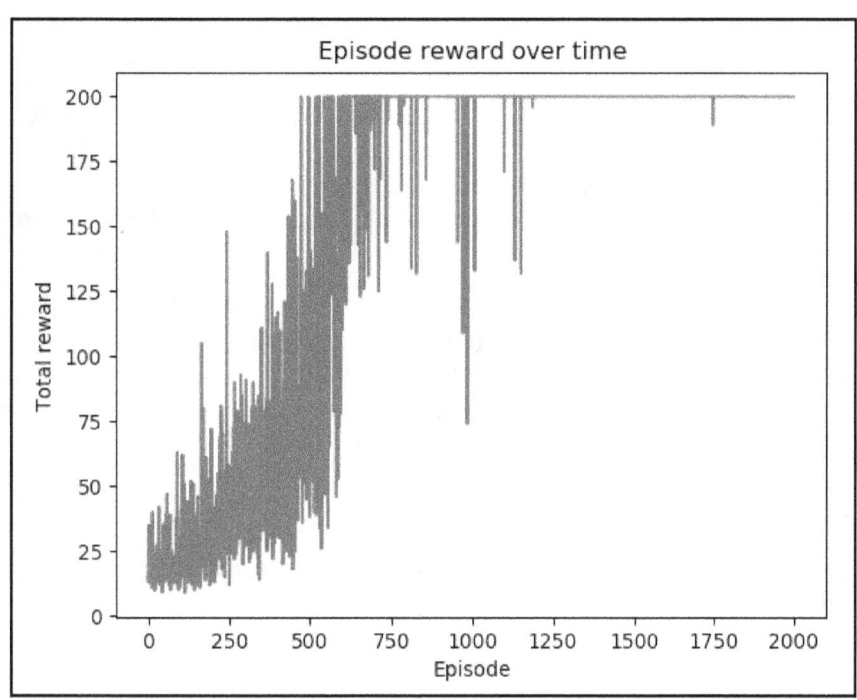

You can see that the performance is very stable after around 1,200 episodes.

With the additional value baseline, we are able to recalibrate the rewards and reduce variance on the gradient estimates.

Implementing the actor-critic algorithm

In the REINFORCE with baseline algorithm, there are two separate components, the policy model and the value function. We can actually combine the learning of these two components, since the goal of learning the value function is to update the policy network. This is what the **actor-critic** algorithm does, and which we are going to develop in this recipe.

The network for the actor-critic algorithm consists of the following two parts:

- **Actor**: This takes in the input state and outputs the action probabilities. Essentially, it learns the optimal policy by updating the model using information provided by the critic.
- **Critic**: This evaluates how good it is to be at the input state by computing the value function. The value guides the actor on how it should adjust.

These two components share parameters of input and hidden layers in the network, as learning is more efficient in this way than learning them separately. Accordingly, the loss function is a summation of two parts, specifically, the negative log likelihood of action measuring the actor, and the mean squared error between the estimated and computed return measuring the critic.

A more popular version of the actor-critic algorithm is **Advantage Actor-Critic (A2C)**. As its name implies, the critic part computes the advantage value, instead of the state-value, which is similar to REINFORCE with baseline. It evaluates how better an action is at a state compared to the other actions, and is known to reduce variance in policy networks.

How to do it...

We develop the actor-critic algorithm in order to solve the CartPole environment as follows:

1. Import all the necessary packages and create a CartPole instance:

```
>>> import gym
>>> import torch
>>> import torch.nn as nn
>>> import torch.nn.functional as F
>>> env = gym.make('CartPole-v0')
```

2. Let's start with the actor-critic neural network model:

```
>>> class ActorCriticModel(nn.Module):
...         def __init__(self, n_input, n_output, n_hidden):
...             super(ActorCriticModel, self).__init__()
...             self.fc = nn.Linear(n_input, n_hidden)
...             self.action = nn.Linear(n_hidden, n_output)
...             self.value = nn.Linear(n_hidden, 1)
...
...         def forward(self, x):
...             x = torch.Tensor(x)
...             x = F.relu(self.fc(x))
...             action_probs = F.softmax(self.action(x), dim=-1)
...             state_values = self.value(x)
...             return action_probs, state_values
```

3. We continue with the __init__ method of the `PolicyNetwork` class using the actor-critic neural network:

```
>>> class PolicyNetwork():
...         def __init__(self, n_state, n_action,
...                     n_hidden=50, lr=0.001):
...             self.model = ActorCriticModel(
...                             n_state, n_action, n_hidden)
...             self.optimizer = torch.optim.Adam(
...                             self.model.parameters(), lr)
...             self.scheduler = torch.optim.lr_scheduler.StepLR(
...                     self.optimizer, step_size=10, gamma=0.9)
```

Note that we use herein a learning rate reducer that allows a dynamic learning rate according to learning progress.

4. Next, we add the `predict` method, which computes the estimated action probabilities and state-value:

```
>>>     def predict(self, s):
...             """
...             Compute the output using the Actor Critic model
...             @param s: input state
...             @return: action probabilities, state_value
...             """
...             return self.model(torch.Tensor(s))
```

5. We now develop the `training` method, which updates the neural network with samples collected in an episode:

```
>>>        def update(self, returns, log_probs, state_values):
...            """
...                Update the weights of the Actor Critic network
...                    given the training samples
...                @param returns: return (cumulative rewards) for
...                    each step in an episode
...                @param log_probs: log probability for each step
...                @param state_values: state-value for each step
...                """
...
...                loss = 0
...                for log_prob, value, Gt in zip(
...                        log_probs, state_values, returns):
...                    advantage = Gt - value.item()
...                    policy_loss = -log_prob * advantage
...                    value_loss = F.smooth_l1_loss(value, Gt)
...                    loss += policy_loss + value_loss
...                self.optimizer.zero_grad()
...                loss.backward()
...                self.optimizer.step()
```

6. The final method for the `PolicyNetwork` class is get_action, which samples an action given a state based on the predicted policy:

```
>>>        def get_action(self, s):
...            """
...                Estimate the policy and sample an action,
...                    compute its log probability
...                @param s: input state
...                @return: the selected action and log probability
...                """
...
...                action_probs, state_value = self.predict(s)
...                action = torch.multinomial(action_probs, 1).item()
...                log_prob = torch.log(action_probs[action])
...                return action, log_prob, state_value
```

It also returns the log probability of the selected action, as well as the estimated state-value.

That's all for the `PolicyNetwork` class!

7. Now, we can move on to developing the main function, training an actor-critic model:

```
>>> def actor_critic(env, estimator, n_episode, gamma=1.0):
...         """
...         Actor Critic algorithm
...         @param env: Gym environment
...         @param estimator: policy network
...         @param n_episode: number of episodes
...         @param gamma: the discount factor
...         """
...         for episode in range(n_episode):
...             log_probs = []
...             rewards = []
...             state_values = []
...             state = env.reset()
...             while True:
...                 action, log_prob, state_value =
...                         estimator.get_action(state)
...                 next_state, reward, is_done, _ = env.step(action)
...                 total_reward_episode[episode] += reward
...                 log_probs.append(log_prob)
...                 state_values.append(state_value)
...                 rewards.append(reward)
...
...                 if is_done:
...                     returns = []
...                     Gt = 0
...                     pw = 0
...                     for reward in rewards[::-1]:
...                         Gt += gamma ** pw * reward
...                         pw += 1
...                         returns.append(Gt)
...                     returns = returns[::-1]
...                     returns = torch.tensor(returns)
...                     returns = (returns - returns.mean()) /
...                                 (returns.std() + 1e-9)
...                     estimator.update(
...                         returns, log_probs, state_values)
...                     print('Episode: {}, total reward: {}'.format(
...                         episode, total_reward_episode[episode]))
...                     if total_reward_episode[episode] >= 195:
...                         estimator.scheduler.step()
...                     break
...
...                 state = next_state
```

8. We specify the size of the policy network (input, hidden, and output layers), the learning rate, and then create a `PolicyNetwork` instance accordingly:

```
>>> n_state = env.observation_space.shape[0]
>>> n_action = env.action_space.n
>>> n_hidden = 128
>>> lr = 0.03
>>> policy_net = PolicyNetwork(n_state, n_action, n_hidden, lr)
```

We set the discount factor as 0.9:

```
>>> gamma = 0.9
```

9. We perform learning with the actor-critic algorithm using the policy network we just developed for 1,000 episodes, and we also keep track of the total rewards for each episode:

```
>>> n_episode = 1000
>>> total_reward_episode = [0] * n_episode
>>> actor_critic(env, policy_net, n_episode, gamma)
```

10. Finally, we display the plot of episode reward over time:

```
>>> import matplotlib.pyplot as plt
>>> plt.plot(total_reward_episode)
>>> plt.title('Episode reward over time')
>>> plt.xlabel('Episode')
>>> plt.ylabel('Total reward')
>>> plt.show()
```

How it works...

As you can see in *Step 2*, the actor and critic share parameters of the input and the hidden layers; the output of the actor consists of the probability of taking individual actions, and the output of the critic is the estimated value of the input state.

In *Step 5*, we compute the advantage value and its negative log likelihood. The loss function in actor-critic is the combination of the negative log likelihood of advantage and the mean squared error between the return and estimated state-value. Note that we use `smooth_l1_loss`, which is a squared term, if the absolute error falls below 1, and an absolute error otherwise.

In *Step 7*, the training function for the actor-critic model carries out the following tasks:

- It runs an episode: for each step in the episode, it samples an action based on the current estimated policy; it stores the reward, log policy, and estimated state-value at each step.
- Once an episode finishes, it calculates the discounted cumulative rewards at each step; it normalizes the resulting returns by subtracting their mean and then dividing them by their standard deviation.
- It updates policy parameters using the returns, log probabilities, and state-values. We also display the total reward for each episode.
- If the total reward for an episode is more than +195, we reduce the learning rate slightly.
- It runs `n_episode` episodes by repeating the aforementioned steps.

You will see the following logs after executing the training in *Step 9*:

```
Episode: 0, total reward: 18.0
Episode: 1, total reward: 9.0
Episode: 2, total reward: 9.0
Episode: 3, total reward: 10.0
Episode: 4, total reward: 10.0
. . .
. . .
Episode: 995, total reward: 200.0
Episode: 996, total reward: 200.0
Episode: 997, total reward: 200.0
Episode: 998, total reward: 200.0
Episode: 999, total reward: 200.0
```

The following plot is the result of *Step 10*:

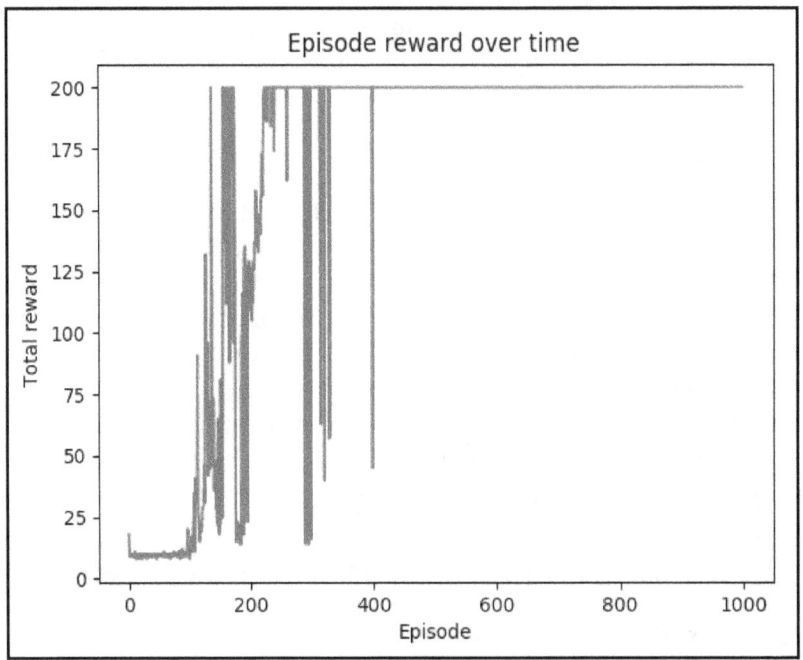

You can see that the rewards after around 400 episodes stay in the maximum value of +200.

In the advantage actor-critic algorithm, we decompose learning into two pieces – actor and critic. Critic in A2C evaluates how good an action is at a state, which guides the actor on how it should react. Again, the advantage value is computed as A(s,a) = Q(s,a) -V(s), which means subtracting state-values from Q values. Actor estimates the action probabilities based on critic's guidance. The introduction of advantage can reduce variance, and hence, A2C is considered a more stable model than the standard actor-critic. As we can see in the CartPole environment, the performance of A2C has been consistent after the training of several hundred episodes. It outperforms REINFORCE with baseline.

Solving Cliff Walking with the actor-critic algorithm

In this recipe, let's solve a more complicated Cliff Walking environment using the A2C algorithm.

Cliff Walking is a typical Gym environment with long episodes without a guarantee of termination. It is a grid problem with a 4 * 12 board. An agent makes a move of up, right, down and left at a step. The bottom-left tile is the starting point for the agent, and the bottom-right is the winning point where an episode will end if it is reached. The remaining tiles in the last row are cliffs where the agent will be reset to the starting position after stepping on any of them, but the episode continues. Each step the agent takes incurs a -1 reward, with the exception of stepping on the cliffs, where a -100 reward incurs.

The state is an integer from 0 to 47, indicating where the agent is located, as illustrated:

0	1	2	3	4	5	6	7	8	9	10	11
12	13	14	15	16	17	18	19	20	21	22	23
24	25	26	27	28	29	30	31	32	33	34	35
36	37	38	39	40	41	42	43	44	45	46	47

Such value does not contain a numerical meaning. For example, being at state 30 does not mean it is 3 times different from being in state 10. Hence, we will first convert it into a one-hot encoded vector before feeding the state to the policy network.

How to do it...

We solve Cliff Walking using the A2C algorithm as follows:

1. Import all the necessary packages and create a CartPole instance:

```
>>> import gym
>>> import torch
>>> import torch.nn as nn
>>> import torch.nn.functional as F
>>> env = gym.make('CliffWalking-v0')
```

2. As the state becomes 48-dimension, we use a more complicated actor-critic neural network with two hidden layers:

```
>>> class ActorCriticModel(nn.Module):
...         def __init__(self, n_input, n_output, n_hidden):
...             super(ActorCriticModel, self).__init__()
...             self.fc1 = nn.Linear(n_input, n_hidden[0])
...             self.fc2 = nn.Linear(n_hidden[0], n_hidden[1])
...             self.action = nn.Linear(n_hidden[1], n_output)
```

```
...        self.value = nn.Linear(n_hidden[1], 1)
...
...    def forward(self, x):
...        x = torch.Tensor(x)
...        x = F.relu(self.fc1(x))
...        x = F.relu(self.fc2(x))
...        action_probs = F.softmax(self.action(x), dim=-1)
...        state_values = self.value(x)
...        return action_probs, state_values
```

Again, the actor and critic share parameters of the input and hidden layers.

3. We continue with the `PolicyNetwork` class using the actor-critic neural network we just developed in *Step 2*. It is the same as the `PolicyNetwork` class in the *Implementing the actor-critic algorithm* recipe.

4. Next, we develop the main function, training an actor-critic model. It is almost the same as the one in the *Implementing the actor-critic algorithm* recipe, with the additional transformation of state into a one-hot encoded vector:

```
>>> def actor_critic(env, estimator, n_episode, gamma=1.0):
...     """
...     Actor Critic algorithm
...     @param env: Gym environment
...     @param estimator: policy network
...     @param n_episode: number of episodes
...     @param gamma: the discount factor
...     """
...     for episode in range(n_episode):
...         log_probs = []
...         rewards = []
...         state_values = []
...         state = env.reset()
...         while True:
...             one_hot_state = [0] * 48
...             one_hot_state[state] = 1
...             action, log_prob, state_value = 
...                 estimator.get_action(one_hot_state)
...             next_state, reward, is_done, _ = env.step(action)
...             total_reward_episode[episode] += reward
...             log_probs.append(log_prob)
...             state_values.append(state_value)
...             rewards.append(reward)
...
...             if is_done:
...                 returns = []
...                 Gt = 0
...                 pw = 0
```

```
...                    for reward in rewards[::-1]:
...                        Gt += gamma ** pw * reward
...                        pw += 1
...                        returns.append(Gt)
...                    returns = returns[::-1]
...                    returns = torch.tensor(returns)
...                    returns = (returns - returns.mean()) /
                                (returns.std() + 1e-9)
...                    estimator.update(
                            returns, log_probs, state_values)
...                    print('Episode: {}, total reward: {}'.format(
                            episode, total_reward_episode[episode]))
...                    if total_reward_episode[episode] >= -14:
...                        estimator.scheduler.step()
...                    break
...
...                state = next_state
```

5. We specify the size of the policy network (input, hidden, and output layers), the learning rate, and then create a `PolicyNetwork` instance accordingly:

```
>>> n_state = 48
>>> n_action = env.action_space.n
>>> n_hidden = [128, 32]
>>> lr = 0.03
>>> policy_net = PolicyNetwork(n_state, n_action, n_hidden, lr)
```

And we set the discount factor as 0.9:

```
>>> gamma = 0.9
```

6. We perform learning with the actor-critic algorithm using the policy network we just developed for 1,000 episodes, and we also keep track of the total rewards for each episode:

```
>>> n_episode = 1000
>>> total_reward_episode = [0] * n_episode
>>> actor_critic(env, policy_net, n_episode, gamma)
```

7. Now, we display the plot of episode reward over time since the 100th episode:

```
>>> import matplotlib.pyplot as plt
>>> plt.plot(range(100, n_episode), total_reward_episode[100:])
>>> plt.title('Episode reward over time')
>>> plt.xlabel('Episode')
>>> plt.ylabel('Total reward')
>>> plt.show()
```

How it works...

You may notice in *Step 4* that we reduce the learning rate slightly if the total reward for an episode is more than -14. A reward of -13 is the maximum value we are able to achieve, by taking the path 36-24-25-26-27-28-29-30-31-32-33-34-35-47.

You will see the following logs after executing the training in *Step 6*:

```
Episode: 0, total reward: -85355
Episode: 1, total reward: -3103
Episode: 2, total reward: -1002
Episode: 3, total reward: -240
Episode: 4, total reward: -118
. . .
. . .
Episode: 995, total reward: -13
Episode: 996, total reward: -13
Episode: 997, total reward: -13
Episode: 998, total reward: -13
Episode: 999, total reward: -13
```

The following plot is the result of *Step 7*:

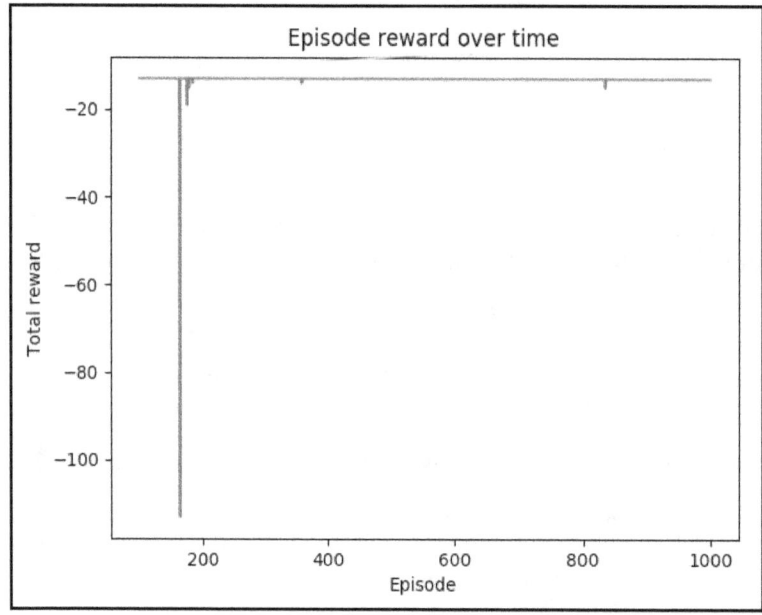

As we can observe, after around the 180th episode, rewards in most episodes achieve the optimal value, -13.

In this recipe, we solved the Cliff Walking problem with the A2C algorithm. As the integer state from 0 to 47 represents the location of the agent in the 4*12 board, which doesn't contain numerical meaning, we first converted it into a one-hot encoded vector of 48 dimensions. To deal with the input of 48 dimensions, we use a slightly more complicated neural network with two hidden layers. A2C has proved to be a stable policy method in our experiment.

Setting up the continuous Mountain Car environment

So far, the environments we have worked on have discrete action values, such as 0 or 1, representing up or down, left or right. In this recipe, we will experience a Mountain Car environment with continuous actions.

Continuous Mountain Car (`https://github.com/openai/gym/wiki/ MountainCarContinuous-v0`) is a Mountain Car environment with continuous actions whose value is from -1 to 1. As shown in the following screenshot, its goal is to get the car to the top of the hill on the right-hand side:

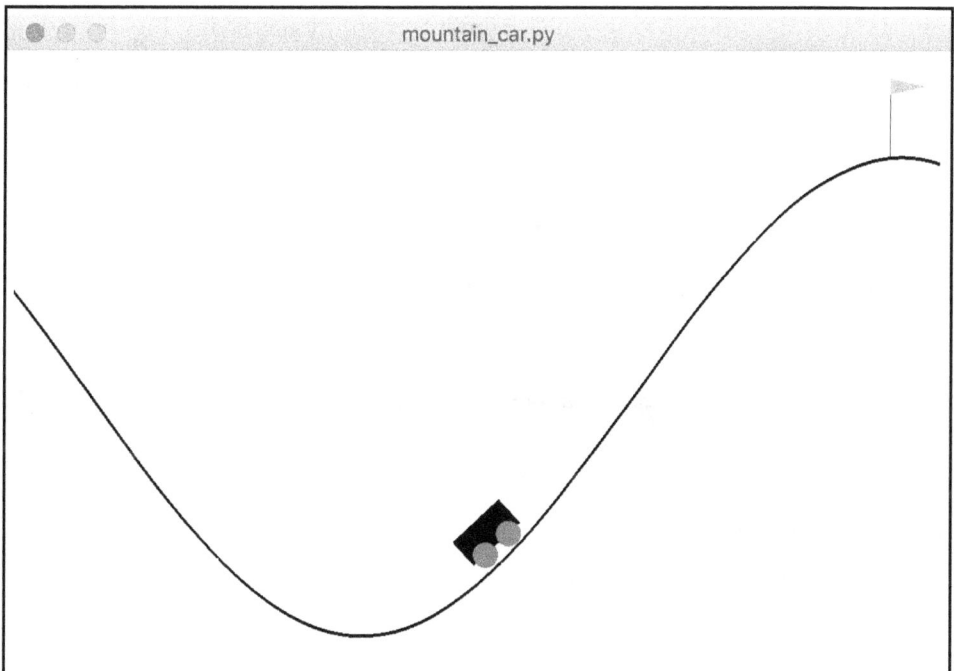

In a one-dimensional track, the car is positioned between -1.2 (leftmost) and 0.6 (rightmost), and the goal (yellow flag) is located at 0.5. The engine of the car is not strong enough to drive it to the top in a single pass, so it has to drive back and forth to build up momentum. Hence, the action is a float that represents the force of pushing the car to the left if it is in a negative value from -1 to 0, or pushing the car to the right if it is in a positive value from 0 to 1.

There are two states of the environment:

- **Position of the car**: This is a continuous variable from -1.2 to 0.6
- **Velocity of the car**: This is a continuous variable from -0.07 to 0.07

The starting state consists of a position between -0.6 to -0.4, and a velocity of 0.

The reward associated with each step is $-a^2$, where a is the action. And there is an additional reward of + 100 for reaching the goal. So, it penalizes the force taken in each step until the car reaches the goal. An episode ends when the car reaches the goal position (obviously), or after 1,000 steps.

How to do it...

Let's simulate the continuous Mountain Car environment by observing the following steps:

1. We import the Gym library and create an instance of the continuous Mountain Car environment:

```
>>> import gym
>>> import torch
>>> env = gym.envs.make("MountainCarContinuous-v0")
```

2. Take a look at the action space:

```
>>> print(env.action_space.low[0])
-1.0
>>> print(env.action_space.high[0])
1.0
```

3. We then reset the environment:

```
>>> env.reset()
array([-0.56756635,   0. ])
```

The car starts with state [-0.56756635, 0.], which means that the initial position is around -0.56 and the velocity is 0. You may see a different initial position as it is randomly generated from -0.6 to -0.4.

4. Let's now take a naive approach: we just take a random action from -1 to 1:

```
>>> is_done = False
>>> while not is_done:
...         random_action = torch.rand(1) * 2 - 1
...         next_state, reward, is_done, info =
env.step(random_action)
...         print(next_state, reward, is_done)
...         env.render()
>>> env.render()
 [-0.5657432    0.00182313] -0.09924464356736849 False
 [-0.5622848    0.00345837] -0.07744002014160288 False
 [-0.55754507   0.00473979] -0.04372991690837722 False
 ......
 ......
```

The state (position and velocity) keeps changing accordingly, and the reward is $-a^2$ for each step.

You will also see in the video that the car is repeatedly moving right and back to the left.

How it works...

As you can imagine, the continuous Mountain Car problem is a challenging environment, even more so than the original discrete one with only three different possible actions. We need to drive the car back and forth to build up momentum with the right amount of force and direction. Furthermore, the action space is continuous, which means that the value lookup / update method (such as the TD method, DQN) will not work. In the next recipe, we will solve the continuous Mountain Car problem with a continuous control version of the A2C algorithm.

Solving the continuous Mountain Car environment with the advantage actor-critic network

In this recipe, we are going to solve the continuous Mountain Car problem using the advantage actor-critic algorithm, a continuous version this time of course. You will see how it differs from the discrete version.

As we have seen in A2C for environments with discrete actions, we sample actions based on the estimated probabilities. How can we model a continuous control, since we can't do such sampling for countless continuous actions? We can actually resort to Gaussian distribution. We can assume that the action values are under a Gaussian distribution:

$$\pi(a|s) = N(\mu, \sigma)$$

Here, the mean, μ, and deviation, σ, are computed from the policy network. With this tweak, we can sample actions from the constructed Gaussian distribution by current mean and deviation. The loss function in continuous A2C is similar to the one we used in discrete control, which is a combination of negative log likelihood computed with the action probabilities under the Gaussian distribution and the advantage values, and the regression error between the actual return values and estimated state-values.

Note that one Gaussian distribution is used to simulate action in one dimension, so, if the action space is in k dimensions, we need to use k Gaussian distributions. In the continuous Mountain Car environment, the action space is one-dimensional. The main difficulty of A2C as regards continuous control is how to construct the policy network, as it computes parameters for the Gaussian distribution.

How to do it...

We solve the continuous Mountain Car problem using continuous A2C as follows:

1. Import all the necessary packages and create a continuous Mountain Car instance:

```
>>> import gym
>>> import torch
>>> import torch.nn as nn
>>> import torch.nn.functional as F
>>> env = gym.make('MountainCarContinuous-v0')
```

2. Let's start with the actor-critic neural network model:

```
>>> class ActorCriticModel(nn.Module):
...       def __init__(self, n_input, n_output, n_hidden):
...           super(ActorCriticModel, self).__init__()
...           self.fc = nn.Linear(n_input, n_hidden)
...           self.mu = nn.Linear(n_hidden, n_output)
...           self.sigma = nn.Linear(n_hidden, n_output)
...           self.value = nn.Linear(n_hidden, 1)
...           self.distribution = torch.distributions.Normal
...
...       def forward(self, x):
...           x = F.relu(self.fc(x))
...           mu = 2 * torch.tanh(self.mu(x))
...           sigma = F.softplus(self.sigma(x)) + 1e-5
...           dist = self.distribution(
...                   mu.view(1, ).data, sigma.view(1, ).data)
...           value = self.value(x)
...           return dist, value
```

3. We continue with the __init__ method of the `PolicyNetwork` class using the actor-critic neural network we just developed:

```
>>> class PolicyNetwork():
...       def __init__(self, n_state, n_action,
...                    n_hidden=50, lr=0.001):
...           self.model = ActorCriticModel(
...                       n_state, n_action, n_hidden)
...           self.optimizer = torch.optim.Adam(
...                       self.model.parameters(), lr)
```

4. Next, we add the `predict` method, which computes the estimated action probabilities and state-value:

```
>>>       def predict(self, s):
...           """
...           Compute the output using the continuous Actor Critic
model
...           @param s: input state
...           @return: Gaussian distribution, state_value
...           """
...           self.model.training = False
...           return self.model(torch.Tensor(s))
```

5. We now develop the training method, which updates the policy network with samples collected in an episode. We will reuse the update method developed in the *Implementing the actor-critic algorithm* recipe and will not repeat it here.

6. The final method for the `PolicyNetwork` class is `get_action`, which samples an action from the estimated Gaussian distribution given a state:

```
>>>        def get_action(self, s):
...            """
...            Estimate the policy and sample an action,
                   compute its log probability
...            @param s: input state
...            @return: the selected action, log probability,
                   predicted state-value
...            """
...            dist, state_value = self.predict(s)
...            action = dist.sample().numpy()
...            log_prob = dist.log_prob(action[0])
...            return action, log_prob, state_value
```

It also returns the log probability of the selected action, and the estimated state-value.

That's all for the `PolicyNetwork` class for continuous control!

Now, we can move on to developing the main function, training an actor-critic model:

```
>>> def actor_critic(env, estimator, n_episode, gamma=1.0):
...         """
...         continuous Actor Critic algorithm
...         @param env: Gym environment
...         @param estimator: policy network
...         @param n_episode: number of episodes
...         @param gamma: the discount factor
...         """
...         for episode in range(n_episode):
...             log_probs = []
...             rewards = []
...             state_values = []
...             state = env.reset()
...             while True:
...                 state = scale_state(state)
...                 action, log_prob, state_value =
                        estimator.get_action(state)
...                 action = action.clip(env.action_space.low[0],
                                    env.action_space.high[0])
...                 next_state, reward, is_done, _ = env.step(action)
...                 total_reward_episode[episode] += reward
...                 log_probs.append(log_prob)
...                 state_values.append(state_value)
...                 rewards.append(reward)
```

```
...                 if is_done:
...                     returns = []
...                     Gt = 0
...                     pw = 0
...                     for reward in rewards[::-1]:
...                         Gt += gamma ** pw * reward
...                         pw += 1
...                         returns.append(Gt)
...                     returns = returns[::-1]
...                     returns = torch.tensor(returns)
...                     returns = (returns - returns.mean()) /
                                      (returns.std() + 1e-9)
...                     estimator.update(
                            returns, log_probs, state_values)
...                     print('Episode: {}, total reward: {}'.format(
                            episode, total_reward_episode[episode]))
...                     break
...                 state = next_state
```

7. The `scale_state` function is used to normalize (standardize) the inputs for faster model convergence. We first randomly generate 10,000 observations and use them to train a scaler:

```
>>> import sklearn.preprocessing
>>> import numpy as np
>>> state_space_samples = np.array(
...         [env.observation_space.sample() for x in range(10000)])
>>> scaler = sklearn.preprocessing.StandardScaler()
>>> scaler.fit(state_space_samples)
```

Once the scaler is trained, we use it in the `scale_state` function to transform new input data:

```
>>> def scale_state(state):
...         scaled = scaler.transform([state])
...         return scaled[0]
```

8. We specify the size of the policy network (input, hidden, and output layers), the learning rate, and then create a `PolicyNetwork` instance accordingly:

```
>>> n_state = env.observation_space.shape[0]
>>> n_action = 1
>>> n_hidden = 128
>>> lr = 0.0003
>>> policy_net = PolicyNetwork(n_state, n_action, n_hidden, lr)
```

We set the discount factor as `0.9`:

```
>>> gamma = 0.9
```

9. We perform continuous control with the actor-critic algorithm using the policy network we just developed for 200 episodes, and we also keep track of the total rewards for each episode:

```
>>> n_episode = 200
>>> total_reward_episode = [0] * n_episode
>>> actor_critic(env, policy_net, n_episode, gamma)
```

11. Now, let's display the plot of episode reward over time:

```
>>> import matplotlib.pyplot as plt
>>> plt.plot(total_reward_episode)
>>> plt.title('Episode reward over time')
>>> plt.xlabel('Episode')
>>> plt.ylabel('Total reward')
>>> plt.show()
```

How it works...

In this recipe, we used Gaussian A2C to solve the continuous Mountain Car environment.

In *Step 2*, the network in our example has one hidden layer. There are three separate components in the output layer. They are the mean and deviation of the Gaussian distribution, and the state-value. The output of the distribution mean is scaled to the range of [-1, 1] (or [-2, 2] in this example), using a tanh activation function. As for the distribution deviation, we use softplus as the activation function to ensure a positive deviation. The network returns the current Gaussian distribution (actor) and estimated state-value (critic).

The training function for the actor-critic model in *Step 7* is quite similar to what we developed in the *Implementing the actor-critic algorithm* recipe. You may notice that we add a value clip to the sampled action in order to keep it within the [-1, 1] range . We will explain what the `scale_state` function does in an upcoming step.

You will see the following logs after executing the training in *Step 10*:

```
Episode: 0, total reward: 89.46417524456328
Episode: 1, total reward: 89.54226159679301
Episode: 2, total reward: 89.91828341346695
Episode: 3, total reward: 90.04199470314816
Episode: 4, total reward: 86.23157467747066
...
```

```
. . .
Episode: 194, total reward: 92.71676277432059
Episode: 195, total reward: 89.97484988523927
Episode: 196, total reward: 89.26063135086025
Episode: 197, total reward: 87.19460382302674
Episode: 198, total reward: 79.86081433777699
Episode: 199, total reward: 88.98075638481279
```

The following plot is the result of *Step 11*:

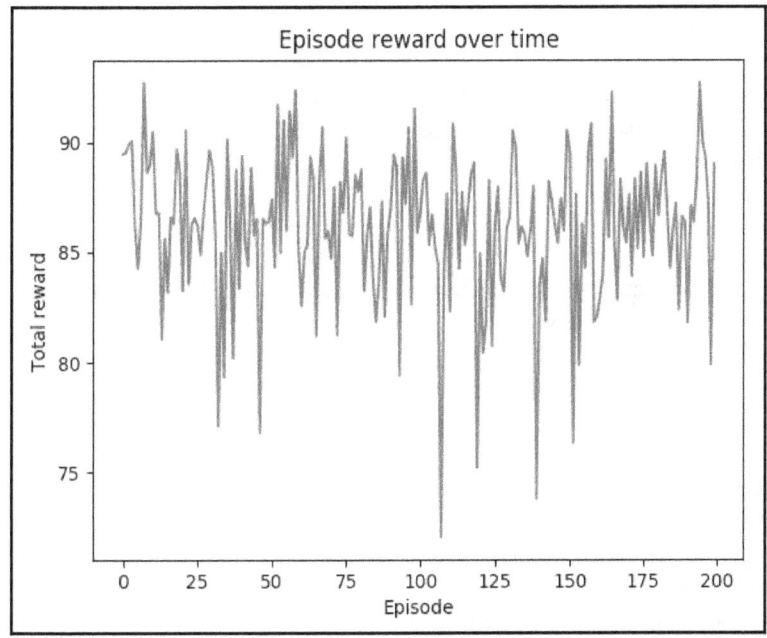

According to the resolved requirements in `https://github.com/openai/gym/wiki/MountainCarContinuous-v0`, getting a reward above +90 is regarded as the environment being solved. We have multiple episodes where we solve the environment.

In continuous A2C, we assume that each dimension of the action space is Gaussian distributed. The mean and deviation of a Gaussian distribution are parts of the output layer of the policy network. The remainder of the output layer is for the estimation of state-value. An action (or set of actions) is (are) sampled from the Gaussian distribution(s) parameterized by the current mean(s) and deviation(s). The loss function in continuous A2C is similar to its discrete version, which is the combination of negative log likelihood computed with the action probabilities under the Gaussian distributions and the advantage values, and the regression error between the actual return values and estimated state-values.

There's more...

So far, we have always modeled policy in a stochastic manner where we sample actions from distributions or computed probabilities. As a bonus section, we will briefly talk about the **Deterministic Policy Gradient (DPG)**, where we model the policy as a deterministic decision. We simply treat the deterministic policy as a special case of stochastic policy by directly mapping input states to actions instead of probabilities of actions. The DPG algorithm generally uses the following two sets of neural networks:

- **Actor-critic network**: This is very similar to the A2C we have experienced, but in a deterministic manner. It predicts state-values and actions to be taken.
- **Target actor-critic network**: This is a periodical copy of the actor-critic network with the purpose of stabilizing learning. Obviously, you don't want to have targets that keep on changing. This network provides time-delayed targets for training.

As you can see, there is not much new in DPG, but a nice combination of A2C and a time-delayed target mechanism. Feel free to implement the algorithm yourself and use it to solve the continuous Mountain Car environment.

See also

If you are not familiar with softplus activation, or want to read more about DPG, please check out the following material:

- Softplus: `https://en.wikipedia.org/wiki/Rectifier_(neural_networks)`
- Original paper of the DFP: `https://hal.inria.fr/file/index/docid/938992/filename/dpg-icml2014.pdf`

Playing CartPole through the cross-entropy method

In this last recipe, by way of a bonus (and fun) section, we will develop a simple, yet powerful, algorithm to solve CartPole. It is based on cross-entropy, and directly maps input states to an output action. In fact, it is more straightforward than all the other policy gradient algorithms in this chapter.

We have applied several policy gradient algorithms to solve the CartPole environment. They use complicated neural network architectures and a loss function, which may be overkill for simple environments such as CartPole. Why don't we directly predict the actions for given states? The idea behind this is straightforward: we model the mapping from state to action, and train it ONLY with the most successful experiences from the past. We are only interested in what the correct actions should be. The objective function, in this case, is the cross-entropy between the actual and predicted actions. In CartPole, there are two possible actions: left and right. For simplicity, we can convert it into a binary classification problem with the following model diagram:

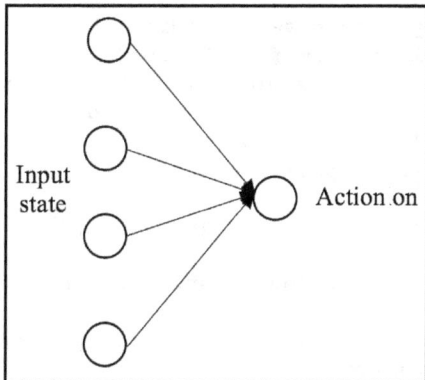

How to do it...

We solve the CartPole problem using cross-entropy as follows:

1. Import all the necessary packages and create a CartPole instance:

```
>>> import gym
>>> import torch
>>> import torch.nn as nn
>>> from torch.autograd import Variable
>>> env = gym.make('CartPole-v0')
```

2. Let's start with the action estimator:

```
>>> class Estimator():
...         def __init__(self, n_state, lr=0.001):
...             self.model = nn.Sequential(
...                             nn.Linear(n_state, 1),
...                             nn.Sigmoid()
...                         )
```

```
...             self.criterion = torch.nn.BCELoss()
...             self.optimizer = torch.optim.Adam(
                            self.model.parameters(), lr)
...
...         def predict(self, s):
...             return self.model(torch.Tensor(s))
...
...         def update(self, s, y):
...             """
...             Update the weights of the estimator given
                    the training samples
...             """
...             y_pred = self.predict(s)
...             loss = self.criterion(
                        y_pred, Variable(torch.Tensor(y)))
...             self.optimizer.zero_grad()
...             loss.backward()
...             self.optimizer.step()
```

3. We now develop the main training function for the cross-entropy algorithm:

```
>>> def cross_entropy(env, estimator, n_episode, n_samples):
...         """
...         Cross-entropy algorithm for policy learning
...         @param env: Gym environment
...         @param estimator: binary estimator
...         @param n_episode: number of episodes
...         @param n_samples: number of training samples to use
...         """
...         experience = []
...         for episode in range(n_episode):
...             rewards = 0
...             actions = []
...             states = []
...             state = env.reset()
...             while True:
...                 action = env.action_space.sample()
...                 states.append(state)
...                 actions.append(action)
...                 next_state, reward, is_done, _ = env.step(action)
...                 rewards += reward
...                 if is_done:
...                     for state, action in zip(states, actions):
...                         experience.append((rewards, state,
action))
...                     break
...                 state = next_state
...
```

```
...         experience = sorted(experience,
                                key=lambda x: x[0], reverse=True)
...         select_experience = experience[:n_samples]
...         train_states = [exp[1] for exp in select_experience]
...         train_actions = [exp[2] for exp in select_experience]
...
...         for _ in range(100):
...             estimator.update(train_states, train_actions)
```

4. We then specify the input size of the action estimator and the learning rate:

```
>>> n_state = env.observation_space.shape[0]
>>> lr = 0.01
```

Then we create an Estimator instance accordingly:

```
>>> estimator = Estimator(n_state, lr)
```

5. We will generate 5,000 random episodes and cherry-pick the best 10,000 (state, action) pairs for training the estimator:

```
>>> n_episode = 5000
>>> n_samples = 10000
>>> cross_entropy(env, estimator, n_episode, n_samples)
```

6. After the model is trained, let's test it out. We use it to play 100 episodes and record the total rewards:

```
>>> n_episode = 100
>>> total_reward_episode = [0] * n_episode
>>> for episode in range(n_episode):
...     state = env.reset()
...     is_done = False
...     while not is_done:
...         action = 1 if estimator.predict(state).item() >= 0.5
else 0
...         next_state, reward, is_done, _ = env.step(action)
...         total_reward_episode[episode] += reward
...         state = next_state
```

7. We then visualize the performance as follows:

```
>>> import matplotlib.pyplot as plt
>>> plt.plot(total_reward_episode)
>>> plt.title('Episode reward over time')
>>> plt.xlabel('Episode')
>>> plt.ylabel('Total reward')
>>> plt.show()
```

How it works...

As you can see in *Step 2*, the action estimator has two layers – input and output layers, followed by a sigmoid activation function, and the loss function is binary cross-entropy.

Step 3 is for training the cross-entropy model. Specifically, for each training episode, we take random actions, accumulate rewards, and record states and actions. After experiencing `n_episode` episodes, we take the most successful episodes (with the highest total rewards) and extract `n_samples` of (state, action) pairs as training samples. We then train the estimator for 100 iterations on the training set we just constructed.

Executing the lines of code in *Step 7* will result in the following plot:

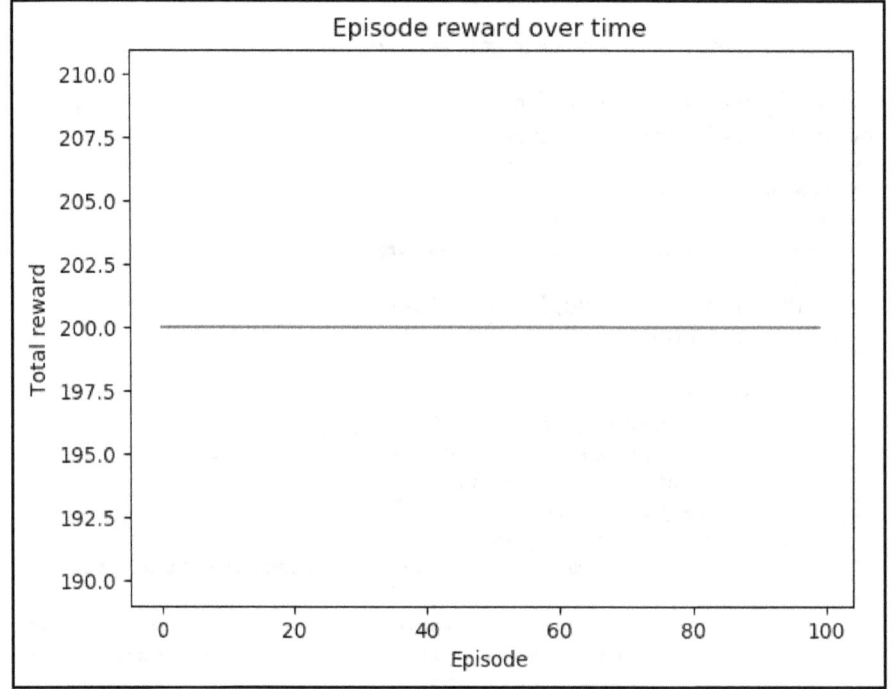

As you can see, there are +200 rewards for all testing episodes!

Cross-entropy is very simple, yet useful, for simple environments. It directly models the relationship between input states and output actions. A control problem is framed into a classification problem where we try to predict the correct action among all the alternatives. The trick is that we only learn from the right experience, which guides the model in terms of what the most rewarding action should be, given a state.

9
Capstone Project – Playing Flappy Bird with DQN

In this very last chapter, we will work on a capstone project—playing Flappy Bird using reinforcement learning. We will apply what we have learned throughout this book to build an intelligent bot. We will also focus on building **Deep Q-Networks** (**DQNs**), fine-tuning model parameters, and deploying the model. Let's see how long the bird can stay in the air.

The capstone project will be built section by section in the following recipes:

- Setting up the game environment
- Building a Deep Q-Network to play Flappy Bird
- Training and tuning the network
- Deploying the model and playing the game

As a result, the code in each recipe is to be built on top of the previous recipes.

Setting up the game environment

To play Flappy Bird with a DQN, we first need to set up the environment.

We'll simulate the Flappy Bird game using Pygame. Pygame (https://www.pygame.org) contains a set of Python modules developed for creating video games. It also includes graphics and sound libraries needed in games. We can install the Pygame package as follows:

```
pip install pygame
```

Flappy Bird is a famous mobile game originally developed by Dong Nguyen. You can try it yourself, using your keyboard, at `https://flappybird.io/`. The aim of the game is to remain alive as long as possible. The game ends when the bird touches the floor or a pipe. So, the bird needs to flap its wings at the right times to get through the random pipes and to avoid falling to the ground. Possible actions include flapping and not flapping. In the game environment, the reward is +0.1 for every step, with the following two exceptions:

- -1 when a collision occurs
- +1 when the bird gets through the gap between two pipes. The original Flappy Bird game is scored based on the number of gaps passed through.

Getting ready

Download the assets of the game environment we need from `https://github.com/yanpanlau/Keras-FlappyBird/tree/master/assets/sprites`. For simplicity, we'll just use the images in the `sprites` folder. Specifically, we will need the following images:

- `background-black.png`: The background image of the screen
- `base.png`: The image for the floor
- `pipe-green.png`: The image for the pipes that the bird needs to stay away from
- `redbird-downflap.png`: The image for the bird when it's flapping down
- `redbird-midflap.png`: The image for the bird when it's not flapping
- `redbird-upflap.png`: The image for the bird when it's flapping up

If you are interested, you can also use audio files to make the game more fun.

How to do it...

We'll develop the Flappy Bird game environment using `Pygame` as follows:

1. We start by developing a utility function that loads images and transforms them into the right format:

```
>>> from pygame.image import load
>>> from pygame.surfarray import pixels_alpha
>>> from pygame.transform import rotate
>>> def load_images(sprites_path):
...     base_image = load(sprites_path +
                              'base.png').convert_alpha()
...     background_image = load(sprites_path +
```

```
                                   'background-black.png').convert()
...        pipe_images = [rotate(load(sprites_path +
                                  'pipe-green.png').convert_alpha(), 180),
...                       load(sprites_path +
                                  'pipe-green.png').convert_alpha()]
...        bird_images = [load(sprites_path +
                                  'redbird-upflap.png').convert_alpha(),
...                       load(sprites_path +
                                  'redbird-midflap.png').convert_alpha(),
...                       load(sprites_path +
                                  'redbird-downflap.png').convert_alpha()]
...        bird_hitmask = [pixels_alpha(image).astype(bool)
                                  for image in bird_images]
...        pipe_hitmask = [pixels_alpha(image).astype(bool)
                                  for image in pipe_images]
...        return base_image, background_image, pipe_images,
                       bird_images, bird_hitmask, pipe_hitmask
```

2. Import all the necessary packages for the environment:

```
>>> from itertools import cycle
>>> from random import randint
>>> import pygame
```

3. Initialize the game and clock and set 30 frames per second as the screen refresh frequency:

```
>>> pygame.init()
>>> fps_clock = pygame.time.Clock()
>>> fps = 30
```

4. Specify the screen size and create a screen accordingly, then add a caption to the screen:

```
>>> screen_width = 288
 >>> screen_height = 512
 >>> screen = pygame.display.set_mode((screen_width,
screen_height))
 >>> pygame.display.set_caption('Flappy Bird')
```

5. We then load necessary images (in the `sprites` folder) with the following function:

```
>>> base_image, background_image, pipe_images, bird_images,
bird_hitmask, pipe_hitmask = load_images('sprites/')
```

6. Get the game variables, including the size of the bird and the pipes, and set 100 as the vertical gap between two pipes:

```
>>> bird_width = bird_images[0].get_width()
>>> bird_height = bird_images[0].get_height()
>>> pipe_width = pipe_images[0].get_width()
>>> pipe_height = pipe_images[0].get_height()
>>> pipe_gap_size = 100
```

7. The flapping movement of the bird rotates through up, middle, down, middle, up, and so on:

```
>>> bird_index_gen = cycle([0, 1, 2, 1])
```

This is just to make the game more fun to watch.

8. After defining all constants, we start with the __init__ method of the game environment's FlappyBird class:

```
>>> class FlappyBird(object):
...     def __init__(self):
...         self.pipe_vel_x = -4
...         self.min_velocity_y = -8
...         self.max_velocity_y = 10
...         self.downward_speed = 1
...         self.upward_speed = -9
...         self.cur_velocity_y = 0
...         self.iter = self.bird_index = self.score = 0
...         self.bird_x = int(screen_width / 5)
...         self.bird_y = int((screen_height - bird_height) / 2)
...         self.base_x = 0
...         self.base_y = screen_height * 0.79
...         self.base_shift = base_image.get_width() -
...                     background_image.get_width()
...         self.pipes = [self.gen_random_pipe(screen_width),
...                     self.gen_random_pipe(screen_width * 1.5)]
...         self.is_flapped = False
```

9. We continue by defining the `gen_random_pipe` method, which generates a pair of pipes (one upper and one lower) in a given horizontal position and random vertical positions:

```
>>>     def gen_random_pipe(self, x):
...         gap_y = randint(2, 10) * 10 + int(self.base_y * 0.2)
...         return {"x_upper": x,
...                 "y_upper": gap_y - pipe_height,
...                 "x_lower": x,
...                 "y_lower": gap_y + pipe_gap_size}
```

The upper and lower pipes are in the y position of `gap_y - pipe_height` and `gap_y + pipe_gap_size` respectively.

10. The next method we develop is `check_collision`, which returns `True` if the bird collides with the base or a pipe:

```
>>>     def check_collision(self):
...         if bird_height + self.bird_y >= self.base_y - 1:
...             return True
...         bird_rect = pygame.Rect(self.bird_x, self.bird_y,
...                                 bird_width, bird_height)
...         for pipe in self.pipes:
...             pipe_boxes = [pygame.Rect(pipe["x_upper"],
...                 pipe["y_upper"], pipe_width,
pipe_height),
...                           pygame.Rect(pipe["x_lower"],
...                 pipe["y_lower"], pipe_width,
pipe_height)]
...             # Check if the bird's bounding box overlaps to
...                 the bounding box of any pipe
...             if bird_rect.collidelist(pipe_boxes) == -1:
...                 return False
...             for i in range(2):
...                 cropped_bbox = bird_rect.clip(pipe_boxes[i])
...                 x1 = cropped_bbox.x - bird_rect.x
...                 y1 = cropped_bbox.y - bird_rect.y
...                 x2 = cropped_bbox.x - pipe_boxes[i].x
...                 y2 = cropped_bbox.y - pipe_boxes[i].y
...                 for x in range(cropped_bbox.width):
...                     for y in range(cropped_bbox.height):
...                         if bird_hitmask[self.bird_index][x1+x,
...                             y1+y] and pipe_hitmask[i][
...                             x2+x, y2+y]:
...                             return True
...         return False
```

11. The last and the most import method we need is `next_step`, which performs an action and returns the updated image frame of the game, the reward received, and whether the episode is over or not:

```
>>>        def next_step(self, action):
...            pygame.event.pump()
...            reward = 0.1
...            if action == 1:
...                self.cur_velocity_y = self.upward_speed
...                self.is_flapped = True
...            # Update score
...            bird_center_x = self.bird_x + bird_width / 2
...            for pipe in self.pipes:
...                pipe_center_x = pipe["x_upper"] +
                                        pipe_width / 2
...                if pipe_center_x < bird_center_x
                                < pipe_center_x + 5:
...                    self.score += 1
...                    reward = 1
...                    break
...            # Update index and iteration
...            if (self.iter + 1) % 3 == 0:
...                self.bird_index = next(bird_index_gen)
...            self.iter = (self.iter + 1) % fps
...            self.base_x = -((-self.base_x + 100) %
                                    self.base_shift)
...            # Update bird's position
...            if self.cur_velocity_y < self.max_velocity_y
                            and not self.is_flapped:
...                self.cur_velocity_y += self.downward_speed
...            self.is_flapped = False
...            self.bird_y += min(self.cur_velocity_y,
                    self.bird_y - self.cur_velocity_y - bird_height)
...            if self.bird_y < 0:
...                self.bird_y = 0
...            # Update pipe position
...            for pipe in self.pipes:
...                pipe["x_upper"] += self.pipe_vel_x
...                pipe["x_lower"] += self.pipe_vel_x
...            # Add new pipe when first pipe is
                    about to touch left of screen
...            if 0 < self.pipes[0]["x_lower"] < 5:
...                self.pipes.append(self.gen_random_pipe(
                                    screen_width + 10))
...            # remove first pipe if its out of the screen
...            if self.pipes[0]["x_lower"] < -pipe_width:
...                self.pipes.pop(0)
...            if self.check_collision():
```

```
...                is_done = True
...                reward = -1
...                self.__init__()
...            else:
...                is_done = False
...            # Draw sprites
...            screen.blit(background_image, (0, 0))
...            screen.blit(base_image, (self.base_x, self.base_y))
...            screen.blit(bird_images[self.bird_index],
...                        (self.bird_x, self.bird_y))
...            for pipe in self.pipes:
...                screen.blit(pipe_images[0],
...                        (pipe["x_upper"], pipe["y_upper"]))
...                screen.blit(pipe_images[1],
...                        (pipe["x_lower"], pipe["y_lower"]))
...            image = pygame.surfarray.array3d(
...                        pygame.display.get_surface())
...            pygame.display.update()
...            fps_clock.tick(fps)
...            return image, reward, is_done
```

That's all for the Flappy Bird environment.

How it works...

In *Step 8*, we define the velocity of the pipe (to the left by 4 units as time goes by), the minimal and maximal vertical velocity of the bird (-8 and 10), its upward and downward acceleration (-9 and 1), its default vertical velocity (0), the starting index of the bird image (0), the initial score, the initial horizontal and vertical position of the bird, the position of the base, and the coordinates of the pipes that are randomly generated using the gen_random_pipe method.

In *Step 11*, by default, the reward for a step is +0.1. If the action is flap, we increase the bird's vertical velocity by its upward acceleration. Then, we check whether the bird happens to get through a pair of pipes. If it does, the game score increases by 1 and the step reward becomes + 1. We update the bird's position, its image index, as well as the pipes' position. A new pair of pipes will be generated if the old pair is about to leave the left-hand side of the screen, and the old pair of pipes will be deleted once it goes offscreen. If a collision occurs, the episode will end and the reward will be -1; the game will also reset. Finally, we'll display the updated frame on the game screen.

Building a Deep Q-Network to play Flappy Bird

Now that the Flappy Bird environment is ready, we can start tackling it by building a DQN model.

As we have seen, a screen image is returned at each step after an action is taken. A CNN is one of the best neural network architectures to deal with image inputs. In a CNN, the convolutional layers are able to effectively extract features from images, which will be passed on to fully connected layers downstream. In our solution, we will use a CNN with three convolutional layers and one fully connected hidden layer. An example of CNN architecture is as follows:

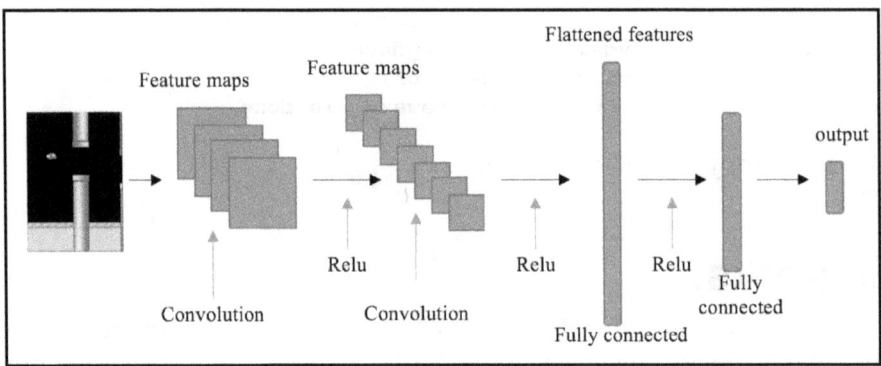

How to do it...

Let's develop a CNN-based DQN model as follows:

1. Import the necessary modules:

```
>>> import torch
>>> import torch.nn as nn
>>> import torch.nn.functional as F
>>> import numpy as np
>>> import random
```

2. We start with the CNN model:

```
>>> class DQNModel(nn.Module):
...     def __init__(self, n_action=2):
```

```
...             super(DQNModel, self).__init__()
...             self.conv1 = nn.Conv2d(4, 32,
...                             kernel_size=8, stride=4)
...             self.conv2 = nn.Conv2d(32, 64, 4, stride=2)
...             self.conv3 = nn.Conv2d(64, 64, 3, stride=1)
...             self.fc = nn.Linear(7 * 7 * 64, 512)
...             self.out = nn.Linear(512, n_action)
...             self._create_weights()
...
...         def _create_weights(self):
...             for m in self.modules():
...                 if isinstance(m, nn.Conv2d) or
...                                 isinstance(m, nn.Linear):
...                     nn.init.uniform(m.weight, -0.01, 0.01)
...                     nn.init.constant_(m.bias, 0)
...
...         def forward(self, x):
...             x = F.relu(self.conv1(x))
...             x = F.relu(self.conv2(x))
...             x = F.relu(self.conv3(x))
...             x = x.view(x.size(0), -1)
...             x = F.relu(self.fc(x))
...             output = self.out(x)
...             return output
```

3. Now develop a DQN with experience replay using the CNN model we just built:

```
>>> class DQN():
...         def __init__(self, n_action, lr=1e-6):
...             self.criterion = torch.nn.MSELoss()
...             self.model = DQNModel(n_action)
...             self.optimizer = torch.optim.Adam(
...                     self.model.parameters(), lr)
```

4. The `predict` method estimates the output Q-values, given an input state:

```
>>>     def predict(self, s):
...         """
...         Compute the Q values of the state for all
...             actions using the learning model
...         @param s: input state
...         @return: Q values of the state for all actions
...         """
...         return self.model(torch.Tensor(s))
```

5. An `update` method updates the weights of the neural network, given a training sample, and returns the current loss:

```
>>>     def update(self, y_predict, y_target):
...         """
...         Update the weights of the DQN given a training sample
...         @param y_predict:
...         @param y_target:
...         @return:
...         """
...         loss = self.criterion(y_predict, y_target)
...         self.optimizer.zero_grad()
...         loss.backward()
...         self.optimizer.step()
...         return loss
```

6. The last part of the DQN class is the `replay` method, which performs experience replay given a collection of past experiences:

```
>>>     def replay(self, memory, replay_size, gamma):
...         """
...         Experience replay
...         @param memory: a list of experience
...         @param replay_size: the number of samples we
...             use to update the model each time
...         @param gamma: the discount factor
...         @return: the loss
...         """
...         if len(memory) >= replay_size:
...             replay_data = random.sample(memory, replay_size)
...             state_batch, action_batch, next_state_batch,
...                 reward_batch, done_batch = zip(*replay_data)
...             state_batch = torch.cat(
...                     tuple(state for state in state_batch))
...             next_state_batch = torch.cat(
...                     tuple(state for state in
next_state_batch))
...             q_values_batch = self.predict(state_batch)
...             q_values_next_batch =
...                     self.predict(next_state_batch)
...             reward_batch = torch.from_numpy(np.array(
...                     reward_batch, dtype=np.float32)[:, None])
...             action_batch = torch.from_numpy(
...                 np.array([[1, 0] if action == 0 else [0, 1]
...                 for action in action_batch],
dtype=np.float32))
```

```
...                    q_value = torch.sum(
                               q_values_batch * action_batch, dim=1)
...                    td_targets = torch.cat(
...                    tuple(reward if terminal else reward +
                               gamma * torch.max(prediction) for
                               reward, terminal, prediction
...                        in zip(reward_batch, done_batch,
                               q_values_next_batch)))
...                    loss = self.update(q_value, td_targets)
...                    return loss
```

That's it for the DQN class. In the next recipe, we will train the DQN model on a number of iterations.

How it works...

In *Step 2*, we put together the backbone of the CNN-based DQN. It has three convolutional layers with various configurations. A ReLU activation function follows each convolutional layer. The resulting feature map from the last convolutional layer is then flattened and fed to a fully-connected hidden layer with 512 nodes, followed by the output layer.

Note that we also set a boundary for the initial random value of the weights and a zero bias so that the model is more likely to converge faster.

Step 6 is for step-wise training with experience replay. If we have enough experiences, we randomly draw a replay_size set of experiences for training. We then convert each experience into a training sample composed of the predicted values and output target values, given an input state. The target values are computed as follows:

- Update the target Q value for the action using the reward and the new Q values, as in: $r + \gamma max_{a'} Q(s', a')$

- If it is a terminal state, the target Q value is updated as r.

And finally, we update the neural network using the selected batch of training samples.

Training and tuning the network

In this recipe, we will train the DQN model to play Flappy Bird.

In each step of the training, we take an action following the epsilon-greedy policy: under a certain probability (epsilon), we will take a random action, flapping or not flapping in our case; otherwise, we select the action with the highest value. We also adjust the value of epsilon for each step as we favor more exploration at the beginning and more exploitation when the DQN model is getting more mature.

As we have seen, the observation for each step is a two-dimensional image of the screen. We need to transform the observation images into states. Simply using one image from a step will not provide enough information to guide the agent as to how to react. Hence, we form a state using images from four adjacent steps. We will first reshape the image into the expected size, then concatenate the image of the current frame with the three previous ones.

How to do it...

We train the DQN model as follows:

1. Import the necessary modules:

```
>>> import random
>>> import torch
>>> from collections import deque
```

2. We start by developing the epsilon-greedy policy:

```
>>> def gen_epsilon_greedy_policy(estimator, epsilon, n_action):
...         def policy_function(state):
...             if random.random() < epsilon:
...                 return random.randint(0, n_action - 1)
...             else:
...                 q_values = estimator.predict(state)
...                 return torch.argmax(q_values).item()
...         return policy_function
```

3. We specify the size of the preprocessed image, the batch size, the learning rate, the gamma , the number of actions, the initial and final epsilon, the number of iterations, and the size of the memory:

```
>>> image_size = 84
>>> batch_size = 32
>>> lr = 1e-6
>>> gamma = 0.99
>>> init_epsilon = 0.1
>>> final_epsilon = 1e-4
>>> n_iter = 2000000
>>> memory_size = 50000
>>> n_action = 2
```

We also save the trained model periodically, as it will be a very long process:

```
>>> saved_path = 'trained_models'
```

Don't forget to create a folder named `trained_models`.

4. We specify the random feed for experimental reproducibility:

```
>>> torch.manual_seed(123)
```

5. We create a DQN model accordingly:

```
>>> estimator = DQN(n_action)
```

We also create a memory queue:

```
>>> memory = deque(maxlen=memory_size)
```

New samples will be appended to the queue, and the old ones will be removed as long as there are more than 50,000 samples in the queue.

6. Next, we initialize a Flappy Bird environment:

```
>>> env = FlappyBird()
```

We then obtain the initial image:

```
>>> image, reward, is_done = env.next_step(0)
```

7. As mentioned before, we should resize the raw image to `image_size *`
   `image_size`:

```
>>> import cv2
 >>> import numpy as np
 >>> def pre_processing(image, width, height):
 ...      image = cv2.cvtColor(cv2.resize(image,
                     (width, height)), cv2.COLOR_BGR2GRAY)
 ...      _, image = cv2.threshold(image, 1, 255, cv2.THRESH_BINARY)
 ...      return image[None, :, :].astype(np.float32)
```

If the `cv2` package is not installed, you can do so with the following command:

```
pip install opencv-python
```

Let's preprocess the image accordingly:

```
>>> image = pre_processing(image[:screen_width, :int(env.base_y)],
image_size, image_size)
```

8. Now, we construct a state by concatenating four images. Since we only have the
   first frame now, we simply replicate it four times:

```
>>> image = torch.from_numpy(image)
>>> state = torch.cat(tuple(image for _ in range(4)))[None, :, :,
:]
```

9. We then work on the training loop for `n_iter` steps:

```
>>> for iter in range(n_iter):
...      epsilon = final_epsilon + (n_iter - iter)
                 * (init_epsilon - final_epsilon) / n_iter
...      policy = gen_epsilon_greedy_policy(
                  estimator, epsilon, n_action)
...      action = policy(state)
...      next_image, reward, is_done = env.next_step(action)
...      next_image = pre_processing(next_image[
         :screen_width, :int(env.base_y)], image_size, image_size)
...      next_image = torch.from_numpy(next_image)
...      next_state = torch.cat((
                  state[0, 1:, :, :], next_image))[None, :, :, :]
...      memory.append([state, action, next_state, reward,
is_done])
...      loss = estimator.replay(memory, batch_size, gamma)
...      state = next_state
...      print("Iteration: {}/{}, Action: {},
                  Loss: {}, Epsilon {}, Reward: {}".format(
                  iter + 1, n_iter, action, loss, epsilon, reward))
```

```
...        if iter+1 % 10000 == 0:
...            torch.save(estimator.model, "{}/{}".format(
                    saved_path, iter+1))
```

After we run that section of code, we'll see the following logs:

```
Iteration: 1/2000000, Action: 0, Loss: None, Epsilon 0.1, Reward:
0.1
 Iteration: 2/2000000, Action: 0, Loss: None, Epsilon
0.09999995005000001, Reward: 0.1
 Iteration: 3/2000000, Action: 0, Loss: None, Epsilon 0.0999999001,
Reward: 0.1
 Iteration: 4/2000000, Action: 0, Loss: None, Epsilon
0.09999985015, Reward: 0.1
 ...
 ...
 Iteration: 201/2000000, Action: 1, Loss: 0.040504034608602524,
Epsilon 0.09999001000000002, Reward: 0.1
 Iteration: 202/2000000, Action: 1, Loss: 0.010011588223278522,
Epsilon 0.09998996005, Reward: 0.1
 Iteration: 203/2000000, Action: 1, Loss: 0.07097195833921432,
Epsilon 0.09998991010000001, Reward: 0.1
 Iteration: 204/2000000, Action: 1, Loss: 0.040418840944767,
Epsilon 0.09998986015000001, Reward: 0.1
 Iteration: 205/2000000, Action: 1, Loss: 0.00999421812593937,
Epsilon 0.09998981020000001, Reward: 0.1
```

The training will take a while. Of course, you can speed up training with the
GPU.

10. Finally, we save the last trained mode:

```
>>> torch.save(estimator.model, "{}/final".format(saved_path))
```

How it works...

In *Step 9*, for each training step, we perform the following tasks:

- Slightly decrease the epsilon, and create an epsilon-greedy policy accordingly.
- Take the action computed using the epsilon-greedy policy.
- Preprocess the resulting image and construct the new state by appending the
  image to those from the previous three steps.
- Record the experience in this step, including the state, the action, the next state,
  the reward received, and whether it ends or not.

- Update the model with experience replay.
- Print out the training status and update the state.
- Save the trained model periodically in order to avoid retraining from scratch.

Deploying the model and playing the game

Now that we've trained the DQN model, let's apply it to play the Flappy Bird game.

Playing the game with the trained model is simple. We will just take the action associated with the highest value in each step. We will play a few episodes to see how it performs. Don't forget to preprocess the raw screen image and construct the state.

How to do it...

We test the DQN model on new episodes as follows:

1. We first load the final model:

```
>>> model = torch.load("{}/final".format(saved_path))
```

2. We run 100 episodes, and we perform the following for each episode:

```
>>> n_episode = 100
>>> for episode in range(n_episode):
...       env = FlappyBird()
...       image, reward, is_done = env.next_step(0)
...       image = pre_processing(image[:screen_width,
                 :int(env.base_y)], image_size, image_size)
...       image = torch.from_numpy(image)
...       state = torch.cat(tuple(image for _ in range(4)))[
                   None, :, :, :]
...       while True:
...           prediction = model(state)[0]
...           action = torch.argmax(prediction).item()
...           next_image, reward, is_done = env.next_step(action)
...           if is_done:
...               break
...           next_image = pre_processing(next_image[:screen_width,
                       :int(env.base_y)], image_size, image_size)
...           next_image = torch.from_numpy(next_image)
...           next_state = torch.cat((state[0, 1:, :, :],
                       next_image))[None, :, :, :]
...           state = next_state
```

Hopefully, you will see something like the following image, where the bird gets through a series of pipes:

How it works...

In *Step 2*, we perform the following tasks for each episode:

- Initialize a Flappy Bird environment.
- Observe the initial image and generate its state.
- Compute the Q-values, given the state, using the model and taking the action with the highest Q-value
- Observe the new image and whether the episode ends or not.
- If the episode continues, compute the state of the next image and assign it to the current state.
- Repeat until the episode ends.

Other Books You May Enjoy

If you enjoyed this book, you may be interested in these other books by Packt:

Hands-On Reinforcement Learning with Python
Sudharsan Ravichandiran

ISBN: 978-1-78883-652-4

- Understand the basics of reinforcement learning methods, algorithms, and elements
- Train an agent to walk using OpenAI Gym and Tensorflow
- Understand the Markov Decision Process, Bellman's optimality, and TD learning
- Solve multi-armed-bandit problems using various algorithms
- Master deep learning algorithms, such as RNN, LSTM, and CNN with applications
- Build intelligent agents using the DRQN algorithm to play the Doom game
- Teach agents to play the Lunar Lander game using DDPG
- Train an agent to win a car racing game using dueling DQN

Python Reinforcement Learning Projects
Rajalingappaa Shanmugamani, Sean Saito, Et al

ISBN: 978-1-78899-161-2

- Train and evaluate neural networks built using TensorFlow for RL
- Use RL algorithms in Python and TensorFlow to solve CartPole balancing
- Create deep reinforcement learning algorithms to play Atari games
- Deploy RL algorithms using OpenAI Universe
- Develop an agent to chat with humans
- Implement basic actor-critic algorithms for continuous control
- Apply advanced deep RL algorithms to games such as Minecraft
- Autogenerate an image classifier using RL

Leave a review - let other readers know what you think

Please share your thoughts on this book with others by leaving a review on the site that you bought it from. If you purchased the book from Amazon, please leave us an honest review on this book's Amazon page. This is vital so that other potential readers can see and use your unbiased opinion to make purchasing decisions, we can understand what our customers think about our products, and our authors can see your feedback on the title that they have worked with Packt to create. It will only take a few minutes of your time, but is valuable to other potential customers, our authors, and Packt. Thank you!

Index

P

Pi
  calculating, with MC method 92, 93, 94
policy evaluation
  performing 57, 58, 59, 60, 61, 62, 63
policy gradient algorithm
  developing 42, 43, 44, 45, 46, 47, 48
Pong
  reference link 250
Pygame
  reference link 301
Python
  about 10
PyTorch
  fundamentals, reviewing 26, 27, 28, 29
  hill-climbing algorithm, implementing 36, 38, 40
  random search algorithm, implementing 30, 31, 32
  reference link 11, 13
  tensor, updating 30
  URL 10

Q

Q-functions
  about 108
  estimating, with gradient descent approximation 201, 202, 203, 204, 205, 206
Q-learning algorithm
  about 134
  developing 133, 134, 135, 137, 138
  developing, with linear function approximation 206, 207, 209, 210
  developing, with neural network function approximation 218, 219, 220, 221
  used, for solving Taxi problem 149, 150
  working 136

R

random search algorithm
  implementing, with PyTorch 30
  working 33
random search approach 30
random search policy
  evaluating 30

implementing 30
  implementing, with PyTorch 31, 32
  total reward, plotting 34, 35
REINFORCE algorithm
  developing, with baseline 270, 271, 272, 274, 275
  implementing 264, 265, 266, 267, 268, 269

S

SARSA algorithm
  developing 145, 146, 148
  used, for solving Taxi problem 155, 156, 158, 159
  working 147
state value function 55, 108
State-Action-Reward-State-Action (SARSA)
  about 145
  developing, with linear function approximation 211, 213, 214
stochastic 43

T

table of environments
  reference link 130, 199
target actor-critic network 296
Taxi problem
  reference link 149
  solving, with Q-learning algorithm 149, 150, 151, 152, 154
  solving, with SARSA algorithm 155, 156, 158, 159
  working 154, 155, 157, 158
temporal difference (TD) 129
tensor operations
  reference link 30
Thompson sampling (TS) algorithm
  about 184
  used, for solving multi-armed bandit problems 183, 185, 186, 188, 189, 190
Torch
  URL 10

U

upper confidence bound (UCB) algorithm
  about 176

used, for solving multi-armed bandit problems
    176, 177, 178
usable ace 100

V

value function 55
value iteration algorithm 68

W

weighted importance sampling
    used, for developing MC control 125, 126, 127

Windy Gridworld environment playground
    developing 140, 142, 144
    reference link 140
    setting up 139, 140
    working 144
working environment
    Anaconda, installing 10
    conda, using 12
    PyTorch, installing 11
    setting up 10, 12
    tensor, creating in PyTorch 12

www.ingramcontent.com/pod-product-compliance
Lightning Source LLC
Chambersburg PA
CBHW080621060326
40690CB00021B/4769